WebGL Beginner's Guide

Become a master of 3D web programming in WebGL and JavaScript

Diego Cantor

Brandon Jones

PUBLISHING

BIRMINGHAM - MUMBAI

WebGL Beginner's Guide

First published: June 2012

Production Reference: 1070612

Published by Packt Publishing Ltd.
Livery Place
35 Livery Street
Birmingham B3 2PB, UK.

ISBN 978-1-84969-172-7

www.packtpub.com

Cover Image by Diego Cantor (diego.cantor@gmail.com)

Credits

Authors
Diego Cantor
Brandon Jones

Reviewers
Paul Brunt
Dan Ginsburg
Andor Salga
Giles Thomas

Acquisition Editor
Wilson D'Souza

Lead Technical Editor
Azharuddin Sheikh

Technical Editors
Manasi Poonthottam
Manali Mehta
Rati Pillai
Ankita Shashi
Manmeet Singh Vasir

Copy Editor
Leonard D'Silva

Project Coordinator
Joel Goveya

Proofreader
Lesley Harrison

Indexer
Monica Ajmera Mehta

Graphics
Valentina D'silva
Manu Joseph

Production Coordinator
Melwyn D'sa

Cover Work
Melwyn D'sa

About the Authors

Diego Hernando Cantor Rivera is a Software Engineer born in 1980 in Bogota, Colombia. Diego completed his undergraduate studies in 2002 with the development of a computer vision system that tracked the human gaze as a mechanism to interact with computers.

Later on, in 2005, he finished his master's degree in Computer Engineering with emphasis in Software Architecture and Medical Imaging Processing. During his master's studies, Diego worked as an intern at the imaging processing laboratory CREATIS in Lyon, France and later on at the Australian E-Health Research Centre in Brisbane, Australia.

Diego is currently pursuing a PhD in Biomedical Engineering at Western University in London, Canada, where he is involved in the development augmented reality systems for neurosurgery.

When Diego is not writing code, he enjoys singing, cooking, travelling, watching a good play, or bodybuilding.

Diego speaks Spanish, English, and French.

Acknowledgement

I would like to thank all the people that in one way or in another have been involved with this project:

My partner Jose, thank you for your love and infinite patience.

My family Cecy, Fredy, and Jonathan.

My mentors Dr. Terry Peters and Dr. Robert Bartha for allowing me to work on this project. Thank you for your support and encouragement.

My friends and collegues Danielle Pace and Chris Russ. Guys your work ethic, professionalism, and dedication are inspiring. Thank you for supporting me during the development of this project.

Brandon Jones, my co-author for the awesome glMatrix library! This is a great contribution to the WebGL world! Also, thank you for your contributions on chapters 7 and 10. Without you this book would not had been a reality.

The technical reviewers who taught me a lot and gave me great feedback during the development of this book: Dan Ginsburg, Giles Thomas, Andor Salga, and Paul Brunt. You guys rock!

The tireless PACKT team: Joel Goveya, Wilson D'souza, Maitreya Bhakal, Meeta Rajani, Azharuddin Sheikh, Manasi Poonthottam, Manali Mehta, Manmeet Singh Vasir, Archana Manjrekar, Duane Moraes, and all the other people that somehow contributed to this project at PACKT publishing.

Brandon Jones has been developing WebGL demos since the technology first began appearing in browsers in early 2010. He finds that it's the perfect combination of two aspects of programming that he loves, allowing him to combine eight years of web development experience and a life-long passion for real-time graphics.

Brandon currently works with cutting-edge HTML5 development at Motorola Mobility.

I'd like to thank my wife, Emily, and my dog, Cooper, for being very patient with me while writing this book, and Zach for convincing me that I should do it in the first place.

About the Reviewers

Paul Brunt has over 10 years of web development experience, initially working on e-commerce systems. However, with a strong programming background and a good grasp of mathematics, the emergence of HTML5 presented him with the opportunity to work with richer media technologies with particular focus on using these web technologies in the creation of games. He was working with JavaScript early on in the emergence of HTML5 to create some early games and applications that made extensive use of SVG, canvas, and a new generation of fast JavaScript engines. This work included a proof of concept platform game demonstration called *Berts Breakdown*.

With a keen interest in computer art and an extensive knowledge of Blender, combined with knowledge of real-time graphics, the introduction of WebGL was the catalyst for the creation of GLGE. He began working on GLGE in 2009 when WebGL was still in its infancy, gearing it heavily towards the development of online games.

Apart from GLGE he has also contributed to other WebGL frameworks and projects as well as porting the JigLib physics library to JavaScript in 2010, demoing 3D physics within a browser for the first time.

Dan Ginsburg is the founder of Upsample Software, LLC, a software company offering consulting services with a specialization in 3D graphics and GPU computing. Dan has co-authored several books including the *OpenGL ES 2.0 Programming Guide* and *OpenCL Programming Guide*. He holds a B.Sc in Computer Science from Worcester Polytechnic Institute and an MBA from Bentley University.

Andor Salga graduated from Seneca College with a bachelor's degree in software development. He worked as a research assistant and technical lead in Seneca's open source research lab (CDOT) for four years, developing WebGL libraries such as Processing.js, C3DL, and XB PointStream. He has presented his work at SIGGRAPH, MIT, and Seneca's open source symposium.

I'd like to thank my family and my wife Marina.

Giles Thomas has been coding happily since he first encountered an ICL DRS 20 at the age of seven. Never short on ambition, he wrote his first programming language at 12 and his first operating system at 14. Undaunted by their complete lack of success, and thinking that the third time is a charm, he is currently trying to reinvent cloud computing with a startup called PythonAnywhere. In his copious spare time, he runs a blog at `http://learningwebgl.com/`

www.PacktPub.com

Support files, eBooks, discount offers, and more

You might want to visit www.PacktPub.com for support files and downloads related to your book.

Did you know that Packt offers eBook versions of every book published, with PDF and ePub files available? You can upgrade to the eBook version at www.PacktPub.com and as a print book customer, you are entitled to a discount on the eBook copy. Get in touch with us at service@packtpub.com for more details.

At www.PacktPub.com, you can also read a collection of free technical articles, sign up for a range of free newsletters and receive exclusive discounts and offers on Packt books and eBooks.

http://PacktLib.PacktPub.com

Do you need instant solutions to your IT questions? PacktLib is Packt's online digital book library. Here, you can access, read and search across Packt's entire library of books.

Why Subscribe?

- ◆ Fully searchable across every book published by Packt
- ◆ Copy and paste, print and bookmark content
- ◆ On demand and accessible via web browser

Free Access for Packt account holders

If you have an account with Packt at www.PacktPub.com, you can use this to access PacktLib today and view nine entirely free books. Simply use your login credentials for immediate access.

Table of Contents

Preface

WebGL is a new web technology that brings hardware-accelerated 3D graphics to the browser without requiring the user to install additional software. As WebGL is based on OpenGL and brings in a new concept of 3D graphics programming to web development, it may seem unfamiliar to even experienced web developers.

Packed with many examples, this book shows how WebGL can be easy to learn despite its unfriendly appearance. Each chapter addresses one of the important aspects of 3D graphics programming and presents different alternatives for its implementation. The topics are always associated with exercises that will allow the reader to put the concepts to the test in an immediate manner.

WebGL Beginner's Guide presents a clear road map to learning WebGL. Each chapter starts with a summary of the learning goals for the chapter, followed by a detailed description of each topic. The book offers example-rich, up-to-date introductions to a wide range of essential WebGL topics, including drawing, color, texture, transformations, framebuffers, light, surfaces, geometry, and more. Each chapter is packed with useful and practical examples that demonstrate the implementation of these topics in a WebGL scene. With each chapter, you will "level up" your 3D graphics programming skills. This book will become your trustworthy companion filled with the information required to develop cool-looking 3D web applications with WebGL and JavaScript.

What this book covers

Chapter 1, Getting Started with WebGL, introduces the HTML5 canvas element and describes how to obtain a WebGL context for it. After that, it discusses the basic structure of a WebGL application. The virtual car showroom application is presented as a demo of the capabilities of WebGL. This application also showcases the different components of a WebGL application.

Chapter 2, Rendering Geometry, presents the WebGL API to define, process, and render objects. Also, this chapter shows how to perform asynchronous geometry loading using AJAX and JSON.

Chapter 3, Lights!, introduces ESSL the shading language for WebGL. This chapter shows how to implement a lighting strategy for the WebGL scene using ESSL shaders. The theory behind shading and reflective lighting models is covered and it is put into practice through several examples.

Chapter 4, Camera, illustrates the use of matrix algebra to create and operate cameras in WebGL. The Perspective and Normal matrices that are used in a WebGL scene are also described here. The chapter also shows how to pass these matrices to ESSL shaders so they can be applied to every vertex. The chapter contains several examples that show how to set up a camera in WebGL.

Chapter 5, Action, extends the use of matrices to perform geometrical transformations (move, rotate, scale) on scene elements. In this chapter the concept of matrix stacks is discussed. It is shown how to maintain isolated transformations for every object in the scene using matrix stacks. Also, the chapter describes several animation techniques using matrix stacks and JavaScript timers. Each technique is exemplified through a practical demo.

Chapter 6, Colors, Depth Testing, and Alpha Blending, goes in depth about the use of colors in ESSL shaders. This chapter shows how to define and operate with more than one light source in a WebGL scene. It also explains the concepts of Depth Testing and Alpha Blending, and it shows how these features can be used to create translucent objects. The chapter contains several practical exercises that put into practice these concepts.

Chapter 7, Textures, shows how to create, manage, and map textures in a WebGL scene. The concepts of texture coordinates and texture mapping are presented here. This chapter discusses different mapping techniques that are presented through practical examples. The chapter also shows how to use multiple textures and cube maps.

Chapter 8, Picking, describes a simple implementation of picking which is the technical term that describes the selection and interaction of the user with objects in the scene. The method described in this chapter calculates mouse-click coordinates and determines if the user is clicking on any of the objects being rendered in the canvas. The architecture of the solution is presented with several callback hooks that can be used to implement logic-specific application. A couple of examples of picking are given.

Chapter 9, Putting It All Together, ties in the concepts discussed throughout the book. In this chapter the architecture of the demos is reviewed and the virtual car showroom application outlined in *Chapter 1, Getting Started with WebGL*, is revisited and expanded. Using the virtual car showroom as the case study, this chapter shows how to import Blender models into WebGL scenes and how to create ESSL shaders that support the materials used in Blender.

Chapter 10, Advanced Techniques, shows a sample of some advanced techniques such as post-processing effects, point sprites, normal mapping, and ray tracing. Each technique is provided with a practical example. After reading this WebGL Beginner's Guide you will be able to take on more advanced techniques on your own.

What you need for this book

- You need a browser that implements WebGL. WebGL is supported by all major browser vendors with the exception of Microsoft Internet Explorer. An updated list of WebGL-enabled browsers can be found here:

  ```
  http://www.khronos.org/webgl/wiki/Getting_a_WebGL_
  Implementation
  ```

- A source code editor that recognizes and highlights JavaScript syntax.

- You may need a web server such as Apache or Lighttpd to load remote geometry if you want to do so (as shown in *Chapter 2, Rendering Geometry*). This is optional.

Who this book is for

This book is written for JavaScript developers who are interested in 3D web development. A basic understanding of the DOM object model, the JQuery library, AJAX, and JSON is ideal but not required. No prior WebGL knowledge is expected.

A basic understanding of linear algebra operations is assumed.

Conventions

In this book, you will find several headings appearing frequently.

To give clear instructions of how to complete a procedure or task, we use:

Time for action – heading

1. Action 1

2. Action 2

3. Action 3

Instructions often need some extra explanation so that they make sense, so they are followed with:

What just happened?

This heading explains the working of tasks or instructions that you have just completed.

You will also find some other learning aids in the book, including:

Have a go hero – heading

These set practical challenges and give you ideas for experimenting with what you have learned.

You will also find a number of styles of text that distinguish between different kinds of information. Here are some examples of these styles, and an explanation of their meaning.

Code words in text are shown as follows: "Open the file ch1_Canvas.html using one of the supported browsers."

A block of code is set as follows:

```
<!DOCTYPE html>
<html>
<head>
    <title> WebGL Beginner's Guide - Setting up the canvas </title>
    <style type="text/css">
    canvas {border: 2px dotted blue;}
    </style>
</head>
<body>
<canvas id="canvas-element-id" width="800" height="600">
Your browser does not support HTML5
</canvas>
</body>
</html>
```

When we wish to draw your attention to a particular part of a code block, the relevant lines or items are set in bold:

```
<!DOCTYPE html>
<html>
<head>
    <title> WebGL Beginner's Guide - Setting up the canvas </title>
    <style type="text/css">
    canvas {border: 2px dotted blue;}
    </style>
</head>
<body>
```

```
<canvas id="canvas-element-id" width="800" height="600">
Your browser does not support HTML5
</canvas>
</body>
</html>
```

Any command-line input or output is written as follows:

```
--allow-file-access-from-files
```

New terms and important words are shown in bold. Words that you see on the screen, in menus or dialog boxes for example, appear in the text like this: "Now switch to camera coordinates by clicking on the **Camera** button."

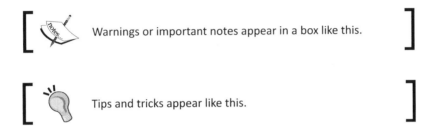

Warnings or important notes appear in a box like this.

Tips and tricks appear like this.

Reader feedback

Feedback from our readers is always welcome. Let us know what you think about this book—what you liked or may have disliked. Reader feedback is important for us to develop titles that you really get the most out of.

To send us general feedback, simply send an e-mail to feedback@packtpub.com, and mention the book title via the subject of your message.

If there is a book that you need and would like to see us publish, please send us a note in the **SUGGEST A TITLE** form on www.packtpub.com or e-mail suggest@packtpub.com.

If there is a topic that you have expertise in and you are interested in either writing or contributing to a book, see our author guide on www.packtpub.com/authors.

Customer support

Now that you are the proud owner of a Packt book, we have a number of things to help you to get the most from your purchase.

Downloading the example code

You can download the example code files for all Packt books you have purchased from your account at `http://www.PacktPub.com`. If you purchased this book elsewhere, you can visit `http://www.PacktPub.com/support` and register to have the files e-mailed directly to you.

Downloading the color images of this book

We also provide you a PDF file that has color images of the screenshots/diagrams used in this book. The color images will help you better understand the changes in the output. You can download this file from `http://www.packtpub.com/sites/default/files/downloads/1727_images.pdf`

Errata

Although we have taken every care to ensure the accuracy of our content, mistakes do happen. If you find a mistake in one of our books—maybe a mistake in the text or the code—we would be grateful if you would report this to us. By doing so, you can save other readers from frustration and help us improve subsequent versions of this book. If you find any errata, please report them by visiting `http://www.packtpub.com/support`, selecting your book, clicking on the **errata submission form** link, and entering the details of your errata. Once your errata are verified, your submission will be accepted and the errata will be uploaded on our website, or added to any list of existing errata, under the Errata section of that title. Any existing errata can be viewed by selecting your title from `http://www.packtpub.com/support`.

Piracy

Piracy of copyright material on the Internet is an ongoing problem across all media. At Packt, we take the protection of our copyright and licenses very seriously. If you come across any illegal copies of our works, in any form, on the Internet, please provide us with the location address or website name immediately so that we can pursue a remedy.

Please contact us at `copyright@packtpub.com` with a link to the suspected pirated material.

We appreciate your help in protecting our authors, and our ability to bring you valuable content.

Questions

You can contact us at `questions@packtpub.com` if you are having a problem with any aspect of the book, and we will do our best to address it.

1
Getting Started with WebGL

In 2007, Vladimir Vukicevic, an American-Serbian software engineer, began working on an OpenGL prototype for the then upcoming HTML `<canvas>` element which he called Canvas 3D. In March, 2011, his work would lead Kronos Group, the nonprofit organization behind OpenGL, to create WebGL: a specification to grant Internet browsers access to Graphic Processing Units (GPUs) on those computers where they were used.

WebGL was originally based on OpenGL ES 2.0 (ES standing for Embedded Systems), the OpenGL specification version for devices such as Apple's iPhone and iPad. But as the specification evolved, it became independent with the goal of providing portability across various operating systems and devices. The idea of web-based, real-time rendering opened a new universe of possibilities for web-based 3D environments such as videogames, scientific visualization, and medical imaging. Additionally, due to the pervasiveness of web browsers, these and other kinds of 3D applications could be taken to mobile devices such as smart phones and tablets. Whether you want to create your first web-based videogame, a 3D art project for a virtual gallery, visualize the data from your experiments, or any other 3D application you could have in mind, the first step will be always to make sure that your environment is ready.

In this chapter, you will:

- ◆ Understand the structure of a WebGL application
- ◆ Set up your drawing area (canvas)
- ◆ Test your browser's WebGL capabilities
- ◆ Understand that WebGL acts as a state machine
- ◆ Modify WebGL variables that affect your scene
- ◆ Load and examine a fully-functional scene

System requirements

WebGL is a web-based 3D Graphics API. As such there is *no* installation needed. At the time this book was written, you will automatically have access to it as long as you have one of the following Internet web browsers:

- Firefox 4.0 or above
- Google Chrome 11 or above
- Safari (OSX 10.6 or above). WebGL is disabled by default but you can switch it on by enabling the **Developer** menu and then checking the **Enable WebGL** option
- Opera 12 or above

To get an updated list of the Internet web browsers where WebGL is supported, please check on the Khronos Group web page following this link:

`http://www.khronos.org/webgl/wiki/Getting_a_WebGL_Implementation`

You also need to make sure that your computer has a graphics card.

If you want to quickly check if your current configuration supports WebGL, please visit this link:

`http://get.webgl.org/`

What kind of rendering does WebGL offer?

WebGL is a 3D graphics library that enables modern Internet browsers to render 3D scenes in a standard and efficient manner. According to Wikipedia, **rendering** is the process of generating an image from a model by means of computer programs. As this is a process executed in a computer, there are different ways to produce such images.

The first distinction we need to make is whether we are using any special graphics hardware or not. We can talk of **software-based rendering** , for those cases where all the calculations required to render 3D scenes are performed using the computer's main processor, its CPU; on the other hand we use the term **hardware-based rendering** for those scenarios where there is a **Graphics Processing Unit (GPU)** performing 3D graphics computations in real time. From a technical point of view, hardware-based rendering is much more efficient than software-based rendering because there is dedicated hardware taking care of the operations. Contrastingly, a software-based rendering solution can be more pervasive due to the lack of hardware dependencies.

A second distinction we can make is whether or not the rendering process is happening locally or remotely. When the image that needs to be rendered is too complex, the render most likely will occur remotely. This is the case for 3D animated movies where dedicated servers with lots of hardware resources allow rendering intricate scenes. We called this **server-based rendering**. The opposite of this is when rendering occurs locally. We called this **client-based rendering**.

WebGL has a client-based rendering approach: the elements that make part of the 3D scene are usually downloaded from a server. However, all the processing required to obtain an image is performed locally using the client's graphics hardware.

In comparison with other technologies (such as Java 3D, Flash, and The Unity Web Player Plugin), WebGL presents several advantages:

- **JavaScript programming**: JavaScript is a language that is natural to both web developers and Internet web browsers. Working with JavaScript allows you to access all parts of the DOM and also lets you communicate between elements easily as opposed to talking to an applet. Because WebGL is programmed in JavaScript, this makes it easier to integrate WebGL applications with other JavaScript libraries such as JQuery and with other HTML5 technologies.

- **Automatic memory management**: Unlike its cousin OpenGL and other technologies where there are specific operations to allocate and deallocate memory manually, WebGL does not have this requisite. It follows the rules for variable scoping in JavaScript and memory is automatically deallocated when it's no longer needed. This simplifies programming tremendously, reducing the code that is needed and making it clearer and easier to understand.

- **Pervasiveness**: Thanks to current advances in technology, web browsers with JavaScript capabilities are installed in smart phones and tablet devices. At the moment of writing, the Mozilla Foundation is testing WebGL capabilities in Motorola and Samsung phones. There is also an effort to implement WebGL on the Android platform.

- **Performance**: The performance of WebGL applications is comparable to equivalent standalone applications (with some exceptions). This happens thanks to WebGL's ability to access the local graphics hardware. Up until now, many 3D web rendering technologies used software-based rendering.

- **Zero compilation**: Given that WebGL is written in JavaScript, there is no need to compile your code before executing it on the web browser. This empowers you to make changes on-the-fly and see how those changes affect your 3D web application. Nevertheless, when we analyze the topic of shader programs, we will understand that we need some compilation. However, this occurs in your graphics hardware, not in your browser.

Structure of a WebGL application

As in any 3D graphics library, in WebGL, you need certain components to be present to create a 3D scene. These fundamental elements will be covered in the first four chapters of the book. Starting from Chapter 5, *Action*, we will cover elements that are not required to have a working 3D scene such as colors and textures and then later on we will move to more advanced topics.

The components we are referring to are as follows:

◆ **Canvas**: It is the placeholder where the scene will be rendered. It is a standard HTML5 element and as such, it can be accessed using the Document Object Model (DOM) through JavaScript.

◆ **Objects**: These are the 3D entities that make up part of the scene. These entities are composed of triangles. In Chapter 2, *Rendering Geometry*, we will see how WebGL handles geometry. We will use WebGL **buffers** to store polygonal data and we will see how WebGL uses these buffers to render the objects in the scene.

◆ **Lights**: Nothing in a 3D world can be seen if there are no lights. This element of any WebGL application will be explored in Chapter 3, *Lights!*. We will learn that WebGL uses **shaders** to model lights in the scene. We will see how 3D objects reflect or absorb light according to the laws of physics and we will also discuss different light models that we can create in WebGL to visualize our objects.

◆ **Camera**: The canvas acts as the viewport to the 3D world. We see and explore a 3D scene through it. In Chapter 4, *Camera*, we will understand the different matrix operations that are required to produce a view perspective. We will also understand how these operations can be modeled as a camera.

This chapter will cover the first element of our list—the canvas. We will see in the coming sections how to create a canvas and how to set up a WebGL context.

Creating an HTML5 canvas

Let's create a web page and add an HTML5 canvas. A **canvas** is a rectangular element in your web page where your 3D scene will be rendered.

Time for action – creating an HTML5 canvas

1. Using your favorite editor, create a web page with the following code in it:

```
<!DOCTYPE html>
<html>
<head>
    <title> WebGL Beginner's Guide - Setting up the canvas </title>
    <style type="text/css">
    canvas {border: 2px dotted blue;}
    </style>
</head>
<body>
<canvas id="canvas-element-id" width="800" height="600">
Your browser does not support HTML5
</canvas>
</body>
</html>
```

Downloading the example code

You can download the example code files for all Packt books you have purchased from your account at http://www.packtpub.com. If you purchased this book elsewhere, you can visit http://www.packtpub.com/support and register to have the files e-mailed directly to you.

2. Save the file as ch1_Canvas.html.

3. Open it with one of the supported browsers.

4. You should see something similar to the following screenshot:

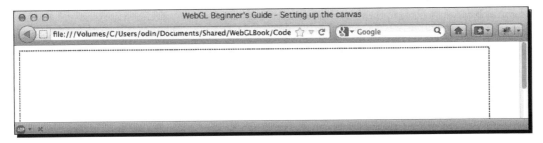

What just happened?

We have just created a simple web page with a canvas in it. This canvas will contain our 3D application. Let's go very quickly to some relevant elements presented in this example.

Defining a CSS style for the border

This is the piece of code that determines the canvas style:

```
<style type="text/css">
canvas {border: 2px dotted blue;}
</style>
```

As you can imagine, this code is not fundamental to build a WebGL application. However, a blue-dotted border is a good way to verify where the canvas is located, given that the canvas will be initially empty.

Understanding canvas attributes

There are three attributes in our previous example:

- **Id**: This is the canvas identifier in the **Document Object Model (DOM)**.
- **Width and height**: These two attributes determine the size of our canvas. When these two attributes are missing, Firefox, Chrome, and WebKit will default to using a 300x150 canvas.

What if the canvas is not supported?

If you see the message on your screen: **Your browser does not support HTML5** (Which was the message we put between `<canvas>` and `</canvas>`) then you need to make sure that you are using one of the supported Internet browsers.

If you are using Firefox and you still see the **HTML5 not supported message**. You might want to be sure that WebGL is enabled (it is by default). To do so, go to Firefox and type `about:config` in the address bar, then look for the property `webgl.disabled`. If is set to `true`, then go ahead and change it. When you restart Firefox and load `ch1_Canvas.html`, you should be able to see the dotted border of the canvas, meaning everything is ok.

In the remote case where you still do not see the canvas, it could be due to the fact that Firefox has blacklisted some graphic card drivers. In that case, there is not much you can do other than use a different computer.

Accessing a WebGL context

A **WebGL context** is a handle (more strictly a JavaScript object) through which we can access all the WebGL functions and attributes. These constitute WebGL's Application Program Interface (API).

We are going to create a JavaScript function that will check whether a WebGL context can be obtained for the canvas or not. Unlike other JavaScript libraries that need to be downloaded and included in your projects to work, *WebGL is already in your browser*. In other words, if you are using one of the supported browsers, you don't need to install or include any library.

Time for action – accessing the WebGL context

We are going to modify the previous example to add a JavaScript function that is going to check the WebGL availability in your browser (trying to get a handle). This function is going to be called when the page is loaded. For this, we will use the standard DOM `onLoad` event.

1. Open the file `ch1_Canvas.html` in your favorite text editor (a text editor that highlight HTML/JavaScript syntax is ideal).

2. Add the following code right below the `</style>` tag:

```
<script>
var gl = null;
function getGLContext(){
var canvas = document.getElementById("canvas-element-id");
    if (canvas == null){
        alert("there is no canvas on this page");
        return;
    }

var names = ["webgl",
             "experimental-webgl",
             "webkit-3d",
             "moz-webgl"];

    for (var i = 0; i < names.length; ++i) {
        try {
           gl = canvas.getContext(names[i]);
        }
        catch(e) {}
        if (gl) break;
    }
    if (gl == null){
        alert("WebGL is not available");
    }
    else{
```

```
        alert("Hooray! You got a WebGL context");
    }
}
    </script>
```

3. We need to call this function on the `onLoad` event. Modify your body tag so it looks like the following:

```
<body onLoad ="getGLContext()">
```

4. Save the file as `ch1_GL_Context.html`.

5. Open the file `ch1_GL_Context.html` using one of the WebGL supported browsers.

6. If you can run WebGL you will see a dialog similar to the following:

What just happened?

Using a JavaScript variable (`gl`), we obtained a reference to a WebGL context. Let's go back and check the code that allows accessing WebGL:

```
var names = ["webgl",
             "experimental-webgl",
             "webkit-3d",
             "moz-webgl"];

for (var i = 0; i < names.length; ++i) {
    try {
        gl = canvas.getContext(names[i]);
    }
    catch(e) {}
    if (gl) break;
}
```

The canvas `getContext` method gives us access to WebGL. All we need to specify a context name that currently can vary from vendor to vendor. Therefore we have grouped them in the possible context names in the `names` array. It is imperative to check on the WebGL specification (you will find it online) for any updates regarding the naming convention.

getContext also provides access to the HTML5 2D graphics library when using 2d as the context name. Unlike WebGL, this naming convention is standard. The HTML5 2D graphics API is completely independent from WebGL and is beyond the scope of this book.

WebGL is a state machine

A WebGL context can be understood as a state machine: once you modify any of its attributes, that modification is permanent until you modify that attribute again. At any point you can query the state of these attributes and so you can determine the current state of your WebGL context. Let's analyze this behavior with an example.

Time for action – setting up WebGL context attributes

In this example, we are going to learn to modify the color that we use to clear the canvas:

1. Using your favorite text editor, open the file ch1_GL_Attributes.html:

```
<html>
<head>
    <title> WebGL Beginner's Guide - Setting WebGL context
attributes </title>
     <style type="text/css">
    canvas {border: 2px dotted blue;}
    </style>

    <script>
     var gl = null;
     var c_width = 0;
     var c_height = 0;

     window.onkeydown = checkKey;

     function checkKey(ev){
       switch(ev.keyCode){
       case 49:{ // 1
            gl.clearColor(0.3,0.7,0.2,1.0);
         clear(gl);
         break;
       }
       case 50:{ // 2
         gl.clearColor(0.3,0.2,0.7,1.0);
         clear(gl);
         break;
```

```
      }
    case 51:{  // 3
      var color = gl.getParameter(gl.COLOR_CLEAR_VALUE);

      // Don't get confused with the following line. It
          // basically rounds up the numbers to one decimal
          cipher
          //just for visualization purposes
      alert('clearColor = (' +
                  Math.round(color[0]*10)/10 +
          ',' + Math.round(color[1]*10)/10+
          ',' + Math.round(color[2]*10)/10+')');

          window.focus();
      break;
    }
    }
  }

  function getGLContext(){
    var canvas = document.getElementById("canvas-element-id");
    if (canvas == null){
        alert("there is no canvas on this page");
        return;
    }

    var names = ["webgl",
                  "experimental-webgl",
                  "webkit-3d",
                  "moz-webgl"];
    var ctx = null;
    for (var i = 0; i < names.length; ++i) {
        try {
            ctx = canvas.getContext(names[i]);
        }
        catch(e) {}
        if (ctx) break;
    }

    if (ctx == null){
      alert("WebGL is not available");
        }
    else{
        return ctx;
    }
  }
```

```
      function clear(ctx){
        ctx.clear(ctx.COLOR_BUFFER_BIT);
            ctx.viewport(0, 0, c_width, c_height);
      }

      function initWebGL(){
        gl = getGLContext();

      }
    </script>
  </head>

  <body onLoad="initWebGL()">
      <canvas id="canvas-element-id" width="800" height="600">
          Your browser does not support the HTML5 canvas element.
      </canvas>
  </body>

  </html>
```

2. You will see that this file is very similar to our previous example. However, there are new code constructs that we will explain briefly. This file contains four JavaScript functions:

Function	Description
checkKey	This is an auxiliary function. It captures the keyboard input and executes code depending on the key entered.
getGLContext	Similar to the one used in the *Time for action – accessing the WebGL context* section. In this version, we are adding some lines of code to obtain the canvas' width and height.
clear	Clear the canvas to the current clear color, which is one attribute of the WebGL context. As was mentioned previously, WebGL works as a state machine, therefore it will maintain the selected color to clear the canvas up to when this color is changed using the WebGL function gl.clearColor (See the checkKey source code)
initWebGL	This function replaces getGLContext as the function being called on the document onLoad event. This function calls an improved version of getGLContext that returns the context in the ctx variable. This context is then assigned to the global variable gl.

3. Open the file `test_gl_attributes.html` using one of the supported Internet web browsers.

4. Press *1*. You will see how the canvas changes its color to green. If you want to query the exact color we used, press *3*.

5. The canvas will maintain the green color until we decided to change the attribute clear color by calling `gl.clearColor`. Let's change it by pressing *2*. If you look at the source code, this will change the canvas clear color to blue. If you want to know the exact color, press *3*.

What just happened?

In this example, we saw that we can change or set the color that WebGL uses to clear the canvas by calling the `clearColor` function. Correspondingly, we used `getParameter` (`gl.COLOR_CLEAR_VALUE`) to obtain the current value for the canvas clear color.

Throughout the book we will see similar constructs where specific functions establish attributes of the WebGL context and the `getParameter` function retrieves the current values for such attributes whenever the respective argument (in our example, `COLOR_CLEAR_VALUE`) is used.

Using the context to access the WebGL API

It is also essential to note here that all of the WebGL functions are accessed through the WebGL context. In our examples, the context is being held by the `gl` variable. Therefore, any call to the WebGL Application Programming Interface (API) will be performed using this variable.

Loading a 3D scene

So far we have seen how to set up a canvas and how to obtain a WebGL context; the next step is to discuss objects, lights, and cameras. However, why should we wait to see what WebGL can do? In this section, we will have a glance at what a WebGL scene look like.

Virtual car showroom

Through the book, we will develop a virtual car showroom application using WebGL. At this point, we will load one simple scene in the canvas. This scene will contain a car, some lights, and a camera.

Time for action – visualizing a finished scene

Once you finish reading the book you will be able to create scenes like the one we are going to play with next. This scene shows one of the cars from the book's virtual car showroom.

1. Open the file `ch1_Car.html` in one of the supported Internet web browsers.

2. You will see a WebGL scene with a car in it as shown in the following screenshot. In *Chapter 2, Rendering Geometry* we will cover the topic of geometry rendering and we will see how to load and render models as this car.

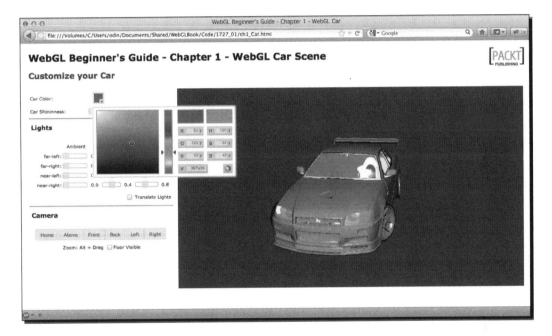

3. Use the sliders to interactively update the four light sources that have been defined for this scene. Each light source has three elements: ambient, diffuse, and specular elements. We will cover the topic about lights in *Chapter 3, Lights!*.

4. Click and drag on the canvas to rotate the car and visualize it from different perspectives. You can zoom by pressing the *Alt* key while you drag the mouse on the canvas. You can also use the arrow keys to rotate the camera around the car. Make sure that the canvas is in focus by clicking on it before using the arrow keys. In *Chapter 4, Camera* we will discuss how to create and operate with cameras in WebGL.

5. If you click on the **Above**, **Front**, **Back**, **Left**, or **Right** buttons you will see an animation that stops when the camera reaches that position. For achieving this effect we are using a JavaScript timer. We will discuss animation in *Chapter 5, Action*.

6. Use the color selector widget as shown in the previous screenshot to change the color of the car. The use of colors in the scene will be discussed in *Chapter 6, Colors, Depth Testing, and Alpha Blending*. Chapters 7-10 will describe the use of textures (*Chapter 7, Textures*), selection of objects in the scene (*Chapter 8, Picking*), how to build the virtual car show room (*Chapter 9, Putting It All Together*) and WebGL advanced techniques (*Chapter 10, Advanced Techniques*).

What just happened?

We have loaded a simple scene in an Internet web browser using WebGL.

This scene consists of:

- A **canvas** through which we see the scene.
- A series of polygonal meshes (**objects**) that constitute the car: roof, windows, headlights, fenders, doors, wheels, spoiler, bumpers, and so on.
- **Light** sources; otherwise everything would appear black.
- A **camera** that determines where in the 3D world is our view point. The camera can be made interactive and the view point can change, depending on the user input. For this example, we were using the left and right arrow keys and the mouse to move the camera around the car.

There are other elements that are not covered in this example such as textures, colors, and special light effects (specularity). Do not panic! Each element will be explained later in the book. The point here is to identify that the four basic elements we discussed previously are present in the scene.

Summary

In this chapter, we have looked at the four basic elements that are always present in any WebGL application: canvas, objects, lights, and camera.

We have learned how to add an HTML5 canvas to our web page and how to set its ID, width, and height. After that, we have included the code to create a WebGL context. We have seen that WebGL works as a state machine and as such, we can query any of its variables using the `getParameter` function.

In the next chapter we will learn how to define, load, and render 3D objects into a WebGL scene.

2

Rendering Geometry

WebGL renders objects following a "divide and conquer" approach. Complex polygons are decomposed into triangles, lines, and point primitives. Then, each geometric primitive is processed in parallel by the GPU through a series of steps, known as the rendering pipeline, in order to create the final scene that is displayed on the canvas.

The first step to use the rendering pipeline is to define geometric entities. In this chapter, we will take a look at how geometric entities are defined in WebGL.

In this chapter, we will:

- ◆ Understand how WebGL defines and processes geometric information
- ◆ Discuss the relevant API methods that relate to geometry manipulation
- ◆ Examine why and how to use JavaScript Object Notation (JSON) to define, store, and load complex geometries
- ◆ Continue our analysis of WebGL as a state machine and describe the attributes relevant to geometry manipulation that can be set and retrieved from the state machine
- ◆ Experiment with creating and loading different geometry models!

Vertices and Indices

WebGL handles geometry in a standard way, independently of the complexity and number of points that surfaces can have. There are two data types that are fundamental to represent the geometry of any 3D object: vertices and indices.

Vertices are the points that define the corners of 3D objects. Each vertex is represented by three floating-point numbers that correspond to the x, y, and z coordinates of the vertex. Unlike its cousin, OpenGL, WebGL does not provide API methods to pass independent vertices to the rendering pipeline, therefore we need to write all of our vertices in a **JavaScript array** and then construct a WebGL vertex buffer with it.

Indices are numeric labels for the vertices in a given 3D scene. Indices allow us to tell WebGL how to connect vertices in order to produce a surface. Just like with vertices, indices are stored in a JavaScript array and then they are passed along to WebGL's rendering pipeline using a WebGL index buffer.

 There are two kind of WebGL buffers used to describe and process geometry: Buffers that contain vertex data are known as **Vertex Buffer Objects** (**VBOs**). Similarly, buffers that contain index data are known as **Index Buffer Objects** (**IBOs**).

Before getting any further, let's examine what WebGL's rendering pipeline looks like and where WebGL buffers fit into this architecture.

Overview of WebGL's rendering pipeline

Here we will see a simplified version of WebGL's rendering pipeline. In subsequent chapters, we will discuss the pipeline in more detail.

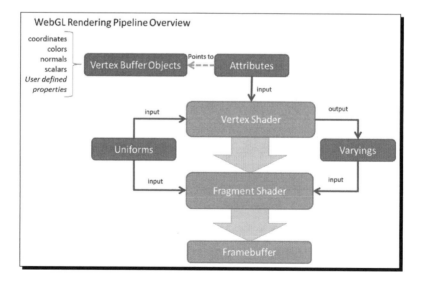

Let's take a moment to describe every element separately.

Vertex Buffer Objects (VBOs)

VBOs contain the data that WebGL requires to describe the geometry that is going to be rendered. As mentioned in the introduction, vertex coordinates are usually stored and processed in WebGL as VBOs. Additionally, there are several data elements such as vertex normals, colors, and texture coordinates, among others, that can be modeled as VBOs.

Vertex shader

The vertex shader is called on each vertex. This shader manipulates *per-vertex* data such as vertex coordinates, normals, colors, and texture coordinates. This data is represented by attributes inside the vertex shader. Each attribute *points to a VBO* from where it reads vertex data.

Fragment shader

Every set of three vertices defines a triangle and each element on the surface of that triangle needs to be assigned a color. Otherwise our surfaces would be transparent.

Each surface element is called a **fragment**. Since we are dealing with surfaces that are going to be displayed on your screen, these elements are more commonly known as **pixels**.

The main goal of the fragment shader is to calculate the color of *individual pixels*. The following diagram explains this idea:

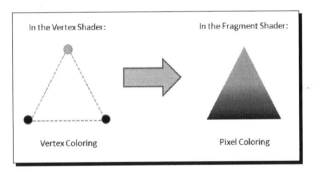

Framebuffer

It is a two-dimensional buffer that contains the fragments that have been processed by the fragment shader. Once all fragments have been processed, a 2D image is formed and displayed on screen. The framebuffer is the final destination of the rendering pipeline.

Attributes, uniforms, and varyings

Attributes, uniforms, and varyings are the three different types of variables that you will find when programming with shaders.

Attributes are input variables used in the vertex shader. For example, vertex coordinates, vertex colors, and so on. Due to the fact that the vertex shader is called on each vertex, the attributes will be *different* every time the vertex shader is invoked.

Uniforms are input variables available for both the vertex shader and fragment shader. Unlike attributes, *uniforms are constant during a rendering cycle*. For example, lights position.

Varyings are used for *passing data* from the vertex shader to the fragment shader.

Now let's create a simple geometric object.

Rendering geometry in WebGL

The following are the steps that we will follow in this section to render an object in WebGL:

1. First, we will define a geometry using JavaScript arrays.

2. Second, we will create the respective WebGL buffers.

3. Third, we will point a vertex shader attribute to the VBO that we created in the previous step to store vertex coordinates.

4. Finally, we will use the IBO to perform the rendering.

Defining a geometry using JavaScript arrays

Let's see what we need to do to create a trapezoid. We need two JavaScript arrays: one for the vertices and one for the indices.

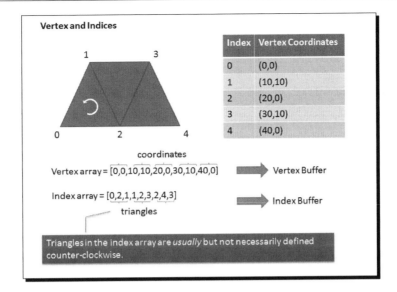

As you can see from the previous screenshot, we have placed the coordinates sequentially in the vertex array and then we have indicated in the index array how these coordinates are used to draw the trapezoid. So, the first triangle is formed with the vertices having indices 0, 1, and 2; the second with the vertices having indices 1, 2, and 3; and finally, the third, with vertices having indices 2, 3, and 4. We will follow the same procedure for all possible geometries.

Creating WebGL buffers

Once we have created the JavaScript arrays that define the vertices and indices for our geometry, the next step consists of creating the respective WebGL buffers. Let's see how this works with a different example. In this case, we have a simple square on the x-y plane (z coordinates are zero for all four vertices):

```
var vertices = [-50.0, 50.0, 0.0,
 -50.0,-50.0, 0.0,
 50.0,-50.0, 0.0,
 50.0, 50.0, 0.0];/* our JavaScript vertex array */
var myBuffer = gl.createBuffer(); /*gl is our WebGL Context*/
```

In the previous chapter, you may remember that WebGL operates as a state machine. Now, when myBuffer is made the *currently bound* WebGL buffer, this means that any subsequent buffer operation will be executed *on this buffer* until it is unbound or another buffer is made the current one with a bound call. We bind a buffer with the following instruction:

```
gl.bindBuffer(gl.ARRAY_BUFFER, myBuffer);
```

The first parameter is the type of buffer that we are creating. We have two options for this parameter:

- gl.ARRAY_BUFFER: Vertex data
- gl.ELEMENT_ARRAY_BUFFER: Index data

In the previous example, we are creating the buffer for vertex coordinates; therefore, we use ARRAY_BUFFER. For indices, the type ELEMENT_ARRAY_BUFFER is used.

> WebGL will always access the currently bound buffer looking for the data. Therefore, we should be careful and make sure that we have always bound a buffer before calling any other operation for geometry processing. If there is no buffer bound, then you will obtain the error INVALID_OPERATION

Once we have bound a buffer, we need to pass along its contents. We do this with the bufferData function:

```
gl.bufferData(gl.ARRAY_BUFFER, new Float32Array(vertices),
gl.STATIC_DRAW);
```

In this example, the vertices variable is a JavaScript array that contains the vertex coordinates. WebGL does not accept JavaScript arrays directly as a parameter for the bufferData method. Instead, WebGL uses **typed arrays**, so that the buffer data can be processed in its native binary form with the objective of speeding up geometry processing performance.

> The specification for typed arrays can be found at: http://www.khronos.org/registry/typedarray/specs/latest/

The typed arrays used by WebGL are Int8Array, Uint8Array, Int16Array, Uint16Array, Int32Array, UInt32Array, Float32Array, and Float64Array.

Please observe that vertex coordinates can be float, but indices are *always* integer. Therefore, we will use `Float32Array` for VBOs and `UInt16Array` for IBOs throughout the examples of this book. These two types represent the largest typed arrays that you can use in WebGL *per rendering call*. The other types can be or cannot be present in your browser, as this specification is not yet final at the time of writing the book.

Since the indices support in WebGL is restricted to 16 bit integers, an index array can only be 65,535 elements in length. If you have a geometry that requires more indices, you will need to use several rendering calls. More about rendering calls will be seen later on in the *Rendering* section of this chapter.

Finally, it is a good practice to unbind the buffer. We can achieve that by calling the following instruction:

```
gl.bindBuffer(gl.ARRAY_BUFFER, null);
```

We will repeat the same calls described here for every WebGL buffer (VBO or IBO) that we will use.

Let's review what we have just learned with an example. We are going to code the `initBuffers` function to create the VBO and IBO for a cone. (You will find this function in the file named `ch2_Cone.html`):

```
var coneVBO = null;   //Vertex Buffer Object
var coneIBO = null;   //Index Buffer Object
function initBuffers() {
  var vertices = [];   //JavaScript Array that populates coneVBO
  var indices  = [];   //JavaScript Array that populates coneIBO;
//Vertices that describe the geometry of a cone
  vertices =[1.5, 0, 0,
    -1.5, 1, 0,
    -1.5, 0.809017,  0.587785,
    -1.5, 0.309017,  0.951057,
    -1.5, -0.309017, 0.951057,
    -1.5, -0.809017, 0.587785,
    -1.5, -1, 0.0,
    -1.5, -0.809017, -0.587785,
    -1.5, -0.309017, -0.951057,
    -1.5, 0.309017,  -0.951057,
    -1.5, 0.809017,  -0.587785];
//Indices that describe the geometry of a cone
  indices = [0, 1, 2,
    0, 2, 3,
    0, 3, 4,
```

```
       0, 4, 5,
       0, 5, 6,
       0, 6, 7,
       0, 7, 8,
       0, 8, 9,
       0, 9, 10,
       0, 10, 1];
   coneVBO = gl.createBuffer();
   gl.bindBuffer(gl.ARRAY_BUFFER, coneVBO);
   gl.bufferData(gl.ARRAY_BUFFER, new Float32Array(vertices),
    gl.STATIC_DRAW);
   gl.bindBuffer(gl.ARRAY_BUFFER, null);
   coneIBO = gl.createBuffer();
   gl.bindBuffer(gl.ELEMENT_ARRAY_BUFFER, coneIBO);
   gl.bufferData(gl.ELEMENT_ARRAY_BUFFER, new Uint16Array(indices),
    gl.STATIC_DRAW);
   gl.bindBuffer(gl.ELEMENT_ARRAY_BUFFER, null);
}
```

If you want to see this scene in action, launch the file ch2_Cone.html in your HTML5 browser.

To summarize, for every buffer, we want to:

◆ Create a new buffer

◆ Bind it to make it the current buffer

◆ Pass the buffer data using one of the typed arrays

◆ Unbind the buffer

Operations to manipulate WebGL buffers

The operations to manipulate WebGL buffers are summarized in the following table:

Method	Description
var aBuffer = createBuffer(void)	Creates the aBuffer buffer
deleteBuffer(Object aBuffer)	Deletes the aBuffer buffer
bindBuffer(ulong target, Object buffer)	Binds a buffer object. The accepted values for target are: ◆ ARRAY_BUFFER (for vertices) ◆ ELEMENT_ARRAY_BUFFER (for indices)

Method	Description
`bufferData(ulong target, Object data, ulong type)`	The accepted values for `target` are: ◆ `ARRAY_BUFFER` (for vertices) ◆ `ELEMENT_ARRAY_BUFFER`(for indices) The parameter `type` is a performance hint for WebGL. The accepted values for `type` are: ◆ `STATIC_DRAW`: Data in the buffer will not be changed (specified once and used many times) `DYNAMIC_DRAW`: Data will be changed frequently (specified many times and used many times) ◆ `STREAM_DRAW`: Data will change on every rendering cycle (specified once and used once)

Associating attributes to VBOs

Once the VBOs have been created, we associate these buffers to vertex shader attributes. Each vertex shader attribute will refer to *one and only one* buffer, depending on the correspondence that is established, as shown in the following diagram:

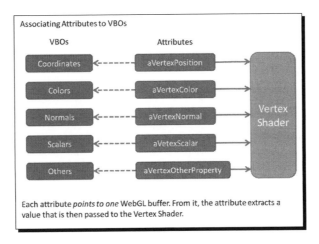

We can achieve this by following these steps:

1. First, we bind a VBO.

2. Next, we point an attribute to the currently bound VBO.

3. Finally, we enable the attribute.

Let's take a look at the first step.

Binding a VBO

We already know how to do this:

```
gl.bindBuffer(gl.ARRAY_BUFFER, myBuffer);
```

where `myBuffer` is the buffer we want to map.

Pointing an attribute to the currently bound VBO

In the next chapter, we will learn to define vertex shader attributes. For now, let's assume that we have the `aVertexPosition` attribute and that it will represent vertex coordinates inside the vertex shader.

The WebGL function that allows pointing attributes to the currently bound VBOs is `vertexAttribPointer`. The following is its signature:

```
gl.vertexAttribPointer(Index,Size,Type,Norm,Stride,Offset);
```

Let us describe each parameter individually:

◆ **Index**: An attribute's index that we are going to map the currently bound buffer to.

◆ **Size**: Indicates the number of values per vertex that are stored in the currently bound buffer.

◆ **Type**: Specifies the data type of the values stored in the current buffer. It is one of the following constants: FIXED, BYTE, UNSIGNED_BYTE, FLOAT, SHORT, or UNSIGNED_SHORT.

◆ **Norm**: This parameter can be set to true or false. It handles numeric conversions that lie out of the scope of this introductory guide. For all practical effects, we will set this parameter to *false*.

◆ **Stride**: If stride is zero, then we are indicating that elements are stored sequentially in the buffer.

◆ **Offset**: The position in the buffer from which we will start reading values for the corresponding attribute. It is usually set to zero to indicate that we will start reading values from the first element of the buffer.

`vertexAttribPointer` defines a pointer for reading information *from the currently bound buffer*. Remember that an error will be generated if there is no VBO currently bound.

Enabling the attribute

Finally, we just need to activate the vertex shader attribute. Following our example, we just need to add:

```
gl.enableVertexAttribArray (aVertexPosition);
```

The following diagram summarizes the mapping procedure:

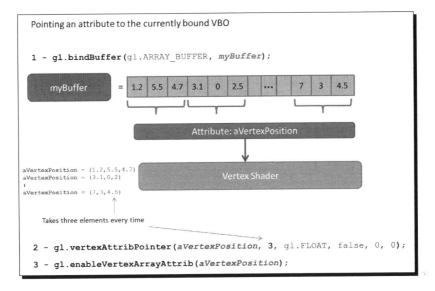

Rendering

Once we have defined our VBOs and we have mapped them to the corresponding vertex shader attributes, we are ready to render!

To do this, we use can use one of the two API functions: `drawArrays` or `drawElements`.

The drawArrays and drawElements functions

The functions `drawArrays` and `drawElements` are used for writing on the framebuffer.

`drawArrays` uses vertex data in the order in which it is defined in the buffer to create the geometry. In contrast, `drawElements` uses indices to access the vertex data buffers and create the geometry.

Both `drawArrays` and `drawElements` will only use **enabled arrays**. These are the *vertex buffer objects that are mapped to active vertex shader attributes.*

In our example, we only have one enabled array: the buffer that contains the vertex coordinates. However, in a more general scenario, *we can have several enabled arrays.* For instance, we can have arrays with information about vertex colors, vertex normals texture coordinates, and any other per-vertex data required by the application. In this case, each one of them would be mapped to an active vertex shader attribute.

Using several VBOs

In the next chapter, we will see how we use a vertex normal buffer in addition to vertex coordinates to create a lighting model for our geometry. In that scenario, we will have two active arrays: vertex coordinates and vertex normals.

Using drawArrays

We will call `drawArrays` when information about indices is not available. In most cases, `drawArrays` is used when the geometry is so simple that defining indices is an overkill; for instance, when we want to render a triangle or a rectangle. In that case, WebGL will create the geometry *in the order in which the vertex coordinates are defined in the VBO.* So if you have contiguous triangles (like in our trapezoid example), you will have to repeat these coordinates in the VBO.

If you need to repeat a lot of vertices to create geometry, probably `drawArrays` is not the best way to go. The more vertex data you duplicate, the more calls you will have on the vertex shader. This could reduce the overall application performance since the same vertices have to go through the pipeline several times. One for each time that they appear repeated in the respective VBO.

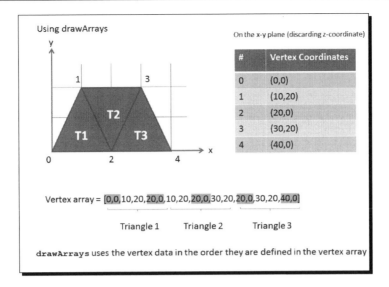

The signature for drawArrays is:

```
gl.drawArrays(Mode, First, Count)
```

Where:

- **Mode**: Represents the type of primitive that we are going to render. Possible values for mode are: gl.POINTS, gl.LINE_STRIP, gl.LINE_LOOP, gl.LINES, gl.TRIANGLE_STRIP, gl.TRIANGLE_FAN, and gl.TRIANGLES (more about this in the next section).

- **First**: Specifies the starting element in the enabled arrays.

- **Count**: The number of elements to be rendered.

From the WebGL specification:

"When drawArrays is called, it uses *count* sequential elements from each enabled array to construct a sequence of geometric primitives, beginning with the element *first*. *Mode* specifies what kinds of primitives are constructed and how the array elements construct those primitives."

Using drawElements

Unlike the previous case where no IBO was defined, `drawElements` allows us to use the IBO, to tell WebGL how to render the geometry. Remember that `drawArrays` *uses VBOs*. This means that the vertex shader will process repeated vertices as many times as they appear in the VBO. Contrastingly, `drawElements` uses indices. Therefore, vertices are processed just once, and can be used as many times as they are defined in the IBO. This feature reduces both the memory and processing required on the GPU.

Let's revisit the following diagram of this chapter:

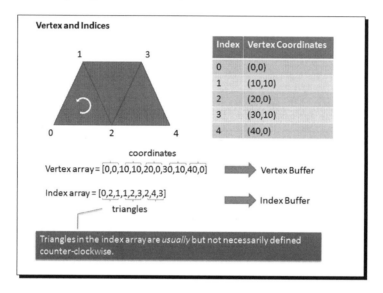

When we use `drawElements`, we need at least two buffers: a VBO and an IBO. The vertex shader will get executed on each vertex in the VBO and then the rendering pipeline will assemble the geometry into triangles using the IBO.

 When using `drawElements`, you need to make sure that the corresponding IBO is currently bound.

The signature for `drawElements` is:

```
gl.drawElements(Mode, Count, Type, Offset)
```

Where:

- **Mode**: Represents the type of primitive that we are going to render. Possible values for mode are `POINTS`, `LINE_STRIP`, `LINE_LOOP`, `LINES`, `TRIANGLE_STRIP`, `TRIANGLE_FAN`, and `TRIANGLES` (more about this later on).

- **Count**: Specifies the number of elements to be rendered.

- **Type**: Specifies the type of the values in indices. Must be `UNSIGNED_BYTE` or `UNSIGNED_SHORT`, as we are handling indices (integer numbers).

- **Offset**: Indicates which element in the buffer will be the starting point for rendering. It is usually the first element (zero value).

WebGL inherits without any change this function from the OpenGL ES 2.0 specification. The following applies:

"When `drawElements` is called, it uses *count* sequential elements from an enabled array, starting at *offset* to construct a sequence of geometric primitives. *Mode* specifies what kinds of primitives are constructed and how the array elements construct these primitives. If more than one array is enabled, each is used."

Putting everything together

I guess you have been waiting to see how everything works together. Let's start with some code. Let's create a simple WebGL program to render a square.

Time for action – rendering a square

Follow the given steps:

1. Open the file `ch_Square.html` in your favorite HTML editor (ideally one that supports syntax highlighting like Notepad++ or Crimson Editor).

2. Let's examine the structure of this file with the help of the following diagram:

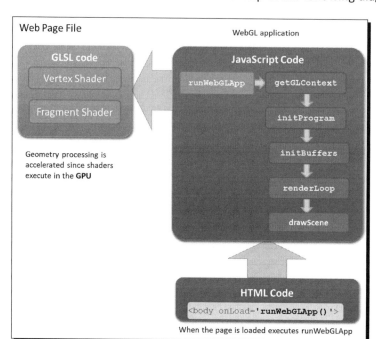

3. The web page contains the following:

- ❑ The script `<script id="shader-fs" type="x-shader/x-fragment">` contains the fragment shader code.

- ❑ The script `<script id="shader-vs" type="x-shader/x-vertex">` contains the vertex shader code. We will not be paying attention to these two scripts as these will be the main point of study in the next chapter. For now, let's notice that we have a fragment shader and a vertex shader.

- ❑ The next script on our web page `<script id="code-js" type="text/javascript">` contains all the JavaScript WebGL code that we will need. This script is divided into the following functions:

❑ **getGLContext**: Similar to the function that we saw in the previous chapter, this function allows us to get a WebGL context for the canvas present in the web page (ch_Square.html).

❑ **initProgram**: This function obtains a reference for the vertex shader and the fragment shader present in the web page (the first two scripts that we discussed) and passes them along to the GPU to be compiled. More about this in the next chapter.

❑ **initBuffers**: Let's take a close look at this function. It contains the API calls to create buffers and to initialize them. In this example, we will be creating a VBO to store coordinates for the square and an IBO to store the indices of the square.

❑ **renderLoop**: This function creates the rendering loop. The application invokes renderLoop periodically to update the scene (using the requestAnimFrame function).

❑ **drawScene**: This function maps the VBO to the respective vertex buffer attribute and enables it by calling enableVertexAttribArray. It then binds the IBO and calls the drawElements function.

❑ Finally, we get to the <body> tag of our web page. Here we invoke runWebGLApp the main function, ,which is executed by the standard JavaScript onLoad event of the *DOM document* with the following instruction:

```
<body onLoad='runWebGLApp()'>
```

4. Open the file ch2_Square.html in the HTML5 browser of your preference (Firefox, Safari, Chrome, or Opera).

5. You will see four tabs showing the code of: **WebGL JS** (JavaScript), **Vertex Shader**, **Fragment Shader**, and **HTML**. You will always need these four elements in your web page to write a WebGL app.

6. If the **WebGL JS** tab is not active, select it.

7. Scroll down to the `initBuffers` function. Please pay attention to the diagram that appears as a comment before the function. This diagram describes how the vertices and indices are organized. You should see something like the following screenshot:

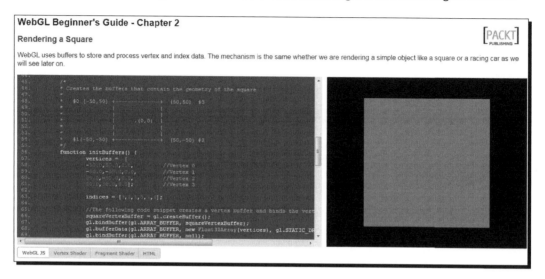

8. Go back to the text editor. If you have closed `ch_Square.html`, open it again.

9. Go to the `initBuffers` function.

10. Modify the buffer array and index array so that the resulting figure is a pentagon instead of a square. To do this, you need to add one vertex to the vertex array and define one more triangle in the index array.

11. Save the file with a different name and open it in the HTML5 browser of your preference to test it.

What just happened?

You have learned about the different code elements that conform to a WebGL app. The `initBufferrs` function has been examined and modified for rendering a different figure.

Have a go hero – changing the square color

Go to the **Fragment Shader** and change the color of your pentagon.

 The format is (red, green, blue, alpha). Alpha is always 1.0 (for now), and the first three arguments are float numbers in the range 0.0 to 1.0.

Remember to save the file after making the changes in your text editor and then open it in the HTML5 browser of your preference to see the changes.

Rendering modes

Let's revisit the signature of the `drawElements` function:

```
gl.drawElements(Mode, Count, Type, Offset)
```

The first parameter determines the type of primitives that we are rendering. In the following time for action section, we are going to see with examples the different rendering modes.

Time for action – rendering modes

Follow the given steps:

1. Open the file `ch_RenderingModes.html` in the HTML5 browser of your preference. This example follows the same structure as discussed in the previous section.

2. Select the **WebGL JS** button and scroll down to the `initBuffer` function.

3. You will see here that we are drawing a trapezoid. However, on screen you will see two triangles! We will see how we did this later.

4. At the bottom of the page, there is a combobox that allows you to select the different rendering modes that WebGL provides, as shown in the following screenshot:

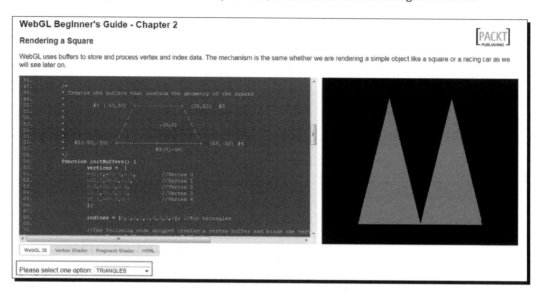

5. When you select any option from this combobox, you are changing the value of the `renderingMode` variable defined at the top of the **WebGL JS** code (scroll up if you want to see where it is defined).

6. To see how each option modifies the rendering, scroll down to the `drawScene` function.

7. You will see there that after binding the IBO `trapezoidIndexBuffer` with the following instruction:

```
gl.bindBuffer(gl.ELEMENT_ARRAY_BUFFER, trapezoidIndexBuffer);
```

you have a switch statement where there is a code that executes, depending on the value of the `renderingMode` variable:

```
case 'TRIANGLES': {
...
}
case 'LINES': {
...
}
case'POINTS': {
...
}
```

8. For each mode, you define the contents of the JavaScript array indices. Then, you pass this array to the currently-bound buffer (`trapezoidIndexBuffer`) by using the `bufferData` function. Finally, you call the `drawElements` function.

9. Let's see what each mode does:

Mode	Example	Description
TRIANGLES		When you use the TRIANGLES mode, WebGL will use the first three indices defined in your IBO for constructing the first triangle, the next three for constructing the second triangle, and so on. In this example, we are drawing two triangles, which can be verified by examining the following `indices` JavaScript array that populates the IBO: `indices = [0,1,2,2,3,4];`
LINES		The LINES mode will instruct WebGL to take each consecutive pair of indices defined in the IBO and draw lines taking the coordinates of the corresponding vertices. For instance `indices = [1,3,0,4,1,2,2,3];` will draw four lines: from vertex number 1 to vertex number 3, from vertex number 0 to vertex number 4, from vertex number 1 to vertex number 2, and from vertex number 2 to vertex number 3.
POINTS		When we use the POINTS mode, WebGL will not generate surfaces. Instead, it will render the vertices that we had defined using the index array. In this example, we will only render vertices number 1, number 2, and number 3 with `indices = [1,2,3];`

Mode	Example	Description
LINE_LOOP	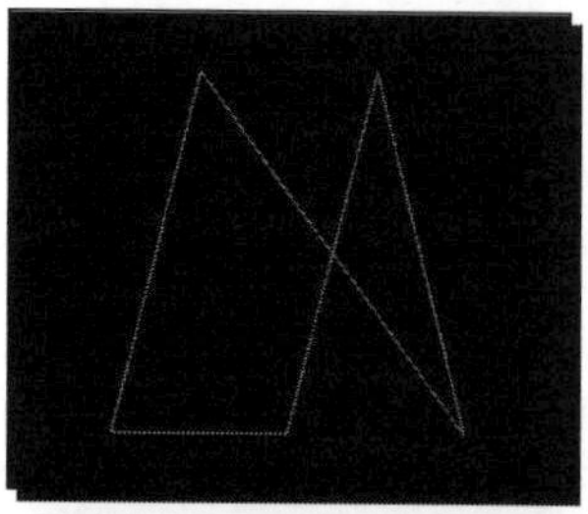	LINE_LOOP draws a closed loop connecting the vertices defined in the IBO to the next one. In our case, it will be indices = [2,3,4,1,0];
LINE_STRIP		It is similar to LINE_LOOP. The difference here is that WebGL does not connect the last vertex to the first one (not a closed loop). The indices JavaScript array will be indices = [2,3,4,1,0];
TRIANGLE_STRIP		TRIANGLE_STRIP draws connected triangles. Every vertex specified after the first three (in our example, vertices number 0, number 1, and number 2) creates a new triangle. If we have indices = [0,1,2,3,4];, then we will generate the triangles: (0,1,2) , (1,2,3), and (2,3,4).
TRIANGLE_FAN		TRIANGLE_FAN creates triangles in a similar way to TRIANGLE_STRIP. However, the first vertex defined in the IBO is taken as the origin of the fan (the only shared vertex among consecutive triangles). In our example, indices = [0,1,2,3,4]; will create the triangles: (0,1,2) and (0,3,4).

Now let's make some changes:

10. Edit the web page (ch_RenderingModes.html) so that when you select the option TRIANGLES, you render the trapezoid instead of two triangles.

You need one extra triangle in the `indices` array.

11. Save the file and test it in the HTML5 browser of your preference.

12. Edit the web page so that you draw the letter 'M' using the option `LINES`.

 You need to define four lines in the `indices` array.

13. Just like before, save your changes and test them in your HTML5 browser.

14. Using the `LINE_LOOP` mode, draw only the boundary of the trapezoid.

What just happened?

We have seen in action through a simple exercise the different rendering modes supported by WebGL. The different rendering modes determine how to interpret vertex and index data to render an object.

WebGL as a state machine: buffer manipulation

There is some information about the state of the rendering pipeline that we can retrieve when we are dealing with buffers with the functions: `getParameter`, `getBufferParameter`, and `isBuffer`.

Just like we did in the previous chapter, we will use `getParameter(parameter)` where parameter can have the following values:

◆ `ARRAY_BUFFER_BINDING`: It retrieves a reference to the currently-bound VBO

◆ `ELEMENT_ARRAY_BUFFER_BINDING`: It retrieves a reference to the currently-bound IBO

Also, we can enquire about the size and the usage of the currently-bound VBO and IBO using `getBufferParameter(type, parameter)` where `type` can have the following values:

◆ `ARRAY_BUFFER`: To refer to the currently bound VBO

◆ `ELEMENT_ARRAY_BUFFER`: To refer to the currently bound IBO

And `parameter` can be:

- ♦ `BUFFER_SIZE`: Returns the size of the requested buffer
- ♦ `BUFFER_USAGE`: Returns the usage of the requested buffer

 Your VBO and/or IBO needs to be bound when you enquire about the state of the currently bound VBO and/or IBO with `getParameter` and `getBufferParameter`.

Finally, `isBuffer(object)` will return `true` if the `object` is a WebGL buffer, `false`, when the buffer is invalid, and an error if the `object` being evaluated is not a WebGL buffer. Unlike `getParameter` and `getBufferParameter`, `isBuffer` does not require any VBO or IBO to be bound.

Time for action – enquiring on the state of buffers

Follow the given steps:

1. Open the file `ch2_StateMachine.html` in the HTML5 browser of your preference.

2. Scroll down to the `initBuffers` method. You will see something similar to the following screenshot:

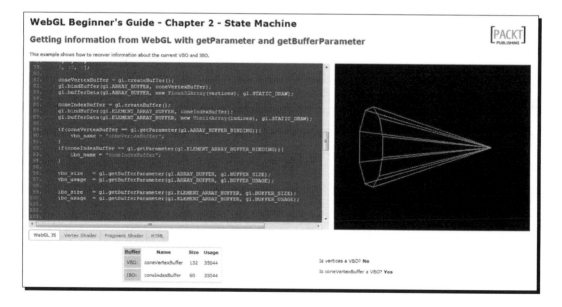

3. Pay attention to how we use the methods discussed in this section to retrieve and display information about the current state of the buffers.

4. The information queried by the `initBuffer` function is shown at the bottom portion of the web page using `updateInfo` (if you look closely at `runWebGLApp` code you will see that `updateInfo` is called right after calling `initBuffers`).

5. At the bottom of the web page (scroll down the web page if necessary), you will see the following result:

Buffer	Name	Size	Usage
VBO:	coneVertexBuffer	132	35044
IBO:	coneIndexBuffer	60	35044

Is vertices a VBO? **No**

Is coneVertexBuffer a VBO? **Yes**

6. Now, open the same file (`ch2_StateMachine.html`) in a text editor.

7. Cut the line:

```
gl.bindBuffer(gl.ARRAY_BUFFER,null);
```

and paste it right before the line:

```
coneIndexBuffer = gl.createBuffer();
```

8. What happens when you launch the page in your browser again?

9. Why do you think this behavior occurs?

What just happened?

You have learned that the currently bound buffer is a state variable in WebGL. The buffer is bound until you unbind it by calling `bindBuffer` again with the corresponding type (`ARRAY_BUFFER` or `ELEMENT_ARRAY_BUFFER`) as the first parameter and with `null` as the second argument (that is, no buffer to bind). You have also learned that you can only query the state of the *currently bound* buffer. Therefore, if you want to query a different buffer, you need to bind it first.

Have a go hero – add one validation

Modify the file so that you can validate and show on screen whether the `indices` array and the `coneIndexBuffer` are WebGL buffers or not.

You will have to modify the table in the HTML body of the file to allocate space for the new validations.

You will have to modify the `updateInfo` function accordingly.

Advanced geometry loading techniques: JavaScript Object Notation (JSON) and AJAX

So far, we have rendered very simple objects. Now let's study a way to load the geometry (vertices and indices) from a file instead of declaring the vertices and the indices every time we call `initBuffers`. To achieve this, we will make asynchronous calls to the web server using AJAX. We will retrieve the file with our geometry from the web server and then we will use the built-in JSON parser to convert the context of our files into JavaScript objects. In our case, these objects will be the `vertices` and `indices` array.

Introduction to JSON – JavaScript Object Notation

JSON stands for **JavaScript Object Notation**. It is a lightweight, text-based, open format used for data interchange. JSON is commonly used as an alternative to XML.

The *JSON format* is language-agnostic. This means that there are parsers in many languages to read and interpret JSON objects. Also, JSON is a subset of the object literal notation of JavaScript. Therefore, we can define JavaScript objects using JSON.

Defining JSON-based 3D models

Let's see how this work. Assume for example that we have the `model` object with two arrays `vertices` and `indices` (does this ring any bells?). Say that these arrays contain the information described in the cone example (`ch2_Cone.html`) as follows:

```
vertices =[1.5, 0, 0,
    -1.5, 1, 0,
    -1.5, 0.809017,  0.587785,
    -1.5, 0.309017,  0.951057,
    -1.5, -0.309017, 0.951057,
    -1.5, -0.809017, 0.587785,
    -1.5, -1, 0,
    -1.5, -0.809017, -0.587785,
    -1.5, -0.309017, -0.951057,
    -1.5, 0.309017,  -0.951057,
    -1.5, 0.809017,  -0.587785];
indices = [0, 1, 2,
```

```
            0, 2, 3,
            0, 3, 4,
            0, 4, 5,
            0, 5, 6,
            0, 6, 7,
            0, 7, 8,
            0, 8, 9,
            0, 9, 10,
            0, 10, 1];
```

Following the JSON notation, we would represent these two arrays as an object, as follows:

```
var model = {
"vertices" : [1.5, 0, 0,
  -1.5, 1, 0,
  -1.5, 0.809017,  0.587785,
  -1.5, 0.309017,  0.951057,
  -1.5, -0.309017, 0.951057,
  -1.5, -0.809017, 0.587785,
  -1.5, -1, 0,
  -1.5, -0.809017, -0.587785,
  -1.5, -0.309017, -0.951057,
  -1.5, 0.309017,  -0.951057,
  -1.5, 0.809017,  -0.587785],
"indices" : [0, 1, 2,
  0, 2, 3,
  0, 3, 4,
  0, 4, 5,
  0, 5, 6,
  0, 6, 7,
  0, 7, 8,
  0, 8, 9,
  0, 9, 10,
  0, 10, 1] };
```

From the previous example, we can infer the following syntax rules:

- The extent of a JSON object is defined by curly brackets {}
- Attributes in a JSON object are separated by comma ,
- There is no comma after the last attribute
- Each attribute of a JSON object has two parts: a **key** and a **value**
- The name of an attribute is enclosed by quotation marks " "

- ◆ Each attribute key is separated from its corresponding value with a colon :
- ◆ Attributes of the type `Array` are defined in the same way you would define them in JavaScript

JSON encoding and decoding

Most modern web browsers support native JSON encoding and decoding through the built-in JavaScript object `JSON`. Let's examine the methods available inside this object:

Method	Description
`var myText = JSON.stringify(myObject)`	We use `JSON.stringify` for converting JavaScript objects to JSON-formatted text.
`var myObject = JSON.parse(myText)`	We use `JSON.parse` for converting text into JavaScript objects.

Let's learn how to encode and decode with the JSON notation.

Time for action – JSON encoding and decoding

Let's create a simple model: a 3D line. Here we will be focusing on how we do JSON encoding and decoding. Follow the given steps:

1. Go to your Internet browser and open the interactive JavaScript console. Use the following table for assistance:

Web browser	Menu option	Shortcut keys (PC / Mac)
Firefox	**Tools	Web Developer	Web Console**	*Ctrl + Shift + K / Command + Alt + K*
Safari	**Develop	Show Web Inspector**	*Ctrl + Shift + C / Command + Alt + C*
Chrome	**Tools	JavaScript Console**	*Ctrl + Shift + J / Command + Alt + J*

2. Create a JSON object by typing:
    ```
    var model = {"vertices":[0,0,0,1,1,1], "indices":[0,1]};
    ```

3. Verify that the `model` is an object by writing:
    ```
    typeof(model)
    ```

4. Now, let's print the `model` attributes. Write this in the console (press *Enter* at the end of each line):
    ```
    model.vertices
    model.indices
    ```

5. Now, let's create a JSON text:

```
var text = JSON.stringify(model)
alert(text)
```

6. What happens when you type `text.vertices`?

As you can see, you get an error message saying that `text.vertices` is not defined. This happens because text is not a JavaScript object but a string with the peculiarity of being written according to JSON notation to describe an object. Everything in it is text and therefore it does not have any fields.

7. Now let's convert the JSON text back to an object. Type the following:

```
var model2 = JSON.parse(text)
typeof(model2)
model2.vertices
```

What just happened?

We have learned to encode and decode JSON objects. The example that we have used is relevant because this is the way we will define our geometry to be loaded from external files. In the next section, we will see how to download geometric models specified with JSON from a web server.

Asynchronous loading with AJAX

The following diagram summarizes the asynchronous loading of files by the web browser using AJAX:

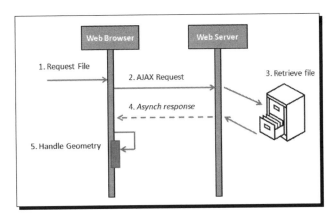

Let's analyze this more closely:

1. **Request file**: First of all, we should indicate the filename that we want to load. Remember that this file contains the geometry that we will be loading from the web server instead of coding the JavaScript arrays (vertices and indices) directly into the web page.

2. **AJAX request**: We need to write a function that will perform the AJAX request. Let's call this function `loadFile`. The code can look like this:

```
function loadFile(name) {
  var request = new XMLHttpRequest();
  var resource = http:// + document.domain + name;
  request.open("GET",resource);
  request.onreadystatechange = function() {
    if (request.readyState == 4) {
      if(request.status == 200 || (request.status == 0 &&
       document.domain.length == 0) {
      handleLoadedGeometry(name,JSON.parse(request.responseText));
       }
      else {
        alert ('There was a problem loading the file :' + name);
        alert ('HTML error code: ' + request.status);
      }
    }
  }
  request.send();
}
```

If the `readyState` is `4`, it means that the file has finished downloading.

More about this function later. Let's say for now that this function will perform the AJAX request.

3. **Retrieve file**: The web server will receive and treat our request as a regular HTTP request. As a matter of fact, the server does not know that this request is *asynchronous* (it is asynchronous for the web browser as it does not wait for the answer). The server will look for our file and whether it finds it or not, it will generate a response. This will take us to step 4.

4. **Asynchronous response**: Once a response is sent to the web browser, the callback specified in the `loadFile` function is invoked. This callback corresponds to the request method `onreadystatechange`. This method examines the answer. If we obtain a status different from `200` (OK according to the HTTP specification), it means that there was a problem. Hopefully the specific error code that we get on the status variable (instead of `200`) can give us a clue about the error. For instance, code `404` means that the resource does not exist. In that case, you would need to

check if there is a typo, or you are requesting a file from a directory different from the directory where the page is located on the web server. Different error codes will give you different alternatives to treat the respective problem. Now if we get a 200 status, we can invoke the handleLoadedGeometry function.

 There is an exception where things can work, even if you do not have a web server. If you are running the example from your computer, the ready state will be 4 but the request status will be 0. This is a valid configuration too.

5. **Handling the loaded model**: In order to keep our code looking pretty, we can create a new function to process the file retrieved from the server. Let's call this handleLoadedGeometry function. Please notice that in the previous segment of code, we used the JSON parser in order to create a JavaScript object from the file before passing it along to the handleLoadedGeometry function. This object corresponds to the second argument (model) as we can see here. The code for the handleLoadedGeometry function looks like this:

```
function handleLoadedGeometry(name,model){
  alert(name + ' has been retrieved from the server');
  modelVertexBuffer = gl.createBuffer();
  gl.bindBuffer(gl.ARRAY_BUFFER, modelVertexBuffer);
  gl.bufferData(gl.ARRAY_BUFFER, new Float32Array(model.vertices),
   gl.STATIC_DRAW);
  modelIndexBuffer = gl.createBuffer();
  gl.bindBuffer(gl.ELEMENT_ARRAY_BUFFER, modelIndexBuffer);
  gl.bufferData(gl.ELEMENT_ARRAY_BUFFER,
   new Uint16Array(model.indices), gl.STATIC_DRAW);
  gl.bindBuffer(gl.ELEMENT_ARRAY_BUFFER, null);
  gl.bindBuffer(gl.ARRAY_BUFFER,null);
}
```

If you look closely, this function is very similar to one of our functions that we saw previously: the initBuffers function. This makes sense because we cannot initialize the buffers until we retrieve the geometry data from the server. Just like initBuffers, we bind our VBO and IBO and pass them the information contained in the JavaScript arrays of our model object.

Setting up a web server

If you *do not* have a web server, we recommend you install a lightweight web server such as lighttpd (http://www.lighttpd.net/).

Please note that if you are using Windows:

1. The installer can be found at `http://en.wlmp-project.net/downloads.php?cat=lighty`

2. Once installed, you should go to the subfolder `bin` and double-click on `Service-Install.exe` to install lighttpd as a Windows service.

3. You should copy Chapter 2's exercises in the subfolder `htdocs` or change *lighttpd's configuration file* to point to *your working directory* (which is the one you have used to run the examples so far).

4. To be able to edit `server.document-root` in the file `conf/lighttpd-inc.conf` you need to run a console with administrative privileges.

Working around the web server requirement

If you have Firefox and do not want to install a web server, you can change `strict_origin_policy` to `false` in `about:config`.

If you are using Chrome and do not want to install a web server, make sure you run it from the command line with the following modifier:

`--allow-file-access-from-files`

Let's use AJAX + JSON to load a cone from our web server.

Time for action – loading a cone with AJAX + JSON

Follow the given steps:

1. Make sure that your web server is running and access the file `ch2_AJAXJSON.html` using your web server.

 You know you are using the web server if the URL in the address bar starts with `localhost/...` instead of `file://...`

2. The folder where you have the code for this chapter should look like this:

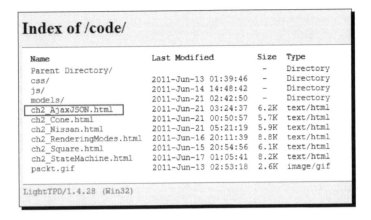

3. Click on `ch2_AjaxJSON.html`.

4. The example will load in your browser and you will see something similar to this:

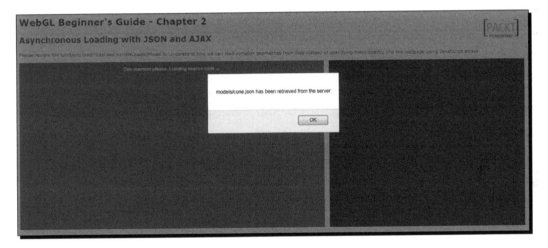

5. When you click on the JavaScript alert, you will see:

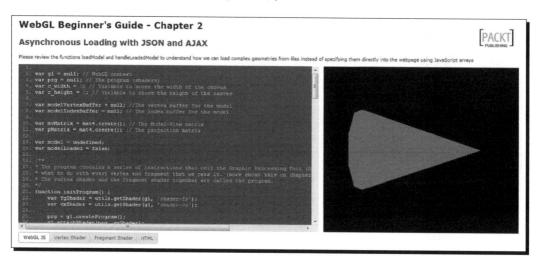

6. As the page says, please review the functions `loadModel` and `handleLoadedModel` to better understand the use of AJAX and JSON in the application.

7. What does the `modelLoaded` variable do? (check the source code).

8. See what happens when you change the color in the file `models/cone.json` and reload the page.

9. Modify the coordinates of the cone in the file `models/cone.json` and reload the page. Here you can verify that WebGL reads and renders the coordinates from the file. If you modify them in the file, the geometry will be updated on the screen.

What just happened?

You learned about using AJAX and JSON to load geometries from a remote location (web server) instead of specifying these geometries (using JavaScript arrays) inside the web page.

Have a go hero – loading a Nissan GTX

Follow the given steps:

1. Open the file `ch2_Nissan.html` using your web server. Again, you should see something like `http://localhost./.../code`

2. You should see something like this:

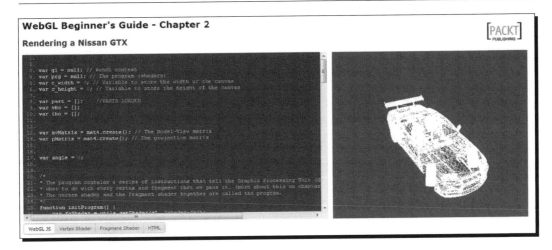

WebGL Beginner's Guide - Chapter 2

Rendering a Nissan GTX

3. The reason we selected the mode LINES instead of the model TRIANGLES (explained previously in this chapter) is to visualize better the structure of this car.

4. Find the line where the rendering mode is being selected and make sure you understand what the code does.

5. Next, go to the drawScene function.

6. In the drawElements instruction, change the mode from gl.LINES to gl.TRIANGLES.

7. Refresh the page in the web browser (*Ctrl + F5* for full refresh).

8. What do you see? Can you hypothesize about the reasons for this? What is your rationale?

When the geometry is complex, the lighting model allows us to visualize it better. Without lights, all our volumes will look opaque and it would be difficult to distinguish their parts (just as in the previous case) when changing from LINES to TRIANGLES.

In the next chapter, we will see how to create a lighting model for our scene. Our work there will be focused on the shaders and how we communicate information back and forth between the WebGL JavaScript API and the attributes, uniforms, and varyings. Do you remember them? We mentioned when we were talking about passing information to the GPU.

Summary

In this chapter, we have discussed how WebGL renders geometry. Remember that there are two kinds of WebGL buffers that deal with geometry rendering: VBOs and IBOs.

WebGL's rendering pipeline describes how the WebGL buffers are used and passed in the form of attributes to be processed by the vertex shader. The vertex shader parallelizes vertex processing in the GPU. Vertices define the surface of the geometry that is going to be rendered. Every element on this surface is known as a fragment. These fragments are processed by the fragment shader. Fragment processing also occurs in parallel in the GPU. When all the fragments have been processed, the framebuffer, a two-dimensional array, contains the image that is then displayed on your screen.

WebGL works as a state machine. As such, properties referring to buffers are available and their values will be dependent on the buffer currently bound.

We also saw that JSON and AJAX are two JavaScript technologies that integrate really well with WebGL, enabling us to load really complex geometries without having to specify them inside our webpage.

In the next chapter, we will learn more about the vertex and fragment shaders and we will see how we can use them to implement light sources in our WebGL scene.

3
Lights!

In WebGL, we make use of the vertex and fragment shaders to create a lighting model for our scene. Shaders allow us to define a mathematical model that governs how our scene is lit. We will study different algorithms and see examples about their implementation.

A basic knowledge of linear algebra will be really useful to help you understand the contents of this chapter. We will use glMatrix, a JavaScript library that handles most of the vector and matrix operation, so you do not need to worry about the details. Nonetheless, it is paramount to have a conceptual understanding of the linear algebra operations that we will discuss.

In this chapter, we will:

- Learn about light sources, normals, and materials
- Learn the difference between shading and lighting
- Use the Goraud and Phong shading methods, and the Lambertian and Phong lighting models
- Define and use uniforms, attributes, and varyings
- Work with ESSL, the shading language for WebGL
- Discuss relevant WebGL API methods that relate to shaders
- Continue our analysis of WebGL as a state machine and describe the attributes relevant to shaders that can be set and retrieved from the state machine

Lights, normals, and materials

In the real world, we see objects because they reflect light. Any object will reflect light depending on the position and relative distance to the light source; the orientation of its surface, which is represented by normal vectors and the material of the object which determines how much light is reflected. In this chapter, we will learn how to combine these three elements in WebGL to model different illumination schemes.

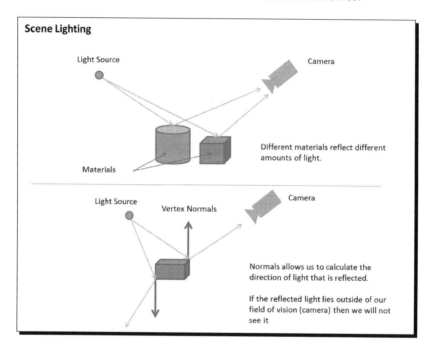

Lights

Light sources can be *positional* or *directional*. A light source is called positional when its location will affect how the scene is lit. For instance, a lamp inside a room falls under this category. Objects far from the lamp will receive very little light and they will appear obscure. In contrast, directional lights refer to lights that produce the same result independent from their position. For example, the light of the sun will illuminate all the objects in a terrestrial scene, regardless of their distance from the sun.

A **positional light** is modeled by a point in space, while a **directional light** is modeled with a vector that indicates its direction. It is common to use a normalized vector for this purpose, given that this simplifies mathematical operations.

Normals

Normals are vectors that are perpendicular to the surface that we want to illuminate. Normals represent the orientation of the surface and therefore they are critical to model the interaction between a light source and the object. *Each vertex has an associated normal vector.*

We make use of a cross product for calculating normals.

[**Cross Product:**
By definition, the cross product of vectors A and B will be perpendicular to both vectors A and B.]

Let's break this down. If we have the triangle conformed by vertices `p0`, `p1`, and `p2`, then we can define the vector `v1` as `p2-p1` and the vector `v2` as `p0-p1`. Then the normal is obtained by calculating the cross product `v1 x v2`. Graphically, this procedure looks something like the following:

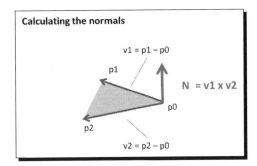

Then we repeat the same calculation for each vertex on each triangle. But, what about the vertices that are shared by more than one triangle? The answer is that each shared vertex normal will receive a contribution from each of the triangles in which the vertex appears.

For example, say that the vertex `p1` is being shared by triangles #1 and #2, and we have already calculated the normals for the vertices of triangle #1. Then, we need to update the `p1` normal by adding up the calculated normal for `p1` on triangle #2. This is a **vector sum**. Graphically, this looks similar to the following:

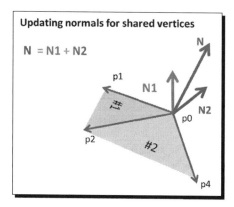

Similar to lights, normals are usually normalized to facilitate mathematical operations.

Materials

The material of an object in WebGL can be modeled by several parameters, including its color and its texture. Material colors are usually modeled as triplets in the RGB space (Red, Green, Blue). Textures, on the other hand, correspond to images that are mapped to the surface of the object. This process is usually called **Texture Mapping**. We will see how to perform texture mapping in *Chapter 7, Textures*.

Using lights, normals, and materials in the pipeline

We mentioned in *Chapter 2, Rendering Geometry*, that WebGL buffers, attributes, and uniforms are used as input variables to the shaders and that varyings are used to carry information between the vertex shader and the fragment shader. Let's revisit the pipeline and see where lights, normals, and materials fit in.

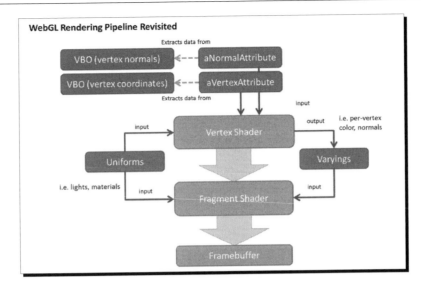

Normals are defined on a vertex-per-vertex basis; therefore normals are modeled in WebGL as a VBO and they are mapped using an attribute, as shown in the preceding diagram. Please notice that attributes are never passed to the fragment shader.

Lights and materials are passed as uniforms. Uniforms are available to both the vertex shader and the fragment shader. This gives us a lot of flexibility to calculate our lighting model because we can calculate how the light is reflected on a vertex-by-vertex basis (vertex shader) or on a fragment-per-fragment basis (fragment shader).

 Remember that the vertex shader and fragment shader together are referred to as the **program**.

Parallelism and the difference between attributes and uniforms

There is an important distinction to make between attributes and uniforms. When a draw call is invoked (using `drawArrays` or `drawElements`), the GPU will launch in parallel several copies of the vertex shader. Each copy will receive a different set of attributes. These attributes are drawn from the VBOs that are mapped to the respective attributes.

On the other hand, all the copies of the vertex shaders will receive the same uniforms, therefore the name, uniform. In other words, uniforms can be seen as constants *per draw call*.

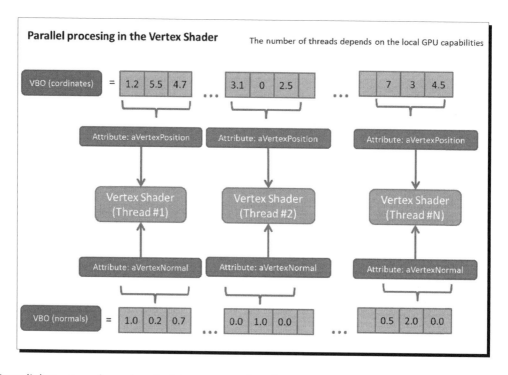

Once lights, normals, and materials are passed to the program, the next step is to determine which *shading* and *lighting* models we will implement. Let's see what this is about.

Shading methods and light reflection models

The terms *shading* and *lighting* are commonly interchanged ambiguously. However, they refer to two different concepts: on one hand, shading refers to the type of *interpolation* that is performed to obtain the final color for every fragment in the scene. We will explain this in a moment. Let's say here as well that the type of shading defines where the final color is calculated—in the vertex shader or in the fragment shader; on the other hand, once the shading model is established, the lighting model determines *how* the normals, materials, and lights are combined to produce the final color. The equations for lighting models use the physical principles of light reflection. Therefore, lighting models are also referred to in literature as *reflection models*.

Shading/interpolation methods

In this section, we will analyze two basic types of interpolation method: Goraud and Phong shading.

Goraud interpolation

The Goraud interpolation method calculates the final color *in the vertex shader*. The vertex normals are used in this calculation. Then the final color for the vertex is carried to the fragment shader using a varying variable. Due to the automatic interpolation of varyings, provided by the rendering pipeline, each fragment will have a color that is a result of interpolating the colors of the enclosing triangle for each fragment.

 The interpolation of varyings is automatic in the pipeline. No programming is required.

Phong interpolation

The Phong method calculates the final color *in the fragment shader*. To do so, each vertex normal is passed along from the vertex shader to the fragment shader using a varying. Because of the interpolation mechanism of varyings included in the pipeline, each fragment will have its own normal. Fragment normals are then used to perform the calculation of the final color in the fragment shader.

The two interpolation models can be summarized by the following diagram:

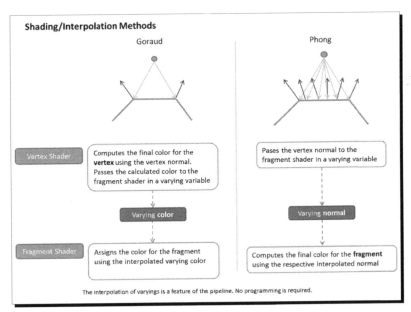

Again, please note here that the shading method does not specify how the final color for every fragment is calculated. It only specifies *where* (vertex or fragment shader) and also the *type of interpolation* (vertex colors or vertex normals).

Light reflection models

As previously mentioned, the lighting model is independent from the shading/interpolation model. The shading model only determines where the final color is calculated. Now it is time to talk about how to perform such calculations.

Lambertian reflection model

Lambertian reflections are commonly used in computer graphics as a model for *diffuse reflections*, which are the kind of reflections where an incident light ray is reflected in many angles instead of only in one angle as it is the case for *specular reflections*.

This lighting model is based on the **cosine emission law** or **Lambert's emission law**. It is named after Johann Heinrich Lambert, from his *Photometria*, published in 1760.

The Lambertian reflection is usually calculated as the dot product between the surface normal (vertex or fragment normal, depending on the interpolation method used) and the negative of the light-direction vector, which is the vector that starts on the surface and ends on the light source position. Then, the number is multiplied by the material and light source colors.

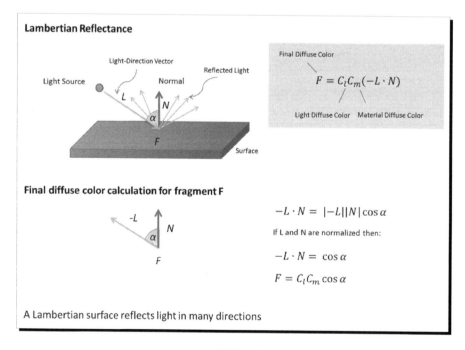

Lambertian Reflectance

Light-Direction Vector

Light Source   Normal   Reflected Light

L N

α

F Surface

Final Diffuse Color

$$F = C_l C_m (-L \cdot N)$$

Light Diffuse Color   Material Diffuse Color

Final diffuse color calculation for fragment F

-L   N

α

F

$$-L \cdot N = |-L||N| \cos \alpha$$

If L and N are normalized then:

$$-L \cdot N = \cos \alpha$$

$$F = C_l C_m \cos \alpha$$

A Lambertian surface reflects light in many directions

Phong reflection model

The Phong reflection model describes the way a surface reflects the light as the sum of three types of reflection: ambient, diffuse, and specular. It was developed by Bui Tuong Phong who published it in his 1973 Ph.D. dissertation.

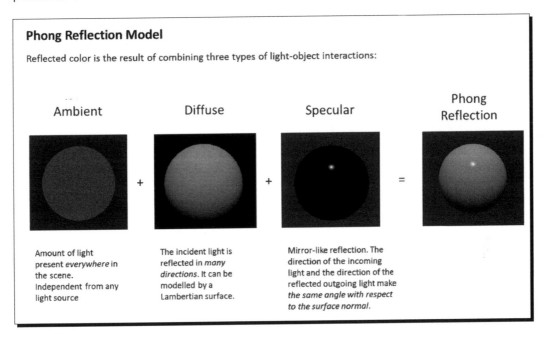

Phong Reflection Model

Reflected color is the result of combining three types of light-object interactions:

Ambient + Diffuse + Specular = Phong Reflection

Amount of light present *everywhere* in the scene. Independent from any light source

The incident light is reflected in *many directions*. It can be modelled by a Lambertian surface.

Mirror-like reflection. The direction of the incoming light and the direction of the reflected outgoing light make *the same angle with respect to the surface normal*.

The *ambient* term accounts for the scattered light present in the scene. This term is independent from any light source and it is the same for all fragments.

The *diffuse* term corresponds to diffuse reflections. Usually a Lambertian model is used for this component.

The *specular* term provides mirror-like reflections. Conceptually, the specular reflection will be at its maximum when we are looking at the object on an angle that is equal to the *reflected* light-direction vector.

This is modeled by the dot product of two vectors, namely, the *eye* vector and the reflected light-direction vector. The eye vector has its origin in the fragment and its end in the view position (camera). The reflected light-direction vector is obtained by reflecting the light-direction vector upon the surface normal vector. When this dot product equals 1 (by working with normalized vectors) then our *camera* will capture the maximum specular reflection.

The dot product is then exponentiated by a number that represents the shininess of the surface. After that, the result is multiplied by the light and material specular components.

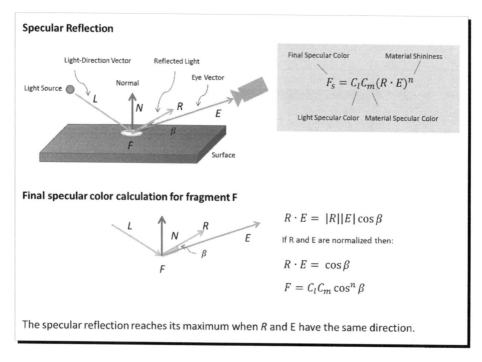

Specular Reflection

$$F_s = C_l C_m (R \cdot E)^n$$

Final specular color calculation for fragment F

$$R \cdot E = |R||E| \cos \beta$$

If R and E are normalized then:

$$R \cdot E = \cos \beta$$

$$F = C_l C_m \cos^n \beta$$

The specular reflection reaches its maximum when *R* and *E* have the same direction.

The ambient, diffuse, and specular terms are added to find the final color of the fragment.

Now it is time for us to learn the language that will allow us to implement the shading and lighting strategies inside the vertex and fragment shaders. This language is called **ESSL**.

ESSL—OpenGL ES Shading Language

OpenGL ES Shading Language (ESSL) is the language in which we write our shaders. Its syntax and semantics are very similar to C/C++. However, it has types and built-in functions that make it easier and more intuitive to manipulate vectors and matrices. In this section, we will cover the basics of ESSL so we can start using it right away.

This section is a summary of the official GLSL ES specification. It is a subset of GLSL (the shading language for OpenGL).

You can find the complete reference at `http://www.khronos.org/registry/gles/specs/2.0/GLSL_ES_Specification_1.0.17.pdf`

Storage qualifier

Variable declarations may have a storage qualifier specified in front of the type:

◆ **attribute**: Linkage between a vertex shader and a WebGL application for per-vertex data. This storage qualifier is only legal inside the vertex shader.

◆ **uniform**: Value does not change across the object being processed, and uniforms form the linkage between a shader and a WebGL application. Uniforms are legal in both the vertex and fragment shaders. If a uniform is shared by the vertex and fragment shader, the respective declarations need to match.

◆ **varying**: Linkage between a vertex shader and a fragment shader for interpolated data. By definition, varyings are necessarily shared by the vertex shader and the fragment shader. The declaration of varyings needs to match between the vertex and fragment shaders.

◆ **const**: a compile-time constant, or a function parameter that is read-only. They can be used anywhere in the code of an ESSL program.

Types

ESSL provides the following basic types:

◆ `void`: For functions that do not return a value or for an empty parameter list

◆ `bool`: A conditional type, taking on values of true or false

◆ `int`: A signed integer

◆ `float`: A single floating-point scalar

◆ `vec2`: A two component floating-point vector

◆ `vec3`: A three component floating-point vector

◆ `vec4`: A four component floating-point vector

◆ `bvec2`: A two component boolean vector

◆ `bvec3`: A three component boolean vector

◆ `bvec4`: A four component boolean vector

◆ `ivec2`: A two component integer vector

◆ `ivec3`: A three component integer vector

◆ `ivec4`: A four component integer vector

◆ `mat2`: A 2×2 floating-point matrix

- ◆ `mat3`: A 3×3 floating-point matrix
- ◆ `mat4`: A 4×4 floating-point matrix
- ◆ `sampler2D`: A handle for accessing a 2D texture
- ◆ `samplerCube`: A handle for accessing a cube mapped texture

So an input variable will have one of the three qualifiers followed by one type. For example, we will declare our `vFinalColor` varying as follows:

```
varying vec4 vFinalColor;
```

This means that the `vFinalColor` variable is a varying vector with four components.

Vector components

We can refer to each one of the components of an ESSL vector by its index.

For example:

`vFinalColor[3]` will refer to the fourth element of the vector (zero-based vectors). However, we can also refer to each component by a letter, as it is shown in the following table:

`{x,y,z,w}`	Useful when accessing vectors representing points or vectors
`{r,g,b,a}`	Useful when accessing vectors representing colors
`{s,t,p,q}`	Useful when accessing vectors that represent texture coordinates

So, for example, if we want to set the *alpha channel* (fourth component) of our variable `vFinalColor` to 1, we can write:

```
vFinalColor[3] = 1.0;
```

or

```
vFinalColor.a = 1.0;
```

We could also do this:

```
vFinalColor.w = 1.0;
```

In all three cases, we are referring to the same fourth component. However, given that `vFinalColor` represents a color, it makes more sense to use the `{r,g,b,a}` notation.

Also, it is possible to use the vector component notation to refer to subsets inside a vector. For example (taken from page *44* in the GLSL ES 1.0.17 specification):

```
vec4 v4;
  v4.rgba;   // is a vec4 and the same as just using v4,
  v4.rgb;    // is a vec3,
  v4.b;      // is a float,
  v4.xy;     // is a vec2,
  v4.xgba;   // is illegal - the component names do not come from
             // the same set.
```

Operators and functions

ESSL also provides many useful operators and functions that simplify vector and matrix operations. According to the specification: the arithmetic binary operators add (+), subtract (-), multiply (*), and divide (/) operate on integer and floating-point typed expressions (including vectors and matrices). The two operands must be the same type, or one can be a scalar float and the other a float vector or matrix, or one can be a scalar integer and the other an integer vector. Additionally, for multiply (*), one can be a vector and the other a matrix with the same dimensional size of the vector. These result in the same fundamental type (integer or float) as the expressions they operate on. If one operand is a scalar and the other is a vector or a matrix, the scalar is applied component-wise to the vector or the matrix, with the final result being of the same type as the vector or the matrix. Dividing by zero does not cause an exception but does result in an unspecified value.

 ◆ $-x$: The negative of the x vector. It produces the same vector in the exact opposite direction.

 ◆ $x+y$: Sum of the vectors x and y. They need to have the same number of components.

 ◆ $x-y$: Subtraction of the vectors x and y. They need to have the same number of components.

 ◆ $x*y$: If x and y are both vectors, then this operator yields a component-wise multiplication. Multiply applied to two matrices return a linear algebraic matrix multiplication, not a component-wise multiplication (for it, you must use the `matrixCompMult` function).

 ◆ x/y: The division operator behaves similarly to the multiply operator.

 ◆ `dot(x,y)`: Returns the dot product (scalar) of two vectors. They need to have the same dimensions.

 ◆ `cross(vec3 x, vec3 y)`: Returns the cross product (vector) of two vectors. They have to be `vec3`.

- ♦ `matrixCompMult (mat x, mat y)`: Component-wise multiplication of matrices. They need to have the same dimensions (`mat2`, `mat3`, or `mat4`).

- ♦ `normalize(x)`: Returns a vector in the same direction but with a length of 1.

- ♦ `reflect(t, n)`: Reflects the vector t along the vector n.

There are many more functions including trigonometry and exponential functions. We will refer to those as we need them in the development of the different lighting models.

Let's see now a quick example of the shaders ESSL code for a scene with the following properties:

- ♦ **Lambertian reflection model**: We account for the diffuse interaction between one light source and our scene. This means that we will use uniforms to define the light properties, the material properties, and we will follow the *Lambert's Emission Law* to calculate the final color for every vertex.

- ♦ **Goraud shading**: We will interpolate vertex colors to obtain fragment colors and therefore we need one `varying` to pass the vertex color information between shaders.

Let's dissect first what the attributes, uniforms, and varyings will be.

Vertex attributes

We start by defining two attributes in the vertex shader. Every vertex will have:

```
attribute vec3 aVertexPosition;
attribute vec3 aVertexNormal;
```

Right after the `attribute` keyword, we find the type of the variable. In this case, this is `vec3`, as each vertex position is determined by three elements (x, y, z). Similarly, the normals are also determined by three elements (x, y, z). Please notice that a position is a *point* in tridimensional space that tells us where the vertex is, while a normal is a *vector* that gives us information about the orientation of the surface that passes along that vertex.

Remember that attributes are only available for use inside the vertex shader.

Uniforms

Uniforms are available to both the vertex shader and the fragment shader. While attributes are different every time the vertex shader is invoked (remember, we process the vertices in parallel, therefore each copy/thread of the vertex shader processes a different vertex). Uniforms are constant throughout a rendering cycle. That is, during a `drawArrays` or `drawElements` WebGL call.

We can use uniforms to pass along information about lights (such as diffuse color and direction), and materials (diffuse color).

For example:

```
uniform vec3 uLightDirection; //incoming light source direction
uniform vec4 uLightDiffuse;   //light diffuse component
uniform vec4 uMaterialDiffuse; //material diffuse color
```

Again, here the keyword `uniform` tells us that these variables are uniforms and the ESSL types `vec3` and `vec4` tell us that these variables have three or four components. In the case of the colors, these components are the red, blue, green, and alpha channels (RGBA) and in the case of the light direction, these components are the x, y, and z coordinates that define the vector in which the light source is directed in the scene.

Varyings

We need to carry the vertex color from the vertex shader to the fragment shader:

```
varying vec4 vFinalColor;
```

As previously mentioned in the section *Storage Qualifier*, the declaration of varyings need to match between the vertex and fragment shaders.

Now let's plug the attributes, uniforms, and varyings into the code and see how the vertex shader and fragment shader look like.

Vertex shader

This is what a vertex shader looks like. On a first look, we identify the attributes, uniforms, and varyings that we will use along with some matrices that we will discuss in a minute. Also we see that the vertex shader has a main function that does not accept parameters and returns void. Inside, we can see some ESSL functions such as normalize and dot and some arithmetical operators.

```
attribute vec3 aVertexPosition;
attribute vec3 aVertexNormal;

uniform mat4 uMVMatrix;
uniform mat4 uPMatrix;
uniform mat4 uNMatrix;

uniform vec3 uLightDirection;
uniform vec4 uLightDiffuse;
uniform vec4 uMaterialDiffuse;
```

```
varying vec4 vFinalColor;

void main(void) {

    vec3 N = normalize(vec3(uNMatrix * vec4(aVertexNormal, 1.0)));
    vec3 L = normalize(uLightDirection);

    float lambertTerm = dot(N,-L);

    vFinalColor = uMaterialDiffuse * uLightDiffuse * lambertTerm;
    vFinalColor.a = 1.0;

    gl_Position = uPMatrix * uMVMatrix * vec4(aVertexPosition, 1.0);
    }
```

There are three uniforms that we have not discussed yet:

```
uniform mat4 uMVMatrix;
uniform mat4 uPMatrix;
uniform mat4 uNMatrix;
```

We can see that these three uniforms are 4x4 matrices. These matrices are required in the vertex shader to calculate the location for vertices and normals whenever we move the camera. There are a couple of operations here that involve using these matrices:

```
vec3 N = vec3(uNMatrix * vec4(aVertexNormal, 1.0));
```

The previous line of code calculates the *transformed normal*.

And:

```
gl_Position = uPMatrix * uMVMatrix * vec4(aVertexPosition, 1.0);
```

This line calculates the *transformed vertex position*. gl_Position is a special output variable that stores the transformed vertex position.

We will come back to these operations in *Chapter 4, Camera*. For now, let's acknowledge that these uniforms and operations deal with camera and world *transformations* (rotation, scale, and translation).

Going back to the code of the main function, we can clearly see that the Lambertian reflection model is being implemented. The dot product of the normalized normal and light direction vector is obtained and then it is multiplied by the light and material diffuse components. Finally, this result is passed into the vFinalColor varying to be used in the fragment shader. Also, as we are calculating the color in the vertex shader and then interpolating the vertex colors for the fragments of every triangle, we are using a Goraud interpolation method.

Fragment shader

The fragment shader is very simple. The first three lines define the precision of the shader. This is mandatory according to the ESSL specification. Similarly, to the vertex shader, we define our inputs; in this case, just one varying variable and then we have the main function.

```
#ifdef GL_SL
precision highp float;
#endif
varying vec4  vFinalColor;

void main(void)  {
  gl_FragColor = vFinalColor;
}
```

We just need to assign the vFinalColor varying to the output variable gl_FragColor.

Remember that the value of the vFinalColor varying will be different from the one calculated in the vertex shader as WebGL will interpolate it by taking the corresponding calculated colors for the vertices surrounding the correspondent fragment (pixel).

Writing ESSL programs

Let's now take a step back and take a look at the big picture. ESSL allows us to implement a lighting strategy provided that we define a shading method and a light reflection model. In this section, we will take a sphere as the object that we want to illuminate and we will see how the selection of a lighting strategy changes the scene.

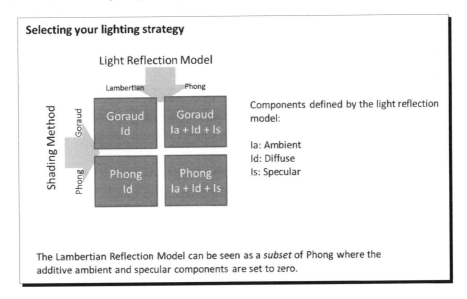

We will see two scenarios for Goraud interpolation: with Lambertian and with Phong reflections; and only one case for Phong interpolation: under Phong shading the Lambertian reflection model is no different from a Phong reflection model where the ambient and specular components are set to zero.

Goraud shading with Lambertian reflections

The Lambertian reflection model only considers the interaction of diffuse material and diffuse light properties. In short, we assign the final color as:

```
Final Vertex Color = Id
```

where the following value is seen:

```
Id = Light Diffuse Property * Material Diffuse Property * Lambert
coefficient
```

Under Goraud shading, the **Lambert coefficient** is obtained by calculating the dot product of the vertex normal and the inverse of the light-direction vector. Both vectors are normalized previous to finding the dot product.

Now let's take a look at the vertex shader and the fragment shader of the example `ch3_Sphere_Goraud_Lambert.html`:

Vertex shader:

```
attribute vec3 aVertexPosition;
attribute vec3 aVertexNormal;
uniform mat4 uMVMatrix;
uniform mat4 uPMatrix;
uniform mat4 uNMatrix;
uniform vec3 uLightDirection;
uniform vec4 uLightDiffuse;
uniform vec4 uMaterialDiffuse;
varying vec4 vFinalColor;
```

```
void main(void) {
  vec3 N = normalize(vec3(uNMatrix * vec4(aVertexNormal, 1.0)));
  vec3 L = normalize(uLightDirection);
  float lambertTerm = dot(N,-L);
    vec4 Id = uMaterialDiffuse * uLightDiffuse * lambertTerm;
  vFinalColor = Id;
  vFinalColor.a = 1.0;
    gl_Position = uPMatrix * uMVMatrix * vec4(aVertexPosition, 1.0);
}
```

Fragment shader:

```
#ifdef GL_ES
precision highp float;
#endif

varying vec4  vFinalColor;

void main(void)  {
  gl_FragColor = vFinalColor;
}
```

We can see that the final vertex color that we process in the vertex shader is carried into a varying variable to the fragment (pixel) shader. However, please remember that the value that arrives to the fragment shader is not the original value that we calculated in the vertex shader. The fragment shader *interpolates* the vFinalColor variable to generate a final color for the respective fragment. This interpolation takes into account the vertices that enclose the current fragment as we saw in *Chapter 2, Rendering Geometry*.

Time for action – updating uniforms in real time

1. Open the file ch3_Sphere_Goraud_Lambert.html in your favorite HTML5 browser.

2. You will see that this example has some widgets at the bottom of the page. These widgets were created using JQuery UI. You can check the code for those in the HTML <body> of the page.

   - **X,Y,Z**: controls the direction of the light. By changing these sliders you will modify the uniform uLightDirection.

   - **Sphere color**: changes the uniform uMaterialDiffuse, which represents the diffuse color of the sphere. Here we use a color selection widget so you can try different colors. The updateObjectColor function receives the updates from the widgets and updates the uMaterialDiffuse uniform.

❑ **Light diffuse term**: changes the uniform `uLightDiffuse`, which represents the diffuse color of the light source. There are no reasons as to why the light color has to be white; however for the sake of simplicity, in this case, we are using a slider instead of a color to restrict the light color to the gray scale. We achieve this by assigning the slider value to the RGB components of `uLightDiffuse` while we keep the alpha channel set to `1.0`. We do this inside the `updateLightDiffuseTerm` function, which receives the slider updates.

3. Try different settings for light source position (which will affect the light-direction vector), the diffuse material, and light properties.

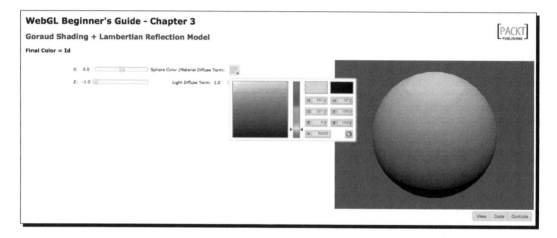

What just happened?

We have seen an example of a simple scene illuminated using Goraud interpolation and a Lambertian reflection model. We have also seen the immediate effects of changing uniform values for the Lambertian lighting model.

Have a go hero – moving light

We have mentioned before that we use matrices to move the camera around the scene. Well, we can also use matrices to move lights!

1. Check the file `ch3_Sphere_Moving.html` using your favorite source code editor. The vertex shader is very similar to the previous diffuse model example. However, there is one extra line:

```
vec4 light = uMVMatrix * vec4(uLightDirection, 0.0);
```

Here we are transforming the `uLightDirection` vector to the light variable. Notice that the uniform `uLightDirection` is a vector with three components (vec3) and that `uMVMatrix` is a 4x4 matrix. In order to do the multiplication, we need to transform this uniform to a four-component vector (vec4). We achieve this with the construct:

```
vec4(uLightDirection, 0.0);
```

The matrix `uMVMatrix` contains the *Model-view-transform*. We will see how all this works in the next chapter. However, for now, let's say that this matrix allows us to update vertices positions and also, as we see in this example, lights positions.

2. Take another look at the vertex shader. In this example, we are rotating the sphere and the light. Every time the `drawScene` function is invoked, we rotate the matrix `mvMatrix` a little bit in the *y axis*:

```
mat4.rotate(mvMatrix, angle * Math.PI / 180, [0, 1, 0]);
```

3. If you examine the code more closely, you will notice that the matrix `mvMatrix` is mapped to the uniform:

```
uMVMatrix:gl.uniformMatrix4fv(prg.uMVMatrix, false, mvMatrix);
```

4. Now run the example in your HTML5 browser. You will see a sphere and a light source rotating on the y-axis:

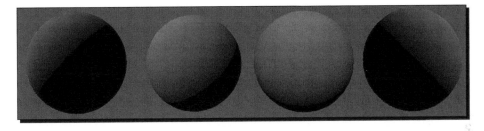

5. Look for the `initLights` function and change the light orientation so the light is pointing in the negative z-axis direction:

```
gl.uniform3f(prg.uLightDirection, 0.0, 0.0, -1.0)
```

6. Save the file and run it again. What happened? Now change the light direction uniform so it points to [-1.0, 0.0, 0.0]. Save the file and run it again on your browser. What happened?

7. Now set the light back to the 45 degree angle by changing the uniform uLightDirection so it goes back to its initial value:

```
gl.uniform3f(prg.uLightDirection, 0.0, 0.0, -1.0)
```

8. Go to drawScene and change the line:

```
mat4.rotate(mvMatrix, angle * Math.PI / 180, [0, 1, 0]);
```

with:

```
mat4.rotate(mvMatrix, angle * Math.PI / 180, [1, 0, 0]);
```

9. Save the file and launch it again in your browser. What happens?

What can you conclude? As you see, the vector that is passed as the third argument to mat4. rotate determines the axis of the rotation. The first component corresponds to the x-axis, the second to the y-axis and the third to the z-axis.

Goraud shading with Phong reflections

In contrast with the Lambertian reflection model, the Phong reflection model considers three properties: the ambient, diffuse, and specular. Following the same analogy that we used in the previous section:

Final Vertex Color = Ia + Id + Is

where:

```
Ia = Light Ambient Property * Material Ambient Property
Id = Light Diffuse Property * Material Diffuse Property * Lambert
coefficient
Is = Light Specular Property * Material Specular Property * specular
coefficient
```

Please notice that:

♦ As we are using Goraud interpolation, we still use vertex normals to calculate the diffuse term. This will change when using Phong interpolation where we will be using fragment normals.

♦ Both light and material have three properties: the ambient, diffuse, and specular colors.

♦ We can see on these equations that Ia, Id, and Is receive contributions from their respective light and material properties.

Based on our knowledge of the Phong reflection model, let's see how to calculate the specular coefficient in ESSL:

```
float specular = pow(max(dot(R, E), 0.0), f );
```

where:

`E` is the view vector or camera vector.

`R` is the reflected light vector.

`f` is the specular exponential factor or *shininess*.

`R` is calculated as:

```
R = reflect(L, N)
```

where `N` is the vertex normal considered and `L` the light direction that we have been using to calculate the Lambert coefficient.

Let's take a look at the ESSL implementation for the vertex and fragment shaders.

Vertex shader:

```
attribute vec3 aVertexPosition;
attribute vec3 aVertexNormal;
uniform mat4 uMVMatrix;
uniform mat4 uPMatrix;
uniform mat4 uNMatrix;
uniform float uShininess;
uniform vec3 uLightDirection;
uniform vec4 uLightAmbient;
uniform vec4 uLightDiffuse;
uniform vec4 uLightSpecular;
uniform vec4 uMaterialAmbient;
uniform vec4 uMaterialDiffuse;
uniform vec4 uMaterialSpecular;
varying vec4 vFinalColor;

void main(void) {

    vec4 vertex = uMVMatrix * vec4(aVertexPosition, 1.0);

vec3 N = vec3(uNMatrix * vec4(aVertexNormal, 1.0));
    vec3 L = normalize(uLightDirection);
    float lambertTerm = clamp(dot(N,-L),0.0,1.0);
```

```
vec4 Ia = uLightAmbient * uMaterialAmbient;
  vec4 Id = vec4(0.0,0.0,0.0,1.0);
  vec4 Is = vec4(0.0,0.0,0.0,1.0);

    Id = uLightDiffuse* uMaterialDiffuse * lambertTerm;

      vec3 eyeVec = -vec3(vertex.xyz);
    vec3 E = normalize(eyeVec);
    vec3 R = reflect(L, N);
    float specular = pow(max(dot(R, E), 0.0), uShininess );
        Is = uLightSpecular * uMaterialSpecular * specular;

  vFinalColor = Ia + Id + Is;
    vFinalColor.a = 1.0;

    gl_Position = uPMatrix * vertex;
  }
```

We can obtain negative dot products for the Lambert term when the geometry of our objects is concave or when the object is in the way between the light source and our point of view, in either case the negative of the light-direction vector and the normals will form an obtuse angle producing a negative dot product, as shown in the following figure:

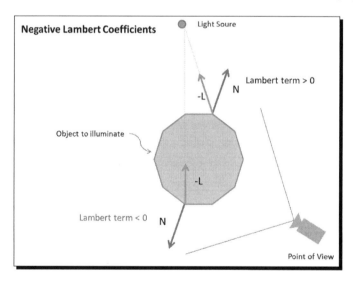

For that reason we are using the ESSL built-in clamp function to restrict the dot product to the positive range. In the case of obtaining a negative dot product, the clamp function will set the lambert term to zero and the respective diffuse contribution will be discarded, generating the correct result.

Given that we are still using Goraud interpolation, the fragment shader is exactly as before:

```
#ifdef GL_ES
precision highp float;
#endif
varying vec4 vFinalColor;

void main(void)
{
  gl_FragColor = vFinalColor;
}
```

In the following section, we will explore the scene and see what it looks like when we have negative Lambert coefficients that have been clamped to the [0,1] range.

Time for action – Goraud shading

1. Open the file `ch3_Sphere_Goraud_Phong.html` in your HTML5 browser. You will see something similar to the following screenshot:

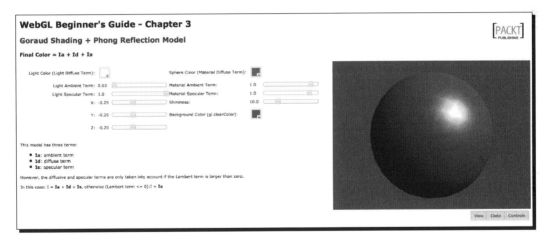

2. The interface looks a little bit more elaborate than the diffuse lighting example. Let's stop here for a moment to explain these widgets:

- **Light color (light diffuse term)**: As mentioned at the beginning of the chapter, we can have a case where our light is not white. We have included a color selector widget here for the light color so you can experiment with different combinations.

- **Light ambient term**: The light ambient property. In this example, a gray value: r = g = b.

❑ **Light specular term**: The light specular property. A gray value: r=g=b.

❑ **X,Y,Z**: The coordinates that define the light orientation.

❑ **Sphere color (material diffuse term)**: The material diffuse property. We have included a color selector so you can try different combinations for the r, g, b channels.

❑ **Material ambient term**: The material ambient property. We have included it just for the sake of it. But as you might have noticed in the diffuse example, this vector is not always used.

❑ **Material specular term**: The material specular property. A gray value.

❑ **Shininess:** The specular exponential factor for the Goraud model.

❑ **Background color (**`gl.clearColor`**)**: This widget simply allows us to change the background color. We used this code in *Chapter 1, Getting started with WebGL*. Now we have a nice color selector widget.

3. Let's prove that when the light source is behind the object, we only see the ambient term.

4. Open the web page (`ch3_Sphere_Goraud_Phong.html`) in a text editor.

5. Look for the `updateLightAmbientTerm` function and replace the line:

   `gl.uniform4fv(prg.uLightAmbient,[la,la,la,1.0]);`

   with:

   `gl.uniform4fv(prg.uLightAmbient,[0.0,la,0.0,1.0]);`

   This will make the ambient property of the light a green color (r = 0, g = la, b=0).

6. Save the file with a new name.

7. Open this new file in your HTML5 browser.

8. Move the light ambient term slider so it is larger than 0.4.

9. Move X close to 0.0

10. See what happens as you move Z towards 1.0. It should be clear then that the light direction is coming behind the object and we are only getting the light ambient term which, in this case, is a color in the green scale (r=0,g=0.3,b=0).

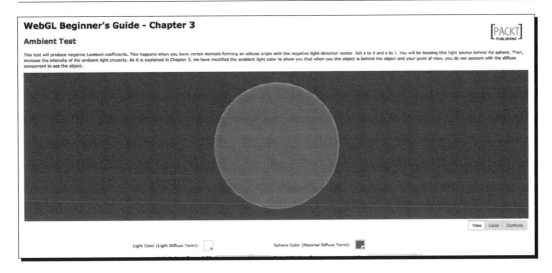

WebGL Beginner's Guide - Chapter 3

Ambient Test

This test will produce negative Lambert coefficients. This happens when you have vertex normals forming an obtuse angle with the negative light-direction vector. Set x to 0 and z to 1. You will be locating this light source behind the sphere. Then, increase the intensity of the ambient light property. As it is explained in Chapter 3, we have modified the ambient light color to show you that when you the object is behind the object and your point of view, you do not account with the diffuse component to see the object.

Light Color (Light Diffuse Term):   Sphere Color (Material Diffuse Term):

11. Go back to the original web page (`ch3_Sphere_Goraud_Phong.html`) in your HTML5 browser.

12. The specular reflection in the Phong reflection model depends on the shininess, the specular property of the material, and the specular property of the light. When the specular property of the material is close to zero (vector [0,0,0,1]), the material *loses* its specular property. Check this behavior with the widgets provided.

13. What happens when the specularity of the material is low and the shininess is high?

14. What happens when the specularity of the material is high and the shininess is low?

15. Using the widgets, try different combinations for the light and material properties.

What just happened?

◆ We have seen how the different parameters of the Phong lighting model interact with each other.

◆ We have modified the light orientation, the properties of the light, and the material to observe different behaviors of the Phong lighting model.

◆ Unlike the Lambertian reflection model, the Goraud lighting model has two extra terms: the ambient and specular components. We have seen how these parameters affect the scene.

Just like the Lambertian reflection model, the Phong reflection model obtains the vertex color in the vertex shader. This color is interpolated in the fragment shader to obtain the final pixel color. This is because, in both cases, we are using Goraud interpolation. Let's now move the heavy processing to the fragment shader and study how we implement the Phong interpolation method.

Phong shading

Unlike the Goraud interpolation, where we calculated the final color for each vertex, the Phong interpolation calculates the final color for every fragment. This means that the calculation of the ambient, diffuse, and specular terms in the Phong model are performed in the fragment shader instead of the vertex shader. As you can imagine, this is more computationally intensive than performing a simple interpolation like in the two previous scenarios where we were using Goraud interpolation. However, we obtain a scene that seems more realistic.

What do we do in the vertex shader then? Well, in this case, we are going to create varyings here that will allow us to do all of the calculations in the fragment shader later on. Think for example of the normals.

Whereas before we had a normal per vertex, now, we need to generate a normal for every pixel so we can calculate the Lambert coefficient for each fragment. We do so by interpolating the normals that we pass to the vertex shader. Nevertheless, the code is very simple. All we need to know is to create a varying that stores the normal for the vertex that we are processing in the vertex shader and obtain the interpolated value in the fragment shader (courtesy of ESSL). That's all! Conceptually, this looks like the following diagram:

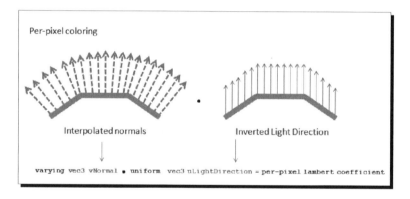

Now let's take a look at the vertex shader under Phong shading:

```
attribute vec3 aVertexPosition;
attribute vec3 aVertexNormal;
uniform mat4 uMVMatrix;
uniform mat4 uPMatrix;
uniform mat4 uNMatrix;
varying vec3 vNormal;
varying vec3 vEyeVec;

void main(void) {
  vec4 vertex = uMVMatrix * vec4(aVertexPosition, 1.0);
```

```
    vNormal = vec3(uNMatrix * vec4(aVertexNormal, 1.0));
    vEyeVec = -vec3(vertex.xyz);
    gl_Position = uPMatrix * uMVMatrix * vec4(aVertexPosition, 1.0);
}
```

In contrast with the Goraud interpolation, the vertex shader looks really simple. There is no final color calculation and we are using two varyings to pass information to the fragment shader. The fragment shader will now look like the following:

```
uniform float uShininess;
uniform vec3 uLightDirection;
uniform vec4 uLightAmbient;
uniform vec4 uLightDiffuse;
uniform vec4 uLightSpecular;
uniform vec4 uMaterialAmbient;
uniform vec4 uMaterialDiffuse;
uniform vec4 uMaterialSpecular;
varying vec3 vNormal;
varying vec3 vEyeVec;

void main(void)
{
 vec3 L = normalize(uLightDirection);
 vec3 N = normalize(vNormal);

 float lambertTerm = dot(N,-L);
 vec4 Ia = uLightAmbient * uMaterialAmbient;
 vec4 Id = vec4(0.0,0.0,0.0,1.0);
 vec4 Is = vec4(0.0,0.0,0.0,1.0);

 if(lambertTerm > 0.0)
 {
  Id = uLightDiffuse * uMaterialDiffuse * lambertTerm;

  vec3 E = normalize(vEyeVec);
  vec3 R = reflect(L, N);
  float specular = pow( max(dot(R, E), 0.0), uShininess);

  Is = uLightSpecular * uMaterialSpecular * specular;
 }

 vec4 finalColor = Ia + Id + Is;
 finalColor.a = 1.0;

 gl_FragColor = finalColor;
}
```

When we pass vectors as varyings, it is possible that they denormalized in the interpolation step. Therefore, you may have noticed that both `vNormal` and `vEyeVec` are normalized before they are used in the fragment shader.

As we mentioned before, under Phong lighting, the Lambertian reflection model can be seen as a Phong reflection model where the ambient and specular components are set to zero. Therefore, we will only cover the general case in the next section where we will see how the sphere scene looks like when using Phong shading and Phong lighting combined.

Time for action – Phong shading with Phong lighting

1. Open the file `ch3 Sphere_Phong.html` in your HTML5 Internet browser. The page will look similar to the following screenshot:

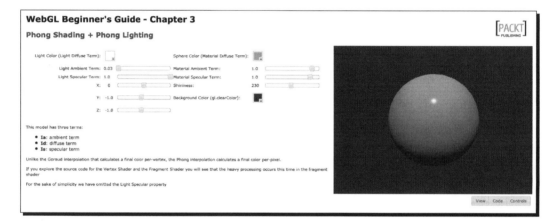

2. The interface is very similar to the Goraud example's interface. Please notice how the Phong shading combined with Phong lighting delivers a more realistic scene.

3. Click on the button **Code**. This will bring up the code viewer area. Check the vertex shader and the fragment shader with the respective buttons that will appear under the code viewer area. As in previous examples, the code has been commented extensively so you can understand every step of the process.

4. Now click on the button **Controls** to go back to the original layout. Modify the different parameters of the Phong lighting model to see the immediate result on the scene to the right.

What just happened?

We have seen the Phong shading and Phong lighting in action. We have explored the source code for the vertex and fragment shaders. We have also modified the different parameters of the model and we have observed the immediate effect of the changes on the scene.

Back to WebGL

It is time to go back to our JavaScript code. Now, how do we close the gap between our JavaScript code and our ESSL code?

First, we need to take a look at how we **create a program** using our WebGL context. Please remember that we refer to both the vertex shader and fragment shader as the program.

Second, we need to know how to **initialize attributes and uniforms**.

Let's take a look at the structure of the web apps that we have developed so far:

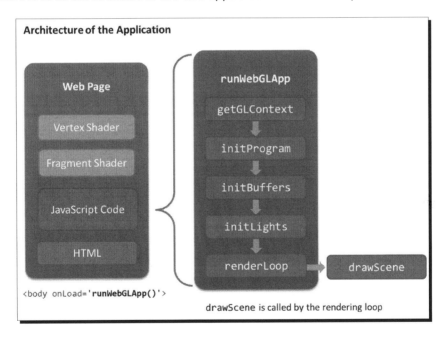

Each application has a vertex shader and a fragment shader embedded in the web page. Then we have a script section where we write all of our WebGL code. Finally, we have the HTML code that defines the page components such as titles and the location of the widgets and the canvas.

In the JavaScript code, we are calling the `runWebGLApp` function on the `onLoad` event of the web page. This is the entry point for our application. The first thing that `runWebGLApp` does is to obtain a WebGL context for the canvas, and then calls a series of functions that initialize the program, the WebGL buffers, and the lights. Finally it gets into a render loop where every time that the loop goes off, the `drawScene` callback is invoked. In this section, we will take a closer look at the `initProgram` and `initLights` functions. `initPrograms` allows creating and compiling a ESSL program while `initLights` allows initializing and passing values to the uniforms defined in the programs. It is inside `initLights` where we will define the light position, direction, and color components (ambient, diffuse, and specular) as well as default values for material properties.

Creating a program

Let's take a step-by-step look at `initProgram`:

```
var prg; //global variable
function initProgram() {
```

First we use the utility function `utils.getShader(WebGLContext, DOM_ID)` to retrieve the contents of the vertex shader and the fragment shader.

```
var fragmentShader= utils.getShader(gl, "shader-fs");
var vertexShader= utils.getShader(gl, "shader-vs");
```

Let's make a small parenthesis here and talk a bit about the `getShader` function. The first parameter of `getShader` is the WebGL context. The second parameter is the DOM ID of the script that contains the source code of the shader that we want to add to the program. Internally, `getShader` reads the source code of the script and it stores it in a local variable named `str`. Then it executes the following piece of code:

```
var shader;
        if (script.type == "x-shader/x-fragment") {
            shader = gl.createShader(gl.FRAGMENT_SHADER);
        } else if (script.type == "x-shader/x-vertex") {
            shader = gl.createShader(gl.VERTEX_SHADER);
        } else {
            return null;
        }

        gl.shaderSource(shader, str);
        gl.compileShader(shader);
```

Basically, the preceding code fragment will create a new shader using the WebGL `createShader` function. Then it will add the source code to it using the `shaderSource` function and finally it will try to compile the shader using the `compileShader` function.

The source code for the `getShader` function is in the file `js/utils.js`, which accompanies this chapter.

Going back to `initProgram`, the program creation occurs in the following lines:

```
prg = gl.createProgram();
gl.attachShader(prg, vertexShader);
gl.attachShader(prg, fragmentShader);
gl.linkProgram(prg);
if (!gl.getProgramParameter(prg, gl.LINK_STATUS)) {
  alert("Could not initialize shaders");
}
gl.useProgram(prg);
```

Here we have used several functions provided by the WebGL context. These are as follows:

WebGL Function	Description
`createProgram()`	Creates a new program (prg)
`attachShader(Object program, Object shader)`	Attaches a shader to the current program
`linkProgram(Object program)`	Creates executable versions of the vertex and fragment shaders that are passed to the GPU
`getProgramParameter(Object program, Object parameter)`	This is part of the WebGL State Machine query mechanism. It allows querying the program parameters. We use this function here to verify whether the program has been successfully linked or not.
`useProgram(Object program)`	It will install the program in the GPU if the program contains valid code (that is, it has been successfully linked).

Finally, we create a **mapping** between JavaScript variables and the program attributes and uniforms. Instead of creating several JavaScript variables here (one per program attribute or uniform), we are attaching properties to the `prg` object. This does not have anything to do with WebGL. It is just a convenience step to keep all of our JavaScript variables as part of the program object.

```
prg.aVertexPosition   = gl.getAttribLocation(prg, "aVertexPosition");
prg.aVertexNormal     = gl.getAttribLocation(prg, "aVertexNormal");
```

```
prg.uPMatrix =gl.getUniformLocation(prg, "uPMatrix");
prg.uMVMatrix = gl.getUniformLocation(prg, "uMVMatrix");
prg.uNMatrix = gl.getUniformLocation(prg, "uNMatrix");


prg.uLightDirection = gl.getUniformLocation(prg, "uLightDirection");
prg.uLightAmbient = gl.getUniformLocation(prg, "uLightAmbient");
prg.uLightDiffuse = gl.getUniformLocation(prg, "uLightDiffuse");
prg.uMaterialDiffuse = gl.getUniformLocation(prg,"uMaterialDiffuse");
}
```

This is all for `initProgram`. Here we have used these WebGL API functions:

WebGL Function	Description
`Var reference = getAttribLocation(Object program,String name)`	This function receives the current program object and a string that contains the name of the attribute that needs to be retrieved. Then this function returns a **reference** to the respective **attribute**.
`var reference= getUniformLocation(Object program,String uniform)`	This function receives the current program object and a string that contains the name of the uniform that needs to be retrieved. Then this function returns a **reference** to the respective **uniform**.

Using this mapping, we can initialize the uniforms and attributes from our JavaScript code, as we will see in the next section.

Initializing attributes and uniforms

Once we have compiled and installed the program, the next step is to initialize the attributes and variables. We will initialize our uniforms using the `initLights` function.

```
function initLights(){
  gl.uniform3fv(prg.uLightDirection, [0.0, 0.0, -1.0]);
  gl.uniform4fv(prg.uLightAmbient, [0.01,0.01,0.01,1.0]);
  gl.uniform4fv(prg.uLightDiffuse, [0.5,0.5,0.5,1.0]);
  gl.uniform4fv(prg.uMaterialDiffuse, [0.1,0.5,0.8,1.0]);


}
```

You can see here that we are using the references obtained with `getUniformLocation` (we did this in `initProgram`).

These are the functions that the WebGL API provides to set and get uniform values:

WebGL Function	Description
`uniform[1234][fi]`	Specifies 1-4 float or int values of a uniform variable
`uniform[1234][fi]v`	Specifies the value of a uniform variable as an array of 1-4 float or int values.
`getUniform(program, reference)`	Retrieves the contents of a uniform variable. The reference parameter has been previously obtained with `getUniformLocation`.

In *Chapter 2, Rendering Geometry,* we saw that there is a three-step process to initialize and use attributes (review the *Associating Attributes to VBOs* section in *Chapter 2, Rendering Geometry*). Let's remember that we:

1. Bind a VBO.
2. Point an attribute to the currently bound VBO.
3. Enable the attribute.

The key piece here is step *2*. We do this with the instruction:

```
gl.vertexAttribPointer(Index,Size,Type,Norm,Stride,Offset);
```

If you check the example `ch3_Wall.html`, you will see that we do this inside the `drawScene` function:

```
gl.vertexAttribPointer(prg.aVertexPosition, 3, gl.FLOAT, false, 0, 0);
gl.vertexAttribPointer(prg.aVertexNormal,3,gl.FLOAT, false, 0,0);
```

Bridging the gap between WebGL and ESSL

Let's see in practice how we integrate our ESSL program to our WebGL code by working on a simple example from scratch.

We have a wall composed of the sections A, B, and C. Imagine that you are facing section B (as shown in the following diagram) and that you have a flashlight on your hand (Frontal View). Intuitively section A and section C will be darker than section B. This fact can be modeled by starting at the color of the center of section B and darkening the color of the surrounding pixels as we move away from the center.

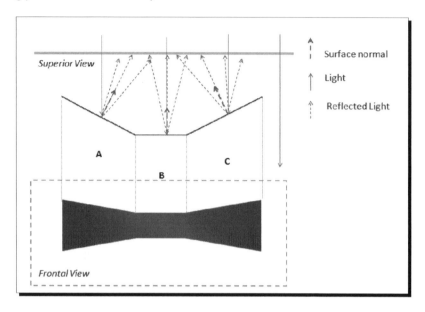

Let's summarize here the code that we need to write:

1. Write the ESSL program. Code the ESSL vertex and fragment shaders. We know how to do this already. For the wall, we are going to select Goraud shading with a Diffuse/Lambertian reflection model.

2. Write the `initProgram` function. We already saw how to do this. We need to make sure that we map all the attributes and uniforms that we had defined in the ESSL code. Including the normals:

   ```
   prg.aVertexNormal= gl.getAttribLocation(prg, "aVertexNormal");
   ```

3. Write `initBuffers`. Here we need to create our geometry: we can represent the wall with eight vertices that define six triangles such as the ones shown in the previous diagram. In `init` buffers, we apply what we learned in *Chapter 2, Rendering Geometry* to set up the appropriate WebGL buffers. This time, we need to set up an additional buffer: the VBO that contain information about normals.

   The code to set up the normals VBO looks like this:

   ```
   var normals = utils.calculateNormals(vertices, indices);
   var normalsBuffer = gl.createBuffer();
   gl.bindBuffer(gl.ARRAY_BUFFER, normalsBuffer);
   ```

```
gl.bufferData(gl.ARRAY_BUFFER, new Float32Array(normals),
gl.STATIC_DRAW);
```

To calculate the normals, we use the following function:

`calculateNormals(vertices, indices)`

You will find this function in the file `js/utils.js`

4. Write `initLights`. We also saw how to do that.

5. There is only a minor but important change to make inside the `drawScene` function. We need to make sure that the normals VBO is bound before we use `drawElements`. The code to do that looks like this:

```
gl.bindBuffer(gl.ARRAY_BUFFER, normalsBuffer);
gl.vertexAttribPointer(prg.aVertexNormal,3,gl.FLOAT, false, 0,0);
```

In the following section, we will explore the functions that we just described for building and illuminating the wall.

Time for action – working on the wall

1. Open the file `ch3_Wall.html` in your HTML5 browse. You will see something similar to the following screenshot:

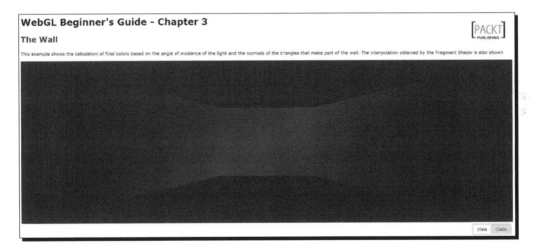

2. Now, open the file again, this time in your favorite text editor (for example, Notepad ++).

3. Go to the vertex shader (Hint: look for the tag `<script id="shader-vs" type="x-shader/x-vertex">`). Make sure that you identify the attributes uniforms and varyings that are declared there.

4. Now go to the fragment shader. Notice that there are no attributes here (Remember: attributes are exclusive of the vertex shader).

5. Go to the `runWebGLApp` function. Verify that we are calling `initProgram` and `initLights` there.

6. Go to `initProgram`. Make sure you understand how the program is built and how we obtain references to attributes and uniforms.

7. Now go to `initLights`. Update the values of the uniforms, as shown here.

```
gl.uniform3fv(prg.uLightDirection, [0.0, 0.0, -1.0]);
gl.uniform4fv(prg.uLightAmbient, [0.1,0.1,0.1,1.0]);
gl.uniform4fv(prg.uLightDiffuse, [0.6,0.6,0.6,1.0]);
gl.uniform4fv(prg.uMaterialDiffuse, [0.6,0.15,0.15,1.0]);
```

8. Please notice that one of the updates consists of changing from `uniform4f` to `uniform4fv` for the uniform `uMaterialDiffuse`.

9. Save the file.

10. Open it again (or reload it) in your HTML5 Internet browser. What happened?

11. Now let's do something a bit more interesting. We are going to create a key listener so every time we hit a key, the light orientation changes.

12. Right after the `initLights` function, write the following code:

```
var azimuth = 0;
var elevation = 0;

document.onkeypress = processKey;
function processKey(ev){

    var lightDirection = gl.getUniform(prg,prg.uLightDirection);
    var incrAzimuth =   10;
    var incrElevation = 10;

    switch(ev.keyCode){
    case 37:{ // left arrow
           azimuth -= incrAzimuth;
           break;
    }
       case 38:{ //up arrow
```

```
                elevation += incrElevation;
                break;
          }
      case 39:{ // right arrow
                azimuth += incrAzimuth;
                break;
      }

        case 40:{ //down arrow
                elevation -= incrElevation;
                break;
          }
      }

      azimuth %= 360;
      elevation %=360;

      var theta = elevation * Math.PI / 180;
      var phi   = azimuth * Math.PI / 180;

      //Spherical to Cartesian coordinate transformation
      lightDirection[0] = Math.cos(theta)* Math.sin(phi);
      lightDirection[1] = Math.sin(theta);
      lightDirection[2] = Math.cos(theta)* -Math.cos(phi);


    gl.uniform3fv(prg.uLightDirection, lightDirection);

}
```

This function processes the arrow keys and changes the light direction accordingly. There is a bit of trigonometry (`Math.cos`, `Math.sin`) `Mat.sin`) there but do not worry. We are just converting the angles (azimuth and elevation) calculated by the entered arrow keys into Cartesian coordinates.

Please notice that we are getting the current light direction using the function:

```
var lightDirection = gl.getUniform(prg,prg.uLightDirection);
```

After processing the key strokes, we can save the updated light direction with:

```
gl.uniform3fv(prg.uLightDirection, lightDirection);
```

13. Save the work and reload the web page:

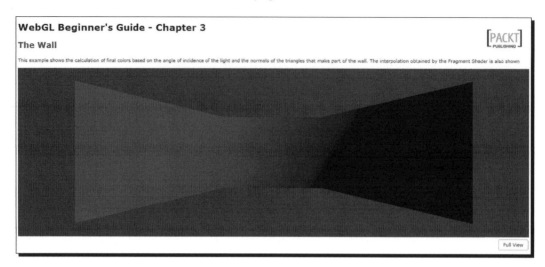

WebGL Beginner's Guide - Chapter 3

The Wall

This example shows the calculation of final colors based on the angle of incidence of the light and the normals of the triangles that make part of the wall. The interpolation obtained by the Fragment Shader is also shown

Full View

14. Use the arrow keys to change the light direction.

15. If you have any problem during the development of the exercise or you just want to verify the final result, please check the file ch3_Wall_Final.html that contains the completed exercise.

What just happened?

In this exercise, we have created a keyboard listener that allows us to update the light orientation so we can move it around the wall and see how it reacts to surface normals. We have also seen how the vertex shader and fragment shader input variables are declared and used. We understood how to build a program by reviewing the initProgram function. We also learned about initializing uniforms on the initLights function. We also studied the getUniform function to retrieve the current value of a uniform.

More on lights: positional lights

Before we finish the chapter, let's revisit the topic of lights. So far we have assumed that our light source is infinitely far away from the scene. This assumption allows us to model the light rays as being parallel to each other. An example of this is sunlight. These lights are called *directional lights*; now we are going to consider the case where the light source is relatively close to the object that it is going to illuminate. Think, for example, of a lamp desk illuminating the document you are reading. These lights are called *positional lights*.

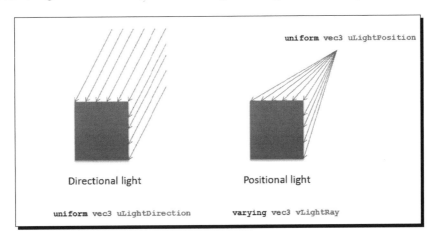

As we experienced before, when working with directional lights, only one variable is required. This is the light direction that we have represented in the uniform `uLightDirection`.

Contrastingly, when working with positional lights, we need to know the location of the light. We can represent it using a uniform that we will name `uLightPosition`. As when using positional lights, the light rays are not parallel to each other, we will need to calculate each light ray separately. We will do this by using a varying that we will name `vLightRay`.

In the following *Time for action* section, we will see how a positional light interacts with a scene.

Time for action – positional lights in action

1. Open the file ch3_Positional Lighting.html in your HTML5 Internet browser. The page will look similar to the following screenshot:

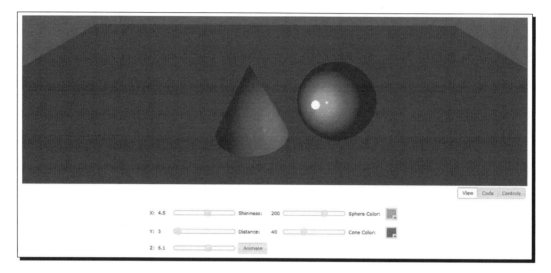

2. The interface of this exercise is very simple. You will notice that there are no sliders to select the ambient and specular properties for the objects or the light source. This has been done deliberately with the objective of focusing on the new element of study—the light position. Unlike in previous exercises, the X, Y, and Z sliders do not represent light direction here. Instead, they allow us to set the light source position. Go ahead and play with them.

3. For clarity, a little sphere representing the position of the light source has been added to the scene. However, this is not generally required.

4. What happens when the light source is located on the surface of the cone or on the surface of the sphere?

5. What happens when the light source is inside the sphere?

6. Now, click on the button **Animate**. As you would expect, the lighting of the scene changes according to the light source and the position of the camera.

7. Let's take a look at the way we calculate the light rays. Click on the **Code** button. Once the code viewer area is displayed, click on the **Vertex Shader** button.

The light ray calculation is performed in the following two lines of code:

```
vec4 light = uMVMatrix * vec4(uLightPosition,1.0);
vLightRay = vertex.xyz-light.xyz;
```

8. The first line allows us to obtain a transformed light position by multiplying the Model-view matrix by the uniform `uLightPosition`. If you check the code in the vertex shader, we also use this matrix for calculating transformed vertices and normals. We will discuss these matrix operations in the next chapter. For now, believe me when I say that this is necessary to obtain transformed vertices, normals, and light positions whenever we move the camera. If you do not believe me, then go ahead and modify this line by removing the matrix from the equation so the line looks like the following:

```
vec4 light = vec4(uLightPosition,1.0);
```

Save the file with a different name and launch it in your HTML5 browser. What is the effect of not transforming the light position? Click on the button **Animate**. What you see is that the camera is moving, but the light source position is not being updated!

9. In the second line of code (*step 7*), we can see that the light ray is calculated as the vector that goes from the transformed light position (light) to the vertex position.

Thanks to the interpolation of varyings that is provided by ESSL, we automatically obtain all the light rays per pixel in the fragment shader.

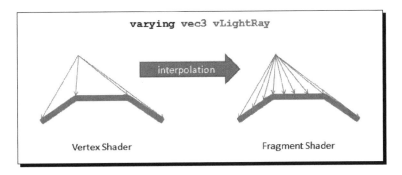

What just happened?

We have studied the difference between directional lights and positional lights. We have also seen the importance of the Model-view matrix for the correct calculation of positional lights when the camera is moving. Also, the procedure to obtain per-vertex light rays has been shown.

Nissan GTS example

We have included in this chapter an example of the Nissan GTS exercise that we saw in *Chapter 2, Rendering Geometry*. This time, we have used a Phong lighting model with a positional light to illuminate the scene. The file where you will find this example is `ch3_Nissan.html`.

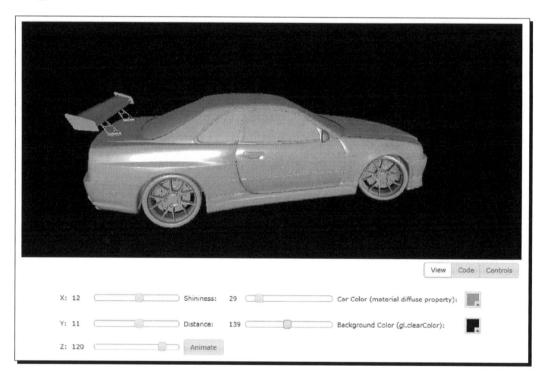

Here you can experiment with different light positions. You can see the nice specular reflections that you obtain thanks to the specularity property of the car and the shininess of the light.

Summary

In this chapter, we have seen how to use the vertex shader and the fragment shader to define a lighting model for our 3D scene. We have learned in detail what light sources, materials, and **normals** are, and how these elements interact to illuminate a WebGL scene. We have also learned the difference between a shading method and a lighting model and have studied the basic Goraud and Phong shading methods and the Lambertian and Phong lighting models. We have also seen several examples of how to implement these shading and lighting models in code using ESSL, and how to communicate between the WebGL code and the ESSL code through attributes and uniforms.

In the following chapter, we will expand on the use of matrices in ESSL and we will see how we use them to represent and move our viewpoint in a 3D scene.

4
Camera

In this chapter, we will learn more about the matrices that we have seen in the source code. These matrices represent transformations that when applied to our scene, allow us to move things around. We have used them so far to set the camera to a distance that is good enough to see all the objects in our scene and also for spinning our Nissan GTS model (Animate button in ch3_Nissan.html). In general, we move the camera and the objects in the scene using matrices.

The bad news is that you will not see a camera object in the WebGL API, only matrices. The good news is that having matrices instead of a camera object gives WebGL a lot of flexibility to represent complex animations (as we will see in *Chapter 5, Action*). In this chapter, we will learn what these matrix transformations mean and how we can use them to define and operate a virtual camera.

In this chapter, we will:

- ◆ Understand the transformations that the scene undergoes from a 3D world to a 2D screen
- ◆ Learn about affine transformations
- ◆ Map matrices to ESSL uniforms
- ◆ Work with the Model-View matrix and the Perspective matrix
- ◆ Appreciate the value of the Normal matrix
- ◆ Create a camera and use it to move around a 3D scene

WebGL does not have cameras

This statement should be shocking! How is it that there are no cameras in a 3D computer graphics technology? Well, let me rephrase this in a more amicable way. WebGL does not have a camera object that you can manipulate. However, we can assume that what we see rendered in the canvas is what our camera captures. In this chapter, we are going to solve the problem of how to represent a camera in WebGL. The short answer is we need 4x4 matrices.

Every time that we move our camera around, we will need to update the objects according to the new camera position. To do this, we need to systematically process each vertex applying a transformation that produces the new viewing position. Similarly, we need to make sure that the object normals and light directions are still consistent after the camera has moved. In summary, we need to analyze two different types of transformations: vertex (points) and normal (vectors).

Vertex transformations

Objects in a WebGL scene go through different transformations before we can see them on our screen. Each transformation is encoded by a 4x4 matrix, as we will see later. How do we multiply vertices that have three components (x,y,z) by a 4x4 matrix? The short answer is that we need to augment the cardinality of our tuples by one dimension. Each vertex then will have a fourth component called the homogenous coordinate. Let's see what they are and why they are useful.

Homogeneous coordinates

Homogeneous coordinates are a key component of any computer graphics program. Thanks to them, it is possible to represent *affine* transformations (rotation, scaling, shear, and translation) and *projective* transformations as 4x4 matrices.

In Homogeneous coordinates, vertices have four components: *x, y, z*, and *w*. The first three components are the vertex coordinates in **Euclidian Space**. The fourth is the perspective component. The 4-tuple (x,y,z,w) take us to a new space: The **Projective Space**.

Homogeneous coordinates make possible to solve a system of linear equations where each equation represents a line that is parallel with all the others in the system. Let's remember here that in Euclidian Space, a system like that does not have solutions, because there are not intersections. However, in Projective Space, this system has a solution—the lines will intersect at infinite. This fact is represented by the perspective component having a value of zero. A good physical analogy of this idea is the image of train tracks: parallel lines that touch in the vanishing point when you look at them.

It is easy to convert from Homogeneous coordinates to non-homogeneous, old-fashioned, Euclidean coordinates. All you need to do is divide the coordinate by *w*:

$$h(x, y, z, w) = v(x / w, y / w, z / w)$$
$$v(x, y, z) = h(x, y, z, 1)$$

Consequently, if we want to go from Euclidian to Projective space, we just add the fourth component *w* and make it 1.

As a matter of fact, this is what we have been doing so far! Let's go back to one of the shaders we discussed in the last chapter: the Phong vertex shader. The code looks like the following:

```
attribute vec3 aVertexPosition;
attribute vec3 aVertexNormal;

uniform mat4 uMVMatrix;
uniform mat4 uPMatrix;
uniform mat4 uNMatrix;

varying vec3 vNormal;
varying vec3 vEyeVec;

void main(void) {
    //Transformed vertex position
    vec4 vertex = uMVMatrix * vec4(aVertexPosition, 1.0);

    //Transformed normal position
    vNormal = vec3(uNMatrix * vec4(aVertexNormal, 0.0));

    //Vector Eye
    vEyeVec = -vec3(vertex.xyz);

    //Final vertex position
    gl_Position = uPMatrix * uMVMatrix * vec4(aVertexPosition, 1.0);
}
```

Please notice that for the `aVertexPosition` attribute, which contains a vertex of our geometry, we create a 4-tuple from the 3-tuple that we receive. We do this with the ESSL construct `vec4()`. ESSL knows that `aVertexPosition` is a `vec3` and therefore we only need the fourth component to create a `vec4`.

To pass from Homogeneous coordinates to Euclidean coordinates, we divide by *w*

To pass from Euclidean coordinates to Homogeneous coordinates, we add *w* =1

Homogeneous coordinates with *w* = 0 represent a point at infinity

There is one more thing you should know about Homogeneous coordinates—while vertices have a Homogeneous coordinate w = 1, vectors have a Homogeneous coordinate w = 0. This is the reason why, in the Phong vertex shader, the line that processes the normals looks like this:

```
vNormal = vec3(uNMatrix * vec4(aVertexNormal, 0.0));
```

To code vertex transformations, we will be using Homogeneous coordinates unless indicated otherwise. Now let's see the different transformations that our geometry undergoes to be displayed on screen.

Model transform

We start our analysis from the object coordinate system. It is in this space where vertex coordinates are specified. Then if we want to translate or move objects around, we use a matrix that encodes these transformations. This matrix is known as the **model matrix**. Once we multiply the vertices of our object by the model matrix, we will obtain new vertex coordinates. These new vertices will determine the position of the object in our 3D world.

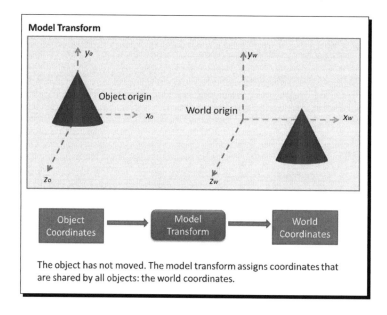

The object has not moved. The model transform assigns coordinates that are shared by all objects: the world coordinates.

While in object coordinates, each object is free to define where its origin is and then specify where its vertices are with respect to this origin, in world coordinates, the origin is shared by all the objects. World coordinates allow us to know where objects are located with respect to each other. It is with the model transform that we determine where the objects are in the 3D world.

View transform

The next transformation, the view transform, shifts the origin of the coordinate system to the view origin. The view origin is where our *eye* or *camera* is located with respect to the world origin. In other words, the view transform switches world coordinates by view coordinates. This transformation is encoded in the **view matrix**. We multiply this matrix by the vertex coordinates obtained by the model transform. The result of this operation is a new set of vertex coordinates whose origin is the view origin. It is in this coordinate system that our camera is going to operate. We will go back to this later in the chapter.

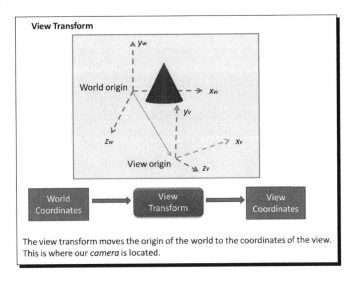

The view transform moves the origin of the world to the coordinates of the view. This is where our *camera* is located.

Projection transform

The next operation is called the projection transform. This operation determines how much of the view space will be rendered and how it will be mapped onto the computer screen. This region is known as the **frustum** and it is defined by six planes (near, far, top, bottom, right, and left planes), as shown in the following diagram:

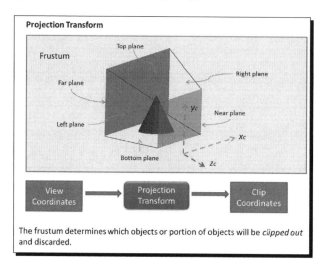

These six planes are encoded in the **Perspective matrix**. Any vertices lying outside of the frustum after applying the transformation are *clipped out* and discarded from further processing. Therefore, the frustum defines, and the projection matrix that encodes the frustum produces, *clipping coordinates*.

The shape and extent of the frustum determines the type of projection from the 3D viewing space to the 2D screen. If the far and near planes have the same dimensions, then the frustum will determine an *orthographic* projection. Otherwise, it will be a *perspective* projection, as shown in the following diagram:

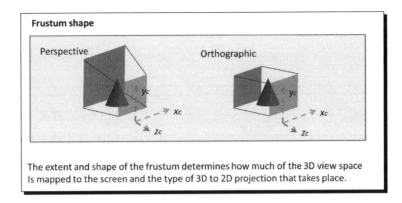

Frustum shape

The extent and shape of the frustum determines how much of the 3D view space Is mapped to the screen and the type of 3D to 2D projection that takes place.

Up to this point, we are still working with Homogeneous coordinates, so the clipping coordinates have four components: x, y, z, and w. The clipping is done by comparing the x, y, and z components against the Homogeneous coordinate w. If any of them is more than, $+w$, or less than, $-w$, then that vertex lies outside the frustum and is discarded.

Perspective division

Once it is determined how much of the viewing space will be rendered, the frustum is mapped into the *near plane* in order to produce a 2D image. The near plane is what is going to be rendered on your computer screen.

Different operative systems and displaying devices can have mechanisms to represent 2D information on screen. To provide robustness for all possible cases, WebGL (also in OpenGL ES) provides an intermediate coordinate system that is independent from any specific hardware. This space is known as the **Normalized Device Coordinates (NDC)**.

Normalized device coordinates are obtained by dividing the clipping coordinates by the w component. This is the reason why this step is known as *perspective division*. Also, please remember that when you divide by the Homogeneous coordinate, we go from projective space (4-components) to Euclidean space (3-components), so NDC only has three components. In the NDC space, the x and y coordinates represent the location of your vertices on a normalized 2D screen, while the z-coordinate encodes depth information, which is the relative location of the objects with respect to the near and far planes. Though, at this point, we are working on a 2D screen, we still keep the depth information. This will allow WebGL to determine later how to display overlapping objects based on their distance to the near plane. When using normalized device coordinates, the depth is encoded in the z-component.

The perspective division transforms the viewing frustum into a cube centered in the origin with minimum coordinates [-1,-1,-1] and maximum coordinates [1,1,1]. Also, the direction of the z-axis is inverted, as shown in the following figure:

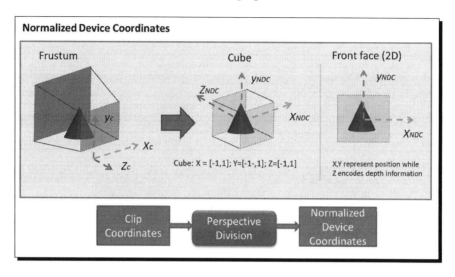

Viewport transform

Finally, NDCs are mapped to **viewport coordinates**. This step maps these coordinates to the available space in your screen. In WebGL, this space is provided by the HTML5 canvas, as shown in the following figure:

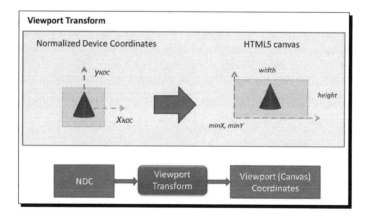

Unlike the previous cases, the viewport transform is not generated by a matrix transformation. In this case, we use the WebGL `viewport` function. We will learn more about this function later in the chapter. Now it is time to see what happens to normals.

Normal transformations

Whenever vertices are transformed, **normal vectors** should also be transformed, so they point in the right direction. We could think of using the Model-View matrix that transforms vertices to do this, but there is a problem: The Model-View matrix will not always keep the perpendicularity of normals.

This problem occurs if there is a unidirectional (one axis) scaling transformation or a shearing transformation in the Model-View matrix. In our example, we have a triangle that has undergone a scaling transformation on the y-axis. As you can see, the normal N' is not normal anymore after this kind of transformation. How do we solve this?

Calculating the Normal matrix

If you are not interested in finding out how we calculate the Normal matrix and just want the answer, please feel free to jump to the end of this section. Otherwise, stick around to see some linear algebra in action!

Let's start from the mathematical definition of perpendicularity. Two vectors are perpendicular if their dot product is zero. In our example:

$$N.S = 0$$

Here, S is the surface vector and it can be calculated as the difference of two vertices, as shown in the previous diagram at the beginning of this section.

Let M be the Model-View matrix. We can use M to transform S as follows:

$$S' = MS$$

This is because S is the difference of two vertices and we use M to transform vertices onto the viewing space.

We want to find a matrix K that allows us to transform normals in a similar way. For the normal N, we want:

$$N' = KN$$

For the scene to be consistent after obtaining N' and S', these two need to keep the perpendicularity that the original vectors N and S had. This is:

$$N'.S' = 0$$

Substituting N' and S':

$$(KN).(MS) = 0$$

A dot product can also be written as a vector multiplication by transposing the first vector, so we have that this still holds:

$$(KN)^T(MS) = 0$$

The transpose of a product is the product of the transposes in the reverse order:

$$N^TK^TMS = 0$$

Grouping the inner terms:

$$N^T(K^TM)S = 0$$

Now remember that $N.S = 0$ so $N^TS = 0$ (again, a dot product can be written as a vector multiplication). This means that in the previous equation, (K^TM) needs to be the identity matrix I, so the original condition of N and S being perpendicular holds:

$$K^TM = I$$

Applying a bit of algebra:

$K^TMM^{-1} = IM^{-1} = M^{-1}$	multiply by the inverse of M on both sides
$K^T(I) = M^{-1}$	because $MM^{-1} = I$
$(K^T)^T = (M^{-1})^T$	transposing on both sides
$K = (M^{-1})^T$	Double transpose of K is the original matrix K.

Conclusions:

- K is the correct matrix transform that keeps the normal vectors being perpendicular to the surface of the object. We call K the **Normal matrix**.

- ◆ *K* is obtained by transposing the inverse of the Model-View matrix (M in this example).
- ◆ We need to use *K* to multiply the normal vectors so they keep being perpendicular to surface when these are transformed.

WebGL implementation

Now let's take a look at how we can implement vertex and normal transformations in WebGL. The following diagram shows the theory that we have learned so far and it shows the relationships between the steps in the theory and the implementation in WebGL.

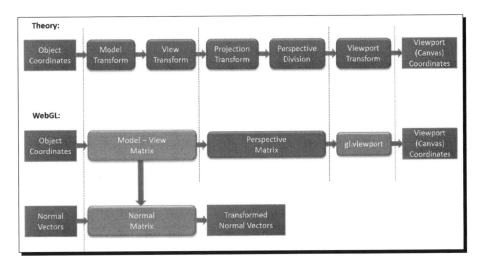

In WebGL, the five transformations that we apply to object coordinates to obtain viewport coordinates are grouped in three matrices and one WebGL method:

1. The **Model-View** matrix that groups the *model* and *view* transform in one single matrix. When we multiply our vertices by this matrix, we end up in view coordinates.

2. The **Normal matrix** is obtained by inverting and transposing the Model-View matrix. This matrix is applied to normal vectors for lighting purposes.

3. The **Perspective matrix** groups the *projection transformation* and *the perspective division*, and as a result, we end up in normalized device coordinates (NDC).

   Finally, we use the operation `gl.viewport` to map NDCs to viewport coordinates:

   `gl.viewport(minX, minY, width, height);`

   The viewport coordinates have their origin in the lower-left corner of the HTML5 canvas.

JavaScript matrices

WebGL does not provide its own methods to perform operations on matrices. All WebGL does is it provides a way to pass matrices to the shaders (as uniforms). So, we need to use a JavaScript library that enables us to manipulate matrices in JavaScript. In this book, we have used `glMatrix` to manipulate matrices. However, there are other libraries available online that can do this for you.

> We used `glMatrix` to manipulate matrices in this book. You can find more information about this library here: `https://github.com/toji/gl-matrix`. And the documentation (linked further down the page) can be found at: `http://toji.github.com/gl-matrix/doc`

These are some of the operations that you can perform with `glMatrix`:

Operation	Syntax	Description
Creation	`var m = mat4.create()`	Creates the matrix m
Identity	`mat4.identity(m)`	Sets m as the identity matrix of rank 4
Copy	`mat4.set(origin,target)`	Copies the matrix `origin` into the matrix `target`
Transpose	`mat4.transpose(m)`	Transposes matrix m
Inverse	`mat4.inverse(m)`	Inverts m
Rotate	`mat4.rotate(m,r,a)`	Rotates the matrix m by r radians around the axis a (this is a 3-element array [x,y,z]).

`glMatrix` also provides functions to perform other linear algebra operations. It also operates on vectors and matrices of rank 3. To get the full list, visit `https://github.com/toji/gl-matrix`

Mapping JavaScript matrices to ESSL uniforms

As the Model-View and Perspective matrices do not change during a single rendering step, they are passed *as uniforms* to the shading program. For example, if we were applying a translation to an object in our scene, we would have to paint the whole object in the new coordinates given by the translation. Painting the whole object in the new position is achieved in exactly one rendering step.

However, before the rendering step is invoked (by calling `drawArrays` or `drawElements`, as we saw in *Chapter 2, Rendering Geometry*), we need to make sure that the shaders have an updated version of our matrices. We have seen how to do that for other uniforms such as light and color properties. The method map JavaScript matrices to uniforms is similar to the following:

First, we get a JavaScript reference to the uniform with:

```
var reference= getUniformLocation(Object program, String uniformName)
```

Then, we use the `reference` to pass the matrix to the shader with:

```
gl.uniformMatrix4fv(WebGLUniformLocation reference, bool transpose,
float[] matrix);
```

`matrix` is the JavaScript matrix variable.

As it is the case for other uniforms, ESSL supports 2, 3, and 4-dimensional matrices:

`uniformMatrix[234]fv(ref,transpose,matrix)`: will load 2x2, 3x3, or 4x4 matrices (corresponding to 2, 3, or 4 in the command name) of floating points into the uniform referenced by ref. The type of ref is `WebGLUniformLocation`. For practical purposes, it is an integer number. According to the specification, the transpose value must be set to `false`. The matrix uniforms are always of floating point type (`f`). The matrices are passed as 4, 9, or 16 element vectors (`v`) and are always specified in a column-major order. The matrix parameter can also be of type `Float32Array`. This is one of JavaScript's typed arrays. These arrays are included in the language to provide access and manipulation of raw binary data, therefore increasing efficiency.

Working with matrices in ESSL

Let's revisit the Phong vertex shader, which was introduced in the last chapter. Please pay attention to the fact that matrices are defined as `uniform mat4`.

In this shader, we have defined three matrices:

◆ `uMVMatrix`: the Model-View matrix

◆ `uPMatrix`: the Perspective matrix

◆ `uNMatrix`: the Normal matrix

```
attribute vec3 aVertexPosition;
attribute vec3 aVertexNormal;

uniform mat4 uMVMatrix;
uniform mat4 uPMatrix;
uniform mat3 uNMatrix;

varying vec3 vNormal;
varying vec3 vEyeVec;

void main(void) {
    //Transformed vertex position
    vec4 vertex = uMVMatrix * vec4(aVertexPosition, 1.0);
```

```
        //Transformed normal vector
        vNormal = uNMatrix * aVertexNormal;

        //Vector Eye
        vEyeVec = -vec3(vertex.xyz);

        //Final vertex position
        gl_Position = uPMatrix * uMVMatrix * vec4(aVertexPosition,
1.0);
    }
```

In ESSL, the multiplication of matrices is straightforward, that is, you do not need to multiply element by element, but as ESSL knows that you are working with matrices, it performs the multiplication for you.

```
        gl_Position = uPMatrix * uMVMatrix * vec4(aVertexPosition, 1.0);
```

The last line of this shader assigns a value to the predefined `gl_Position` variable. This will contain the clipping coordinates for the vertex that is currently being processed by the shader. We should remember here that the shaders work in parallel: each vertex is processed by an instance of the vertex shader.

To obtain the clipping coordinates for a given vertex, we need to multiply first by the Model-View matrix and then by the Projection matrix. To achieve this, we need to multiply to the left (because matrix multiplication is not commutative).

Also, notice that we have had to augment the `aVertexPosition` attribute by including the Homogeneous coordinate. This is because we have always defined our geometry in Euclidean space. Luckily, ESSL lets us do this just by adding the missing component and creating a vec4 on the fly. We need to do this because both the Model-View matrix and the Perspective matrix are described in homogeneous coordinates (4 rows by 4 columns).

Now that we have seen how to map JavaScript matrices to ESSL uniforms in our shaders, let's talk about how to operate with the three matrices: the Model-View matrix, the Normal matrix, and the Perspective matrix.

The Model-View matrix

This matrix allows us to perform *affine transformations* in our scene. **Affine** is a mathematical name to describe transformations that *do not change* the structure of the object that undergoes such transformations. In our 3D world scene, such transformations are rotation, scaling, reflection shearing, and translation. Luckily for us, we do not need to understand how to represent such transformations with matrices. We just have to use one of the many JavaScript matrix libraries that are available online (such as `glMatrix`).

You can find more information on how transformation matrices work in any linear algebra book. Look for *affine transforms in computer graphics*.

Understanding the structure of the Model-View matrix is of no value if you just want to apply transformations to the scene or to objects in the scene. For that effect, you just use a library such as `glMatrix` to do the transformations on your behalf. However, the structure of this matrix could be invaluable information when you are trying to troubleshoot your 3D application.

Let's take a look.

Spatial encoding of the world

By default, when you render a scene, you are looking at it from the origin of the world in the negative direction of the z-axis. As shown in the following diagram, the z-axis is coming out of the screen (which means that you are looking at the negative z-axis).

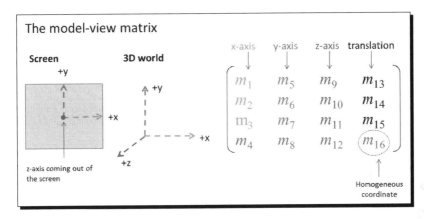

From the center of the screen to the right, you will have the positive x-axis and from the center of the screen up, you will have the positive y-axis. This is the initial configuration and it is the reference for affine transformations.

In this configuration, the Model-View matrix is the **identity matrix** of rank four.

The first three rows of the Model-View matrix contain information about rotations and translations that are affecting the world.

Rotation matrix

The intersection of the first three rows with the first three columns defines the 3x3 Rotation matrix. This matrix contains information about rotations around the standard axis. In the initial configuration, this corresponds to:

$$[m_1, m_2, m_3] = [1, 0, 0] = \text{x-axis}$$

$$[m_5, m_6, m_7] = [0, 1, 0] = \text{y-axis}$$

$$[m_9, m_{10}, m_{11}] = [0, 0, 1] = \text{z-axis}$$

Translation vector

The intersection of the first three rows with the last column defines a three-component Translation vector. This vector indicates how much the origin, and for the same sake, the world, have been translated. In the initial configuration, this corresponds to:

$$\begin{bmatrix} m_{13} \\ m_{14} \\ m_{15} \end{bmatrix} = \begin{bmatrix} 0 \\ 0 \\ 0 \end{bmatrix} = \text{origin (no translation)}$$

The mysterious fourth row

The fourth row does not bear any special meaning.

◆ Elements m_4, m_8, m_{12} are always zero.

◆ Element m_{16} (the homogeneous coordinate) will always be 1.

As we described at the beginning of this chapter, there are no cameras in WebGL. However, all the information that we need to operate a camera (mainly rotations and translations) can be extracted from the Model-View matrix itself!

The Camera matrix

Let's say, for a moment, that we do have a camera in WebGL. A camera should be able to rotate and translate to explore this 3D world. For example, think of a first person shooter game where you have to walk through levels killing zombies. As we saw in the previous section, a 4x4 matrix can encode rotations and translations. Therefore, our hypothetical camera could also be represented by one such matrix.

Assume that our camera is located at the origin of the world and that it is oriented in a way that it is looking towards the negative z-axis direction. This is a good starting point—we already know what transformation represents such a configuration in WebGL (identity matrix of rank 4).

For the sake of analysis, let's break the problem down into two sub-problems: camera translation and camera rotation. We will have a practical demo on each one.

Camera translation

Let's move the camera to [0 ,0, 4] in world coordinates. This means 4 units from the origin on the positive z-axis.

Remember that we do not know at this point of a matrix to move the camera, we only know how to move *the world* (with the Model-View matrix). If we applied:

```
mat4.translate(mvMatrix, [0,0,4]);
```

In such a case, the world would be translated 4 units on the positive z-axis and as the camera position has not been changed (as we do not know a matrix to do this), it would be located at [0,0,-4], which is exactly the opposite of what we wanted in the first place!

Now, say that we applied the translation in the opposite direction:

```
mat4.translate(mvMatrix, [0,0,-4]);
```

In such a case, the world would be moved 4 units on the negative z-axis and then the camera would be located at [0,0,4] in the new world coordinate system.

We can see here that translating the camera is *equivalent* to translating the world in the *opposite* direction.

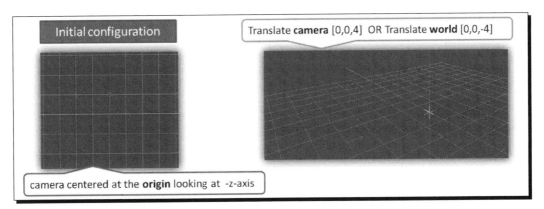

In the following section, we are going to explore translations both in world space and in camera space.

Time for action – exploring translations: world space versus camera space

1. Open `ch4_ModelView_Translation.html` in your HTML5 browser:

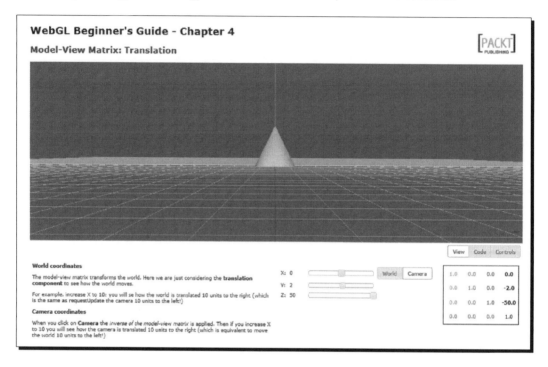

2. We are looking from a distance at the positive z-axis at a cone located at the origin of the world. There are three sliders that will allow you to translate either the world or the camera on the x, y, and z axis, respectively. The world space is activated by default.

3. Can you tell by looking at the World-View matrix on the screen where the origin of the world is? Is it [0,0,0]? (Hint: check where we define translations in the Model-View matrix).

4. We can think of the canvas as the image that our camera sees. If the world center is at [0,-2,-50], where is the camera?

5. If we want to see the cone closer, we would have to move the center of the world towards the camera. We know that the camera is far on the positive z-axis of the world, so the translation will occur on the z-axis. Given that you are on world coordinates, do we need to increase or decrease the z-axis slider? Go ahead and try your answer.

6. Now switch to camera coordinates by clicking on the **Camera** button. What is the translation component of this matrix? What do you need to do if you want to move the camera closer to the cone? What does the final translation look like? What can you conclude?

7. Go ahead and try to move the camera on the x-axis and the y-axis. Check what the correspondent transformations would be on the Model-View matrix.

What just happened?

We saw that the camera translation is the inverse of the Model-View matrix translation. We also learned where to find translation information in a transformation matrix.

Camera rotation

Similarly, if we want to rotate the camera, say, 45 degrees to the right, this would be equivalent to rotating the world 45 degrees to the left. Using `glMatrix` to achieve this, we write the following:

```
mat4.rotate(mvMatrix,45 * Math.PI/180, [0,1,0]);
```

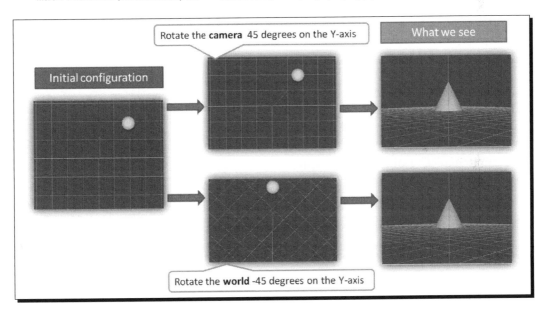

Let's see this behavior in action!

Similar to the previous section where we explored translations, in the following time for action, we are going to play with rotations in both world and camera spaces.

Time for action – exploring rotations: world space versus camera space

1. Open ch4_ModelView_Rotation.html in your HTML5 browser:

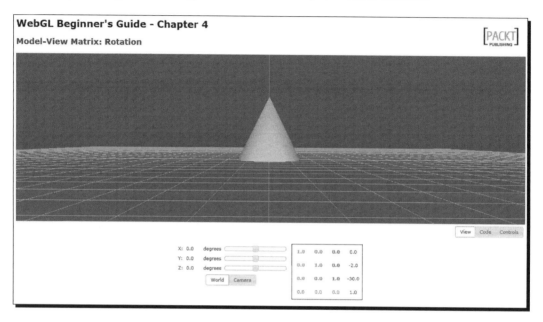

2. Just like in the previous example, we will see:

- ❏ A cone at the origin of the world
- ❏ The camera is located at [0,2,50] in world coordinates
- ❏ Three sliders that will allows us to rotate either the world or the camera
- ❏ Also, we have a matrix where we can see the result of different rotations

3. Let's see what happens to the axis after we apply a rotation. With the **World** coordinates button selected, rotate the world 90 degrees around the x-axis. What does the Model-View matrix look like?

4. Let's see where the axes end up after a 90 degree rotation around the x-axis:

- ❏ By looking at the first column, we can see that the x-axis has not changed. It is still [1,0,0]. This makes sense as we are rotating around this axis.
- ❏ The second column of the matrix indicates where the y-axis is after the rotation. In this case, we went from [0,1,0] , which is the original

configuration, to [0,0,1], which is the axis that is coming out of the screen. This is the z-axis in the initial configuration. This makes sense as now we are looking from above, down to the cone.

❑ The third column of the matrix indicates the new location of the z-axis. It changed from [0,0,1], which as we know is the z-axis in the standard spatial configuration (without transforms), to [0,-1,0], which is the negative portion of the y-axis in the original configuration. This makes sense as we rotated around the x-axis.

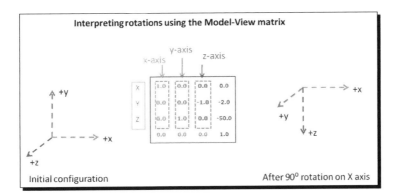

5. As we just saw, understanding the Rotation matrix (3x3 upper-left corner of the Model-View matrix) is simple: the first three columns are always telling us where the axis is.

6. Where are the axis in this transformation:

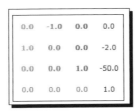

Check your answer by using the sliders to achieve the rotation that you believe produce this matrix.

7. Now let's see how rotations work in **Camera** space. Click on the **Camera** button.

8. Start increasing the angle of rotation in the **X** axis by incrementing the slider position. What do you notice?

9. Go ahead and try different rotations in camera space using the sliders.

10. Are the rotations *commutative*? That is, do you get the same result if you rotate, for example, 5 degrees on the **X** axis and 90 degrees on the **Z** axis, compared to the case where you rotate 90 degrees on the **Z** axis and then you rotate 5 degrees on the **X** axis?

11. Now, go back to **World** space. Please check that when you are in **World** space, you need to reverse the rotations to obtain the same pose. So, if you were applying 5 degrees on the **X** axis and 90 degrees on the **Z** axis. Check that when you apply -5 degrees on the X axis and -90 degrees on the Z axis you obtain the same image as in point 10.

What just happened?

We just saw that the Camera matrix rotation is the inverse of the Model-View matrix rotation. We also learned how to identify the orientation of our world or camera upon analysis of the rotation matrix (3x3 upper-left corner of the correspondent transformation matrix).

Have a go hero – combining rotations and translations

1. The file ch4_ModelView.html contains the combination of rotations and translations. When you open it your HTML5 browser, you see something like the following:

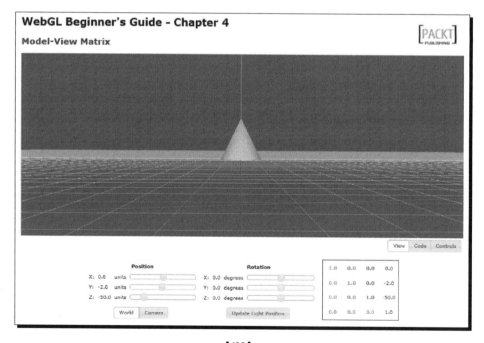

2. Try different configurations of rotations and translations in both **World** and **Camera** spaces.

The Camera matrix is the inverse of the Model-View matrix

We can see through these two scenarios that a Camera matrix would require being the exact Model-View matrix opposite. In linear algebra, we know this as the **inverse** of a matrix.

The inverse of a matrix is such that when multiplying it by the original matrix, we obtain the identity matrix. In other words, if M is the Model-View matrix and C is the Camera matrix, we have the following:

$$MC = I$$

$$M^{-1}MC = M^{-1}$$

$$C = M^{-1}$$

We can create the Camera matrix using `glMatrix` by writing something like the following:

```
var cMatrix = mat4.create();
mat4.inverse(mvMatrix,cMatrix);
```

Thinking about matrix multiplications in WebGL

Please do not skip this section. If you want to, just put a sticker on this page so you remember where to go when you need to debug Model-View transformations. I spent so many nights trying to understand this (sigh) and I wish I had had a book like this to explain this to me.

 Before moving forward, we need to know that in WebGL, the matrix operations are written in the *reverse order* in which they are applied to the vertices.

Here is the explanation. Assume, for a moment, that you are writing the code to rotate/ move the world, that is, you rotate your vertices around the origin and then you move away. The final transformation would look like this:

$$RTv$$

Here, R is the 4x4 matrix encoding pure rotation, T is the 4x4 matrix encoding pure translation, and v corresponds to the vertices present in your scene (in homogeneous coordinates).

Now, if you notice, the first transformation that we actually apply to the vertices is the translation and then we apply the rotation! Vertices need to be multiplied first by the matrix that is to the left. In this scenario, that matrix is *T*. Then, the result needs to be multiplied by *R*.

This fact is reflected in the order of the operations (here `mvMatrix` is the Model-View matrix):

```
mat4.identity(mvMatrix)
mat4.translate(mvMatrix, position); mat4.rotateX(mvMatrix,rotation[0]
*Math.PI/180);
mat4.rotateY(mvMatrix,rotation[1]*Math.PI/180);
mat4.rotateZ(mvMatrix,rotation[2]*Math.PI/180);
```

Now if we were working in camera coordinates and we wanted to apply the same transformation as before, we need to apply a bit of linear algebra first:

$M = RT$	The Model-View matrix *M* is the result of multiplying rotation and translation together
$C = M^{-1}$	We know that the Camera matrix is the inverse of the Model-View matrix
$C = (RT)^{-1}$	By substitution
$C = T^{-1}R^{-1}$	Inverse of a matrix product is the reverse product of the inverses

Luckily for us, when we are working in camera coordinates in the chapter's examples, we have the inverse translation and the inverse rotation already calculated in the global variables `position` and `rotation`. Therefore, we would write something like this in the code (here `cMatrix` is the Camera matrix):

```
mat4.identity(cMatrix);
mat4.rotateX(cMatrix,rotation[0]*Math.PI/180);
mat4.rotateY(cMatrix,rotation[1]*Math.PI/180);
mat4.rotateZ(cMatrix,rotation[2]*Math.PI/180);
mat4.translate(cMatrix,position);
```

Basic camera types

The following are the camera types that we will discuss in this chapter.

- Orbiting camera
- Tracking camera

Orbiting camera

Up to this point, we have seen how we can generate rotations and translations of the world in the world or camera coordinates. However, in both cases, we are always generating the rotations around the center of the world. This could be ideal for many cases where we are orbiting around a 3D object such as our Nissan GTX model. You put the object at the center of the world, then you can examine the object at different angles (rotation) and then you move away (translation) to see the result. Let's call this type of camera an **orbiting camera**.

Tracking camera

Now, going back to the example of the first person shooting game, we need to have a camera that is able to look up when we want to see if there are enemies above us. Just the same, we should be able to look around left and right (rotations) and then move in the direction in which our camera is pointing (translation). This camera type can be designated as a **first-person** camera. This same type is used when the game follows the main character. Therefore, it is also known as a **tracking camera**.

To implement first-person cameras, we need to set up the rotations on the camera axis instead of using the world origin.

Rotating the camera around its location

When we multiply matrices, the order in which matrices are multiplied is relevant. Say, for instance, that we have two 4x4 matrices. Let R be the first matrix and let's assume that this matrix encodes pure rotation; let T be the second matrix and let's assume that T encodes pure translation. Now:

$$RT \neq TR$$

In other words, the order of the operations affects the result. It is not the same to rotate around the origin and then translate away from it (orbiting camera), as compared to translating the origin and then rotating around it (tracking camera)!

So in order to set the location of the camera as the center for rotations, we just need to invert the order in which the operations are called. This is equivalent to converting from an orbiting camera to a tracking camera.

Translating the camera in the line of sight

When we have an orbiting camera, the camera will be always looking towards the center of the world. Therefore, we will always use the z-axis to move to and from the object that we are examining. However, when we have a tracking camera, as the rotation occurs at the camera location, we can end up looking to any position in the world (which is ideal if you want to move around it and explore it). Then, we need to know the direction in which the camera is pointing to in world coordinates (camera axis). We will see how to obtain this next.

Camera model

Just like its counterpart, the Model-View matrix, the Camera matrix encodes information about the camera axes orientation. As we can see in the figure, the upper-left 3x3 matrix corresponds to the camera axes:

◆   The first column corresponds to the x-axis of the camera. We will call it the **Right vector.**

◆   The second column is the y-axis of the camera. This will be the **Up vector.**

◆   The third column determines the vector in which the camera can move back and forth. This is the z-axis of the camera and we will call it the **Camera axis.**

Due to the fact that the Camera matrix is the inverse of the Model-View matrix, the upper-left 3x3 rotation matrix contained in the Camera matrix gives us the orientation of the camera axes in world space. This is a plus, because it means that we can tell the orientation of our camera in world space, just by looking at the columns of this 3x3 rotation matrix (And we know now what each column means).

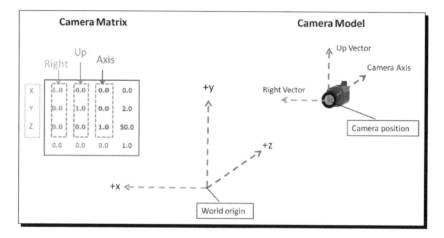

In the following section, we will play with orbiting and tracking cameras and we will see how we can change the camera position using mouse gestures, page widgets (sliders), and also we will have a graphical representation of the resulting Model-View matrix. In this exercise, we will integrate both rotations and translations and we will see how they behave under the two basic types of cameras that we are studying.

Time for action – exploring the Nissan GTX

1. Open the file `ch4_CameraTypes.html` in your HTML5 browser. You will see something like the following:

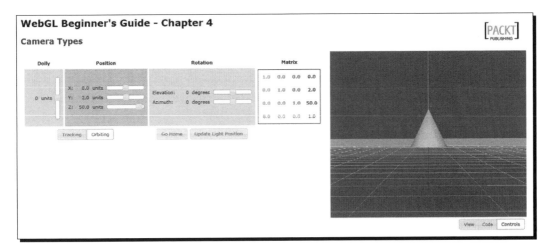

2. Go around the world using the sliders in **Tracking** mode. Cool eh?

3. Now, change the camera type to **Orbiting** mode and do the same.

4. Now, please check that besides the slider controls, both in **Tracking** and **Orbiting** mode, you can use your mouse and keyboard to move around the world.

5. In this exercise, we have implemented a camera using two new classes:

- ❑ `Camera`: to manipulate the camera.
- ❑ `CameraInteractor`: to connect the camera to the canvas. It will receive mouse and keyboard events and it will pass them along to the camera.

If you are curious, you can see the source code of these two classes in `/js/webgl`. We have applied the concepts explained in this chapter to build these two classes.

6. So far, we have seen a cone in the center of the world. Let's change that for something more interesting to explore.

7. Open the file `ch4_CameraTypes.html` in your source code editor.

8. Go to the `load` function. Let's add the car to the scene. Rewrite the contents of this function so it looks like the following:

```
function load() {
    Floor.build(2000,100);
    Axis.build(2000);
    Scene.addObject(Floor);
    Scene.addObject(Axis);
    Scene.loadObjectByParts('models/nissan_gts/pr','Nissan',178);
}
```

You will see that we have increased the size of the axis and the floor so we can see them. We do need to do this because the car is an object much larger than the original cone.

9. There are some steps that we need to take in order to be able to see the car correctly. First we need to make sure that we have a large enough view volume. Go to the `initTransforms` function and update this line:

```
mat4.perspective(30, c_width / c_height, 0.1, 1000.0, pMatrix);
```

With this:

```
mat4.perspective(30, c_width / c_height, 10, 5000.0, pMatrix);
```

10. Do the same in the `updateTransforms` function.

11. Now, let's change the type of our camera so when we load the page, we have an orbiting camera by default. In the `configure` function, change this line:

```
camera = new Camera(CAMERA_TRACKING_TYPE);
```

With:

```
camera = new Camera(CAMERA_ORBIT_TYPE);
```

12. Another thing we need to take into account is the location of the camera. For a large object like this car, we need to be far away from the center of the world. For that purpose, go to the `configure` function and change:

```
camera.goHome([0,2,50]);
```

Add:

```
camera.goHome([0,200,2000]);
```

13. Let's modify the lighting of our scene so it fits better in the model we are displaying. In the function `configure` function, right after this line:

```
interactor = new CameraInteractor(camera, canvas);
```

Write:

```
gl.uniform4fv(prg.uLightAmbient,   [0.1,0.1,0.1,1.0]);
gl.uniform3fv(prg.uLightPosition,  [0, 0, 2120]);
gl.uniform4fv(prg.uLightDiffuse,   [0.7,0.7,0.7,1.0]);
```

14. Save the file with a different name and then load this new file in your HTML5 Internet browser. You should see something like the following screenshot:

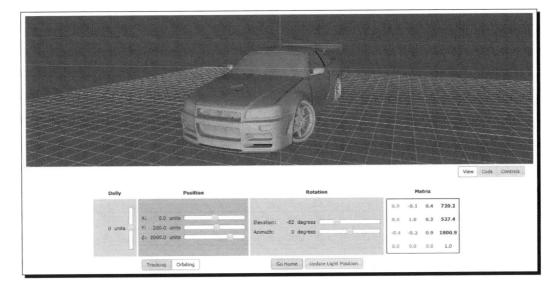

15. Using the mouse, keyboard, or/and the sliders, explore the new scene.
Hint: use orbiting mode to explore the car from different angles.

16. See how the Camera matrix is updated when you move around the scene.

17. You can see what the final exercise looks like by opening the file `ch4_NissanGTR.html`.

What just happened?

We added mouse and keyboard interaction to our scene. We also experimented with the two basic camera types—tracking and orbiting cameras. We modified the settings of our scene to visualize a complex model.

Have a go hero – updating light positions

Remember that when we move the camera, we are applying the inverse transformation to the world. If we do not update the light position, then the light source will be located at the same static point, *regardless* of the final transformation applied to the world.

This is very convenient when we are moving around or exploring an object in the scene. We will always be able to see if the light is located on the same axis of the camera. This is the case for the exercises in this chapter. Nevertheless, we can simulate the case when the camera movement is independent from the light source. To do so, we need to calculate the new light position whenever we move the camera. We do this in two steps:

First, we calculate the light direction. We can do this by simply calculating the difference vector between our target and our origin. Say that the light source is located at [0,2,50]. If we want to direct our light source towards the origin, we calculate the vector [0,0,0] - [0,2,50] (target - origin). This vector has the correct orientation of the light when we target the origin. We repeat the same procedure if we have a different target that needs to be lit. In that case, we just use the coordinates of the target and from them we subtract the location of the light.

As we are directing our light source towards the origin, we can find the direction of the light just by inverting the light position. If you notice, we do this in ESSL in the vertex shader:

```
vec3 L = normalize(-uLightPosition);
```

Now as L is a vector, if we want to update the direction of the light, then we need to use the Normal matrix, discussed earlier in this chapter, in order to update this vector under any world transformation. This step is optional in the vertex shader:

```
if(uUpdateLight){
  L = vec3(uNMatrix*vec4(L,0.0));
}
```

In the previous fragment of code, L is augmented to 4-components, so we can use the direct multiplication provided by ESSL. (Remember that uNMatrix is a 4x4 matrix and as such, the vectors that are transformed by it need to be 4-dimensional). Also, please bear in mind that, as explained in the beginning of the chapter, vectors have their homogeneous coordinate always set to zero, while vertices have their homogeneous coordinate set to one.

After the multiplication, we reduce the result to 3-components before assigning the result back to L.

You can test the effects of updating the light position by using the button **Update Light Position**, provided in the files ch4_NissanGTR.html and ch4_CameraTypes.html.

We connect a global variable that keeps track of the state of this button with the uniform
`uUpdateLight`.

1. Edit `ch4_NissanGTR.html` and set the light position to a different location.
   To do this, edit the `configure` function. Go to:

   `gl.uniform3fv(prg.uLightPosition, [0, 0, 2120]);`

   Try different light positions:

   ❑ `[2120,0,0]`

   ❑ `[0,2120,0]`

   ❑ `[100,100,100]`

2. For each option, save the file and try it with and without updating the light position
   (use the button **Update Light Position**).

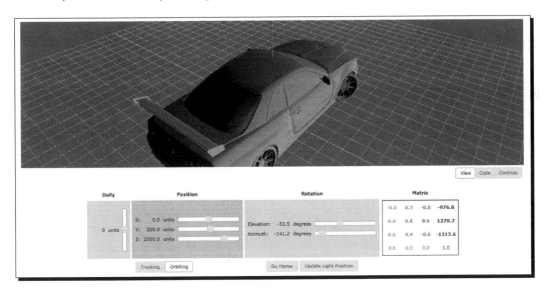

3. For a better visualization, use an **Orbiting** camera.

The Perspective matrix

At the beginning of the chapter, we said that the Perspective matrix combines the
projection transformation and the perspective division. These two steps combined
take a 3D scene and converts it into a cube that is then mapped to the 2D canvas
by the viewport transformation.

In practice, the Perspective matrix determines the geometry of the image that is captured by the camera. In a real world camera, the lens of the camera would determine how distorted the final images are. In a WebGL world, we use the Perspective matrix to simulate that. Also, unlike in the real world where our images are always affected by perspective, in WebGL, we can pick a different representation: the orthographic projection.

Field of view

The Perspective matrix determines the **Field of View (FOV)** of the camera, that is, how much of the 3D space will be captured by the camera. The field of view is a measure given in degrees and the term is used interchangeably with the term **angle of view**.

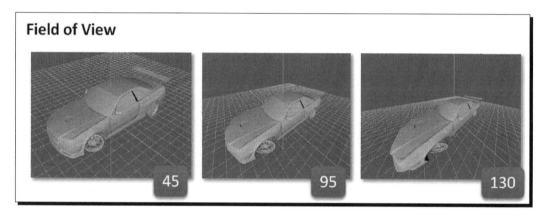

Perspective or orthogonal projection

A perspective projection assigns more space to details that are closer to the camera than the details that are farther from it. In other words, the geometry that is close to the camera will appear bigger than the geometry that is farther from it. This is the way our eyes see the real world. Perspective projection allows us to assess the distance because it gives our brain a *depth cue*.

In contrast, an orthogonal projection uses parallel lines; this means that will look the same size regardless of their distance to the camera. Therefore, the depth cue is lost when using orthogonal projection.

Using `glMatrix`, we can set up the perspective or the orthogonal projection by calling `mat4.persective` or `mat4.ortho` respectively. The signatures for these methods are:

Function	Description (Taken from the documentation of the library)
`mat4.perspective(fovy, aspect, near, far, dest)`	Generates a perspective projection matrix with the given bounds Parameters: `fovy` - vertical field of view `aspect` - aspect ratio—typically viewport width/ height `near, far` - near and far bounds of the frustum `dest` - Optional, `mat4` frustum matrix will be written into Returns: `dest` if specified, a new `mat4` otherwise
`mat4.ortho(left, right, bottom, top, near, far, dest)`	Generates an orthogonal projection matrix with the given bounds: Parameters: `left, right` - left and right bounds of the frustum `bottom, top` - bottom and top bounds of the frustum `near, far` - near and far bounds of the frustum `dest` - Optional, `mat4` frustum matrix will be written into Returns: `dest` if specified, a new `mat4` otherwise.

In the following *time for action* section, we will see how the field of view and the perspective projection affects the image that our camera captures. We will experiment perspective and orthographic projections for both orbiting and tracking cameras.

Time for action – orthographic and perspective projections

1. Open the file `ch4_ProjectiveModes.html` in your HTML5 Internet browser.

2. This exercise is very similar to the previous one. However, there are two new buttons: Perspective and Orthogonal. As you can see, Perspective is activated by default.

3. Change the camera type to **Orbiting**.

4. Change the projective mode to **Orthographic**.

5. Explore the scene. Notice the lack of depth cues that is characteristic of orthogonal projections:

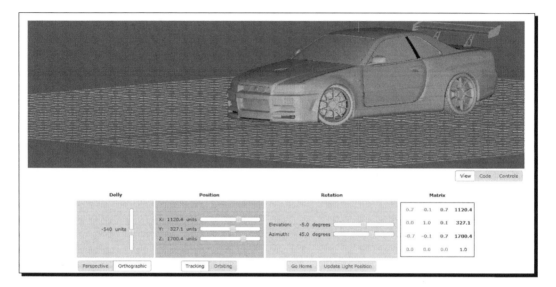

6. Now switch to **Perspective** mode:

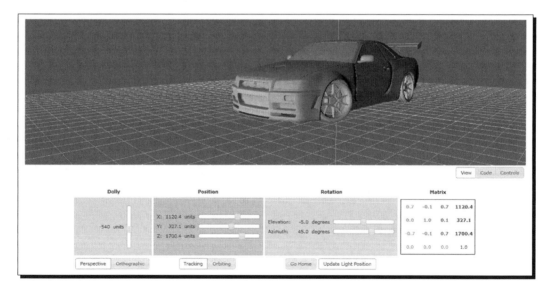

7. Explore the source code. Go to the `updateTransforms` function:

```
function updateTransforms(){
    if (projectionMode == PROJ_PERSPECTIVE){
        mat4.perspective(30, c_width / c_height, 10, 5000,
pMatrix);
    }
    else{
        mat4.ortho(-c_width, c_width, -c_height, c_height, -5000,
5000, pMatrix);
    }
}
```

8. Please take a look at the parameters that we are using to set up the projective view.

9. Let's modify the field of view. Create a global variable right before the `updateTransforms` function:

```
var fovy = 30;
```

10. Let's use this variable instead of the hardcoded value:

Replace:

```
mat4.perspective(30, c_width / c_height, 10, 5000, pMatrix);
```

With:

```
mat4.perspective(fovy, c_width / c_height, 10, 5000, pMatrix);
```

11. Now let's update the camera interactor to update this variable. Open the file `/js/webgl/CameraInteractor.js` in your source code editor.

Append these lines to `CameraInteractor.prototype.onKeyDown` inside `if (!this.ctrl){`:

```
else if (this.key == 87) {  //w
    if(fovy<120) fovy+=5;
    console.info('FovY:'+fovy);
}
else if (this.key == 78) { //n
    if(fovy>15) fovy-=5;
    console.info('FovY:'+fovy);
}
```

Please make sure that you are inside the `if` section.

If these instructions are already there, do not write them again. Just make sure you understand that the goal here is to update the global `fovy` variable that refers to the field of view in perspective mode.

12. Save the changes made to `CameraInteractor.js`.

13. Save the changes made to `ch4_ProjectiveModes.html`. Use a different name. You can see the final result in the file `ch4_ProjectiveModesFOVY.html`.

14. Open the renamed file in your HTML5 Internet browser. Try different fields of view by pressing `w` or `n` repeatedly. Can you replicate these scenes:

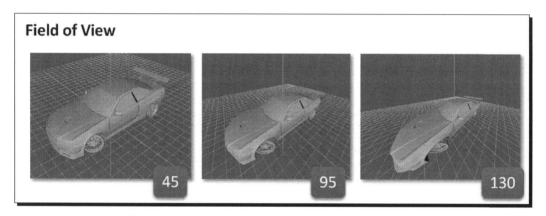

Field of View

45   95   130

15. Notice that as you increase the field of view, your camera will capture more of the 3D space. Think of this as the lens of a real-world camera. With a wide-angle lens, you capture more space with the trade-off of deforming the objects as they move towards the boundaries of your viewing box.

What just happened?

We experimented with different configurations for the Perspective matrix and we saw how these configurations produce different results in the scene.

Have a go hero – integrating the Model-view and the projective transform

Remember that once we have applied the Model-View transformation to the vertices, the next step is to transform the view coordinates to NDC coordinates:

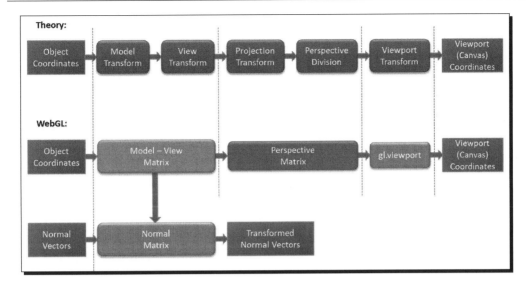

We do this by a simple multiplication using ESSL in the vertex shader:

```
gl_Position = uPMatrix * uMVMatrix * vec4(aVertexPosition,1.0);
```

The predefined variable, `gl_Position`, stores the NDC coordinates for each vertex of every object defined in the scene.

In the previous multiplication, we augment the shader attribute, `aVertexPosition`, to a 4-component vertex because our matrices are 4x4. Unlike normals, vertices have a homogeneous coordinate equal to one (w=1).

After this step, WebGL will convert the computed clipping coordinates to normalized device coordinates and from there to canvas coordinates using the WebGL `viewport` function. We are going to see what happens when we change this mapping.

1. Open the file `ch4_NisanGTS.html` in your source code editor.

2. Go to the `draw` function. This is the rendering function that is invoked every time we interact with the scene (by using the mouse, the keyboard, or the widgets on the page).

3. Change this line:

```
gl.viewport(0, 0, c_width, c_height);
```

Make it:

```
gl.viewport(0, 0, c_width/2, c_height/2);
gl.viewport(c_width/2,c_height/2, c_width, c_height);
gl.viewport(50, 50, c_width-100, c_height-100);
```

4. For each option, save the file and open it on your HTML5 browser.

5. What do you see? Please notice that you can interact with the scene just like before.

Structure of the WebGL examples

We have improved the structure of the code examples in this chapter. As the complexity of our WebGL applications increases, it is wise to have a good, maintainable, and clear design. We have left this section at the end of the chapter so you can use it as a reference when working on the exercises.

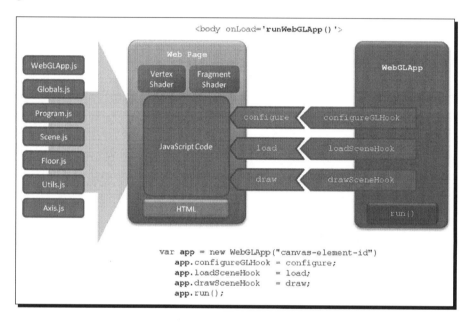

Just like in previous exercises, our entry point is the `runWebGLApp` function which is called when the page is loaded. There we create an instance of `WebGLApp`, as shown in the previous diagram.

WebGLApp

This class encapsulates some of the utility functions that were present in our examples in previous chapters. It also declares a clear and simple life cycle for a WebGL application. `WebGLApp` has three function hooks that we can map to functions in our web page. These hooks determine what functions will be called for each stage in the life cycle of the app. In the examples of this chapter, we have created the following mappings:

- **configureGLHook**: which points to the configure function in the web page
- **loadSceneHook**: which is mapped to the load function in the webpage
- **drawSceneHook**: which corresponds to the draw function in the webpage

A function hook can be described as a pointer to a function. In JavaScript, you can write:

```
function foo(){alert("function foo invoked");}
var hook = foo;
hook();
```

This fragment of code will execute foo when hook() is executed. This allows a pluggable behavior that is more difficult to express in fully typed languages.

WebGLApp will use the function hooks to call configure, load, and draw in our page in that order.

After setting these hooks, the run method is invoked.

The source code for WebGLApp and other supporting objects can be found in /js/webgl

Supporting objects

We have created the following objects, each one in its own file:

- **Globals.js**: Contains the global variables used in the example.
- **Program.js**: Creates the program using the shader definitions. Provides the mapping between JavaScript variables (prg.*) and program attributes and uniforms.
- **Scene.js**: Maintains a list of objects to be rendered. Contains the AJAX/JSON functionality to retrieve remote objects. It also allows adding local objects to the scene.
- **Floor.js**: Defines a grid on the X-Z plane. This object is added to the Scene to have a reference of where the floor is.
- **Axis.js**: Represents the axis in world space. When added to the scene, we will have a reference of where the origin is.

- ◆ WebGLApp.js: Represents a WebGL application. It has three function hooks that define the configuration stage, the scene loading stage, and the rendering stage. These hooks can be connected to functions in our web page.

- ◆ Utils.js: Utility functions such as obtaining a gl context.

 You can refer to Globals.js to find the global variables used in this example (the definition of the JavaScript matrices is there) and Program.js to find the prg.* JavaScript variables that map to attributes and uniforms in the shaders.

Life-cycle functions

The following are the functions that define the life-cycle of a WebGLApp application:

Configure

The configure function sets some parameters of our gl context, such as the color for clearing the canvas, and then it calls the initTransforms function.

Load

The load function sets up the objects Floor and Axis. These two locally-created objects are added to the Scene by calling the addObject method. After that, a remote object (AJAX call) is loaded using the Scene.loadObject method.

Draw

The draw function calls updateTransforms to calculate the matrices for the new position (that is, when we move), then iterates over the objects in the Scene to render them. Inside this loop, it calls setMatrixUniforms for every object to be rendered.

Matrix handling functions

The following are the functions that initialize, update, and pass matrices to the shaders:

initTransforms

As you can see, the Model-View matrix, the Camera matrix, the Perspective matrix, and the Normal matrix are set up here:

```
function initTransforms(){

    mat4.identity(mvMatrix);
    mat4.translate(mvMatrix, home);
```

```
        displayMatrix(mvMatrix);

        mat4.identity(cMatrix);
        mat4.inverse(mvMatrix,cMatrix);

        mat4.identity(pMatrix);
        mat4.perspective(30, c_width / c_height, 0.1, 1000.0, pMatrix);

        mat4.identity(nMatrix);
        mat4.set(mvMatrix, nMatrix);
        mat4.inverse(nMatrix);
        mat4.transpose(nMatrix);

        coords = COORDS_WORLD;
    }
```

updateTransforms

In `updateTransforms`, we use the contents of the global variables `position` and `rotation` to update the matrices. This is, of course, if the `requestUpdate` variable is set to `true`. We set `requestUpdate` to `true` from the GUI controls. The code for these is located at the bottom of the webpage (for instance, check the file `ch4_ModelView_Rotation.html`).

```
    function updateTransforms(){

        mat4.perspective(30, c_width / c_height, 0.1, 1000.0, pMatrix);
        if (coords == COORDS_WORLD){
                mat4.identity(mvMatrix);
                mat4.translate(mvMatrix, position);
                mat4.rotateX(mvMatrix,rotation[0]*Math.PI/180);
                mat4.rotateY(mvMatrix,rotation[1]*Math.PI/180);
                mat4.rotateZ(mvMatrix,rotation[2]*Math.PI/180);
        }
        else{
                mat4.identity(cMatrix);
                mat4.rotateX(cMatrix,rotation[0]*Math.PI/180);
                mat4.rotateY(cMatrix,rotation[1]*Math.PI/180);
                mat4.rotateZ(cMatrix,rotation[2]*Math.PI/180);
                mat4.translate(cMatrix,position);
        }
    }
```

setMatrixUniforms

This function performs the mapping:

```
function setMatrixUniforms(){

    if (coords == COORDS_WORLD){
        mat4.inverse(mvMatrix, cMatrix);
        displayMatrix(mvMatrix);
        gl.uniformMatrix4fv(prg.uMVMatrix, false, mvMatrix);
    }
    else{
        mat4.inverse(cMatrix, mvMatrix);
        displayMatrix(cMatrix);

    }

    gl.uniformMatrix4fv(prg.uPMatrix, false, pMatrix);
    gl.uniformMatrix4fv(prg.uMVMatrix, false, mvMatrix);
    mat4.transpose(cMatrix, nMatrix);
    gl.uniformMatrix4fv(prg.uNMatrix, false, nMatrix);
}
```

Summary

Let's summarize what we have learned in this chapter:

There is no camera object in WebGL. However, we can build one using the Model-View matrix.

3D objects undergo several transformations to be displayed on a 2D screen. These transformations are represented as 4x4 matrices.

Scene transformations are affine. Affine transformations are constituted by a linear transformation followed by a translation. WebGL groups affine transforms in three matrices: the Model-View matrix, the Perspective matrix, and the Normal matrix and one WebGL operation: `gl.viewport()`.

Affine transforms are applied in projective space so they can be represented by 4x4 matrices. To work in projective space, vertices need to be augmented to contain an extra term, namely, w, which is called the perspective coordinate. The 4-tuple (x,y,z,w) is called homogeneous coordinates. Homogeneous coordinates allows representation of lines that intersect on infinity by making the perspective coordinate $w = 0$. Vectors always have a homogeneous coordinate $w = 0$; While points have a homogenous coordinate, namely, $w = 1$ (unless they are at infinity, in which case $w=0$).

By default, a WebGL scene is viewed from the world origin in the negative direction of the z-axis. This can be altered by changing the Model-View matrix.

The Camera matrix is the inverse of the Model-View matrix. Camera and World operations are opposite. There are two basic types of camera—orbiting and tracking camera.

Normals receive special treatment whenever the object suffers an affine transform. Normals are transformed by the Normal matrix, which can be obtained from the Model-View matrix.

The Perspective matrix allows the determining of two basic projective modes, namely, orthographic projection and perspective projection.

5
Action

So far, we have seen static scenes where all interactions are done by moving the camera. The camera transformation is applied to all objects in the 3D scene, therefore we call it a global transform. However, objects in 3D scenes can have actions on their own. For instance, in a racing car game, each car has its own speed and trajectory. In a first-person shooting game your enemies can hide behind barricades then come and fight you or run away. In general, each one of these actions is modeled as a matrix transformation that is attached to the corresponding actor in the scene. These are called local transforms. In this chapter we will study different techniques to make use of local transforms.

In this chapter, we will discuss the following topics:

- ◆ Global versus local transformations
- ◆ Matrix stacks and using them to perform animation
- ◆ Using JavaScript timers to do time-based animation
- ◆ Parametric curves
- ◆ Interpolation

In the previous chapter, we saw that when we apply the same transformation to all the objects in our scene we move the world. This global transformation allowed us to create two different kinds of cameras. Once we have applied the camera transform to all the objects in the scene, each one of them could update its position; representing, for instance, targets that are moving in a first-person shooting game, or the position of other competitors in a car racing game.

This can be achieved by modifying the current Model-View transform for each object. However, if we modified the Model-View matrix, how could we make sure that these modifications do not affect other objects? After all, we only have one Model-View matrix, right?

The solution to this dilemma is to use matrix stacks.

Matrix stacks

A **matrix stack** provides a way to apply local transforms to individual objects in our scene while at the same time we keep the global transform (camera transform) coherent for all of them. Let's see how it works.

Each rendering cycle (each call to our `draw` function) requires calculating the scene matrices to react to camera movements. We are going to update the Model-View matrix for each object in our scene before passing the matrices to the shading program (as attributes). We do this in three steps as follows:

♦ Step 1: Once the global Model-View matrix (camera transform) has been calculated, we proceed to save it in a stack. This step will allow us to recover the original matrix once we had applied to any local transforms.

♦ Step 2: Calculate an updated Model-View matrix for each object in the scene. This update consists of multiplying the original Model-View matrix by a matrix that represents the rotation, translation, and/or scaling of each object in the scene. The updated Model-View matrix is passed to the program and the respective object then appears in the location indicated by its local transform.

♦ Step 3: We recover the original matrix from the stack and then we repeat steps 1 to 3 for the next object that needs to be rendered.

The following diagram shows this three-step procedure for one object:

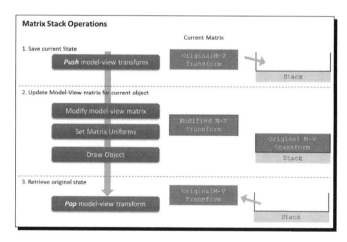

Animating a 3D scene

To animate a scene is nothing else than applying the appropriate local transformations to objects in it. For instance, if we have a cone and a sphere and we want to move them, each one of them will have a corresponding local transformation that will describe its location, orientation, and scale. In the previous section, we saw that matrix stacks allow recovering the original Model-View transform so we can apply the correct local transform for the next object to be rendered.

Knowing how to move objects with local transforms and matrix stacks, the question that needs to be addressed is: *When?*

If we calculated the position that we want to give to the cone and the sphere of our example every time we called the `draw` function, this would imply that the animation rate would be dependent on how fast our rendering cycle goes. A slower rendering cycle would produce choppy animations and a too fast rendering cycle would create the illusion of objects jumping from one side to the other without smooth transitions.

Therefore, it is important to make the animation independent from the rendering cycle. There are a couple of JavaScript elements that we can use to achieve this goal: The `requestAnimFrame` function and JavaScript timers.

requestAnimFrame function

The `window.requestAnimFrame()` function is currently being implemented in HTML5-WebGL enabled Internet browsers. This function is designed such that it calls the rendering function (whatever function we indicate) in a safe way only when the browser/tab window is in focus. Otherwise, there is no call. This saves precious CPU, GPU, and memory resources.

Using the `requestAnimFrame` function, we can obtain a rendering cycle that goes as fast as the hardware allows and at the same time, it is automatically suspended whenever the window is out of focus. If we used `requestAnimFrame` to implement our rendering cycle, we could use then a JavaScript timer that fires up periodically calculating the elapsed time and updating the animation time accordingly. However, the function is a feature that is still in development.

 To check on the status of the `requestAnimFrame` function, please refer to the following URL:
`https://developer.mozilla.org/en/DOM/window.requestAn`
`imationFrame#AutoCompatibilityTable`.

JavaScript timers

We can use two JavaScript timers to isolate the rendering rate from the animation rate.

In our previous code examples, the rendering rate is controlled by the class `WebGLApp`. This class invokes the `draw` function, defined in our page, periodically using a JavaScript timer.

Unlike the `requestAnimFrame` function, JavaScript timers keep running in the background even when the page is not in focus. This is not optimal performance for your computer given that you are allocating resources to a scene that you are not even looking. To mimic some of the `requestAnimFrame` intelligent behavior provided for this purpose, we can use the `onblur` and `onfocus` events of the JavaScript `window` object.

Let's see what we can do:

Action (What)	Goal (Why)	Method (How)
Pause the rendering	To stop the rendering until the window is in focus	Clear the timer calling `clearInterval` in the `window.onblur` function
Slow the rendering	To reduce resource consumption but make sure that the 3D scene keeps evolving even if we are not looking at it	We can clear current timer calling `clearInterval` in the `window.onblur` function and create a new timer with a more relaxed interval (higher value)
Resume the rendering	To activate the 3D scene at full speed when the browser window recovers its focus	We start a new timer with the original render rate in the `window.onfocus` function

By reducing the JavaScript timer rate or clearing the timer, we can handle hardware resources more efficiently.

 The source code for WebGLApp is located in the file `/js/webgl/WebGLApp.js` that accompanies this chapter. In WebGLApp you can see how the `onblur` and `onfocus` events have been used to control the rendering timer as described previously.

Timing strategies

In this section, we will create the second JavaScript timer that will allow controlling the animation. As previously mentioned, a second JavaScript timer will provide independency between how fast your computer can render frames and how fast we want the animation to go. We have called this property the `animation rate`.

However, before moving forward you should know that there is a caveat when working with timers: *JavaScript is not a multi-threaded language*.

This means that if there are several asynchronous events occurring at the same time (blocking events) the browser will queue them for their posterior execution. Each browser has a different mechanism to deal with blocking event queues.

There are two blocking event-handling alternatives for the purpose of developing an animation timer.

Animation strategy

The first alternative is to calculate the elapsed time inside the timer callback. The pseudo-code looks like the following :

```
var initialTime = undefined;
var elapsedTime = undefined;
var animationRate   = 30; //30 ms
function animate(deltaT){
    //calculate object positions based on deltaT
}
function onFrame(){
    elapsedTime = (new Date).getTime() - initialTime;
    if (elapsedTime < animationRate) return; //come back later
    animate(elapsedTime);
    initialTime = (new Date).getTime();
}
function startAnimation(){
  setInterval(onFrame,animationRate/1000);
}
```

Doing so, we can guarantee that the animation time is independent from how often the timer callback is actually executed. If there are big delays (due to other blocking events) this method can result in **dropped frames**. This means the object's positions in our scene will be immediately moved to the current position that they should be in according to the elapsed time (between consecutive animation timer callbacks) and then the intermediate positions are to be ignored. The motion on screen may jump but often a dropped animation frame is an acceptable loss in a real-time application, for instance, when we move one object from point A to point B over a given period of time. However, if we were using this strategy when shooting a target in a 3D shooting game, we could quickly run into problems. Imagine that you shoot a target and then there is a delay, next thing you know the target is no longer there! Notice that in this case where we need to calculate a collision, we cannot afford to miss frames, because the collision could occur in any of the frames that we would drop otherwise without analyzing. The following strategy solves that problem.

Simulation strategy

There are several applications such as the shooting game example where we need all the intermediate frames to assure the integrity of the outcome. For example, when working with collision detection, physics simulations, or artificial intelligence for games. In this case, we need to update the object's positions at a constant rate. We do so by directly calculating the next position for the objects inside the timer callback.

```
var animationRate = 30; //30 ms
var deltaPosition = 0.1
function animate(deltaP){
    //calculate object positions based on deltaP
}
function onFrame(){
    animate(deltaPosition);
}
function startAnimation(){
    setInterval(onFrame,animationRate/1000);
}
```

This may lead to **frozen frames** when there is a long list of blocking events because the object's positions would not be timely updated.

Combined approach: animation and simulation

Generally speaking, browsers are really efficient at handling blocking events and in most cases the performance would be similar regardless of the chosen strategy. Then, deciding to calculate the elapsed time or the next position in timer callbacks will then depend on your particular application.

Nonetheless, there are some cases where it is desirable to combine both animation and simulation strategies. We can create a timer callback that calculates the elapsed time and updates the animation as many times as required per frame. The pseudocode looks like the following:

```
var initialTime = undefined;
var elapsedTime = undefined;
var animationRate = 30; //30 ms
var deltaPosition = 0.1;
function animate(delta){
  //calculate object positions based on delta
}

function onFrame(){
    elapsedTime = (new Date).getTime() - initialTime;
```

```
    if (elapsedTime < animationRate) return; //come back later!

    var steps = Math.floor(elapsedTime / animationRate);
    while(steps > 0){
        animate(deltaPosition);
        steps -= 1;
    }
    initialTime = (new Date).getTime();
}

function startAnimation(){
    initialTime = (new Date).getTime();
    setInterval(onFrame,animationRate/1000);
}
```

You can see from the preceding code snippet that the animation will always update at a fixed rate, no matter how much time elapses between frames. If the app is running at 60 Hz, the animation will update once every other frame, if the app runs at 30 Hz the animation will update once per frame, and if the app runs at 15 Hz the animation will update twice per frame. The key is that by always moving the animation forward a fixed amount it is far more stable and deterministic.

The following diagram shows the responsibilities of each function in the call stack for the combined approach:

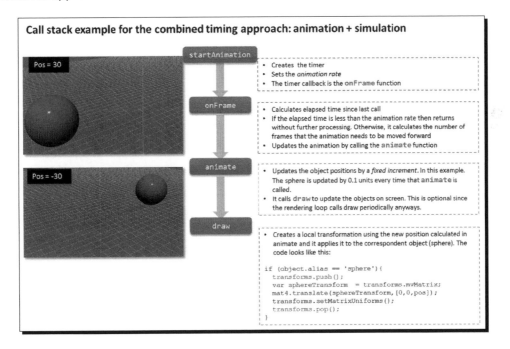

This approach can cause issues if for whatever reason an animation step actually takes longer to compute than the fixed step, but if that is occurring, you really ought to simplify your animation code or put out a recommended minimum system spec for your application.

Web Workers: Real multithreading in JavaScript

Though it is beyond the scope of this book, you may want to know that if performance is really critical to you and you need to ensure that a particular update loop always fires at a consistent rate then you could use **Web Workers**.

Web Workers is an API that allows web applications to spawn background processes running scripts in parallel to their main page. This allows for thread-like operation with message-passing as the coordination mechanism.

You can find the Web Workers specification at the following URL: `http://dev.w3.org/html5/workers/`

Architectural updates

Let's review the structure of the examples developed in the book. Each web page includes several scripts. One of them is `WebGLApp.js`. This script contains the `WebGLApp` object.

WebGLApp review

The `WebGLApp` object defines three function hooks that control the life cycle of the application. As shown in the diagram, we create a `WebGLApp` instance inside the `runWebGLApp` function. Then, we connect the `WebGLApp` hooks to the `configure`, `load`, and `draw` functions that we coded. Also, please notice that the `runWebGLApp` function is the entry point for the application and it is automatically invoked using the `onload` event of the web page.

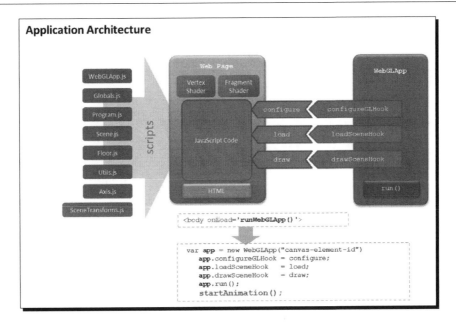

Adding support for matrix stacks

The diagram also shows a new script: SceneTransforms.js. This file contains the SceneTransforms objects that encapsulate the matrix-handling operations including matrix stacks operations push and pop. The SceneTransforms object replaces the functionality provided in *Chapter 4*, *Camera*, by the initTransforms, updateTransforms, and setMatrixUniforms functions.

You can find the source code for SceneTransforms in js/webgl/SceneTransforms.js.

Configuring the rendering rate

After setting the connections between the WebGLApp hooks and our configure, load and draw functions, WebGLApp.run() is invoked. This call creates a JavaScript timer that is triggered every 500 ms. The callback for this timer is the draw function. Up to now a refresh rate of 500 ms was more than acceptable because we did not have any animations. However, this is a parameter that you could tweak later on to optimize your rendering speed. To do so please change the value of the constant WEBGLAPP_RENDER_RATE. This constant is defined in the source code for WebGLApp.

You can find the source code for WebGLApp in js/webgl/WebGLApp.js.

Creating an animation timer

As shown in the previous architecture diagram, we have added a call to the new `startAnimation` function inside the `runWebGLApp` function. This causes the animation to start when the page loads.

Connecting matrix stacks and JavaScript timers

In the following *Time for action* section, we will take a look at a simple scene where we have animated a cone and a sphere. In this example, we are using matrix stacks to implement local transformations and JavaScript timers to implement the animation sequence.

Time for action – simple animation

1. Open `ch5_SimpleAnimation.html` using your WebGL-enabled Internet browser of choice.

2. Move the camera around and see how the objects (sphere and cone) move independently of each other (local transformations) and from the camera position (global transformation).

3. Move the camera around pressing the left mouse button and holding it while you drag the mouse.

4. You can also dolly the camera by clicking the left mouse button while pressing the *Alt* key and then dragging the mouse.

5. Now change the camera type to **Tracking**. If for any reason you lose your bearings, click on **go home**.

6. Let's examine the source code to see how we have implemented this example. Open `ch5_SimpleAnimation.html` using the source code editor of your choice.

7. Take a look at the functions `startAnimation`, `onFrame`, and `animate`. Which timing strategy are we using here?

8. The global variables `pos_sphere` and `pos_cone` contain the position of the sphere and the cone respectively. Scroll up to the `draw` function. Inside the main `for` loop where each object of the scene is rendered, a different local transformation is calculated depending on the current object being rendered. The code looks like the following:

```
transforms.calculateModelView();
transforms.push();
if (object.alias == 'sphere'){
    var sphereTransform  = transforms.mvMatrix;
    mat4.translate(sphereTransform,[0,0,pos_sphere]);
}
else if (object.alias == 'cone'){
    var coneTransform = transforms.mvMatrix;
    mat4.translate(coneTransform, [pos_cone,0,0]);
}
transforms.setMatrixUniforms();
transforms.pop();
```

Using the `transforms` object (which is an instance of `SceneTransforms`) we obtain the global Model-View matrix by calling `transforms.calculateModelView()`. Then, we push it into a matrix stack by calling the `push` method. Now we can apply any transform that we want, knowing that we can retrieve the global transform so it is available for the next object on the list. We actually do so at the end of the code snippet by calling the `pop` method. Between the `push` and `pop` calls, we determine which object is currently being rendered and depending on that, we use the global `pos_sphere` or `pos_cone` to apply a translation to the current Model-View matrix. By doing so, we create a local transform.

9. Take a second look at the previous code. As you saw at the beginning of this exercise, the cone is moving in the x axis while the sphere is moving in the z axis. What do you need to change to animate the cone in the y axis? Test your hypothesis by modifying this code, saving the web page, and opening it again on your HTML5 web browser.

10. Let's go now back to the `animate` function. What do we need to modify here to make the objects to move faster? Hint: take a look at the global variables that this function uses.

What just happened?

In this exercise, we saw a simple animation of two objects. We examined the source code to understand the call stack of functions that make the animation possible. At the end of this call stack, there is a `draw` function that takes the information of the calculated object positions and applies the respective local transforms.

Have a go hero – simulating dropped and frozen frames

1. Open the ch5_DroppingFrames.html file using your HTML5 web browser. Here you will see the same scene that we analyzed in the previous *Time for action* section. You can see here that the animation is not smooth because we are simulating dropping frames.

2. Take a look at the source code in an editor of your choice. Scroll to the animate function. You can see that we have included a new variable: simulationRate. In the onFrame function, this new variable calculates how many simulation steps need to be performed when the time elapsed is around 300 ms (animationRate). Given that the simulationRate is 30 ms this will produce a total of 10 simulation steps. These steps can be more if there are unexpected delays and the elapsed time is considerably higher. This is the behavior that we expect.

3. In this section we want you to experiment with different values for the animationRate and simulationRate variables to answer the following questions:

    ❏ How do we get rid of the dropping frames issue?

    ❏ How can we simulate frozen frames?

 Hint: the calculated steps should always be zero.

    ❏ What is the relationship between the animationRate and the simulationRate variables when simulating frozen frames?

Parametric curves

There are many situations where we don't know the exact position that an object will have at a given time but we know an equation that describe its movement. These equations are known as parametric curves and are called like that because the position depends on one parameter: the time.

There are many examples of parametric curves. We can think for instance of a projectile that we shoot on a game, a car that is going downhill or a bouncing ball. In each case, there are equations that describe the motion of these objects under ideal conditions. The next diagram shows the parametric equation that describes free fall motion.

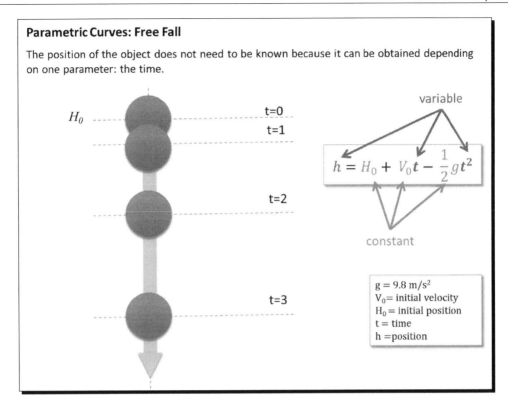

Parametric Curves: Free Fall

The position of the object does not need to be known because it can be obtained depending on one parameter: the time.

variable

$$h = H_0 + V_0 t - \frac{1}{2} g t^2$$

constant

$g = 9.8 \text{ m/s}^2$
$V_0 = \text{initial velocity}$
$H_0 = \text{initial position}$
$t = \text{time}$
$h = \text{position}$

We are going to use parametric curves for animating objects in a WebGL scene. In this example, we will model a set of bouncing balls.

 The complete source code for this exercise can be found in `/code/ch5_BouncingBalls.html`.

Initialization steps

We will create a global variable that will store the time (simulation time).

```
var sceneTime = 0;
```

We also create the global variables that regulate the animation:

```
var animationRate = 15; /* 15 ms */
var elapsedTime = undefined;
var initialTime = undefined;
```

The `load` function is updated to load a bunch of balls using the same geometry (same JSON file) but adding it several times to the scene object. The code looks like this:

```
function load(){

    Floor.build(80,2);
    Axis.build(82);
    Scene.addObject(Floor);

    for (var i=0;i<NUM_BALLS;i++){
        var pos = generatePosition();
        ball.push(new BouncingBall(pos[0],pos[1],pos[2]));
        Scene.loadObject('models/geometry/ball.json','ball'+i);
    }
}
```

Notice that here we also populate an array named `ball[]`. We do this so that we can store the ball positions every time the global time changes. We will talk in depth about the bouncing ball simulation in the next *Time for action* section. For the moment, it is worth mentioning that it is on the `load` function that we load the geometry and initialize the ball array with the initial ball positions.

Setting up the animation timer

The `startAnimation` and `onFrame` functions look exactly as in the previous examples:

```
function onFrame() {
  elapsedTime = (new Date).getTime() - initialTime;
  if (elapsedTime < animationRate) { return;} //come back later
  var steps = Math.floor(elapsedTime / animationRate);
    while(steps > 0){
        animate();
        steps -= 1;
    }
  initialTime = (new Date).getTime();
}

function startAnimation(){
  initialTime = (new Date).getTime();
  setInterval(onFrame,animationRate/1000); // animation rate
}
```

Running the animation

The `animate` function passes the `sceneTime` variable to the `update` method of every ball in the ball array. Then, `sceneTime` is updated by a fixed amount. The code looks like this:

```
function animate(){
    for (var i = 0; i<ball.length; i++){

        ball[i].update(sceneTime);
    }
    sceneTime += 33/1000;  //simulation time
  draw();
}
```

Again, parametric curves are really helpful because we do not need to know beforehand the location of every object that we want to move. We just apply a parametric equation that gives us the location based on the current time. This occurs for every ball inside its `update` method.

Drawing each ball in its current position

In the `draw` function, we use matrix stack to save the state of the Model-View matrix before applying a local transformation for each one of the balls. The code looks like this:

```
transforms.calculateModelView();
transforms.push();
if (object.alias.substring(0,4) == 'ball'){
    var index = parseInt(object.alias.substring(4,8));
    var ballTransform  = transforms.mvMatrix;
    mat4.translate(ballTransform,ball[index].position);
    object.diffuse = ball[index].color;
}
transforms.setMatrixUniforms();
transforms.pop();
```

The trick here is to use the number that makes part of the ball alias to look up the respective ball position in the ball array. For example, if the ball being rendered has the alias `ball32` then this code will look for the current position of the ball whose `index` is `32` in the `ball` array. This one-to-one correspondence between the ball alias and its location in the ball array was established in the `load` function.

In the following *Time for action* section, we will see the bouncing balls animation working. We will also discuss some of the code details.

Time for action – bouncing ball

1. Open `ch5_BouncingBalls.html` in your HTML5-enabled Internet browser.

2. The orbiting camera is activated by default. Move the camera and you will see how all the objects adjust to the global transform (camera) and yet they keep bouncing according to its local transform (bouncing ball).

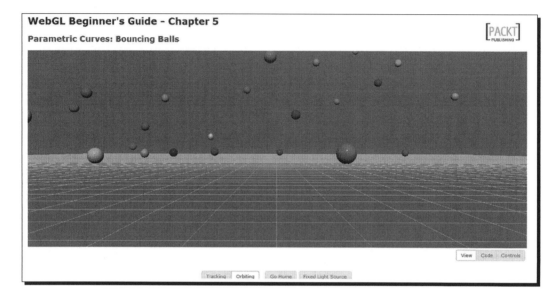

3. Let's explain here a little bit more in detail how we keep track of each ball.

- First of all let's define some global variables and constants:

```
var ball = [];          //Each element of this array is a ball
var BALL_GRAVITY = 9.8;  //Earth acceleration 9.8 m/s2
var NUM_BALLS = 50;      //Number of balls in this
simulation
```

- Next, we need to initialize the ball array. We use a for loop in the `load` function to achieve it:

```
for (var i=0;i<NUM_BALLS;i++){
      ball.push(new BouncingBall());
      Scene.loadObject('models/geometry/ball.
json','ball'+i);
}
```

❑ The `BouncingBall` function initializes the simulation variables for each ball in the ball array. One of this attributes is the position, which we select randomly. You can see how we do this by using the `generatePosition` function.

❑ After adding a new ball to the ball array, we add a new ball object (geometry) to the `Scene` object. Please notice that the alias that we create includes the current index of the ball object in the ball array. For example, if we are adding the 32nd ball to the array, the alias that the corresponding geometry will have in the `Scene` will be `ball32`.

❑ The only other object that we add to the scene here is the `Floor` object. We have used this object in previous exercises. You can find the code for the `Floor` object in `/js/webgl/Floor.js`.

4. Now let's talk about the `draw` function. Here, we go through the elements of the `Scene` and retrieve each object's alias. If the alias starts with the word `ball` then we know that the reminder of the alias corresponds to its index in the ball array. We could have probably used an associative array here to make it look nicer but it does not really change the goal. The main point here is to make sure that we can associate the simulation variables for each ball with the corresponding object (geometry) in the `Scene`.

It is important to notice here that for each object (ball geometry) in the scene, we extract the current position and the color from the respective `BouncingBall` object in the `ball` array.

Also, we alter the current Model-View matrix for each ball using a matrix stack to handle local transformations, as previously described in this chapter. In our case, we want the animation for each ball to be independent from the camera transform and from each other.

5. Up to this point, we have described how the bouncing balls are created (`load`) and how they are rendered (`draw`). None of these functions modify the current position of the balls. We do that using `BouncingBall.update()`. The code there uses the animation time (global variable named `sceneTime`) to calculate the position for the bouncing ball. As each `BouncingBall` has its own simulation parameters, we can calculate the position for each given position when a `sceneTime` is given. In short, the ball position is a function of time and as such, it falls into the category of motion described by parametric curves.

6. The `BouncingBall.update()` method is called inside the `animate` function. As we saw before, this function is invoked by the animation timer each time the timer is up. You can see inside this function how the simulation variables are updated in order to reflect the current state of that ball in the simulation.

What just happened?

We have seen how to handle several object local transformations using the matrix stack strategy while we keep global transformation consistent through each rendering frame.

In the bouncing ball example, we have used an animation timer for the animation that is independent from the rendering timer.

The bouncing ball `update` method shows how parametric curves work.

Optimization strategies

If you play a little and increase the value of the global constant NUM_BALLS from 50 to 500, you will start noticing degradation in the frame rate at which the simulation runs as shown in the following screenshot:

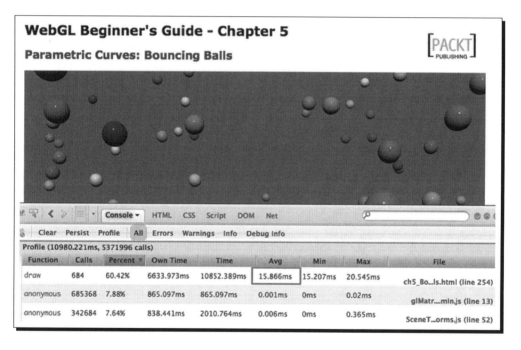

Depending on your computer, the average time for the `draw` function can be higher than the frequency at which the animation timer callback is invoked. This will result in dropped frames. We need to make the draw function faster. Let's see a couple of strategies to do this.

Optimizing batch performance

We can use geometry caching as a way to optimize the animation of a scene full of similar objects. This is the case of the bouncing balls example. Each bouncing ball has a different position and color. These features are unique and independent for each ball. However, all balls share the same geometry.

In the `load` function, for `ch5_BouncingBalls.html` we created 50 vertex buffer objects (VBOs) one for each ball. Additionally, the same geometry is loaded 50 times, and on every rendering loop (`draw` function) a different VBO is bound every time, despite of the fact that the geometry is the same for all the balls!

In `ch5_BouncingBalls_Optimized.html` we modified the functions `load` and `draw` to handle geometry caching. In the first place, the geometry is loaded just once (`load` function):

```
Scene.loadObject('models/geometry/ball.json','ball');
```

Secondly, when the object with alias `'ball'` is the current object in the rendering loop (`draw` function), the delegate `drawBalls` function is invoked. This function sets some of the uniforms that are common to all bouncing balls (so we do not waste time passing them every time to the program for every ball). After that, the `drawBall` function is invoked. This function will set up those elements that are unique for each ball. In our case, we set up the program uniform that corresponds to the ball color, and the Model-View matrix, which is unique for each ball too because of the local transformation (ball position).

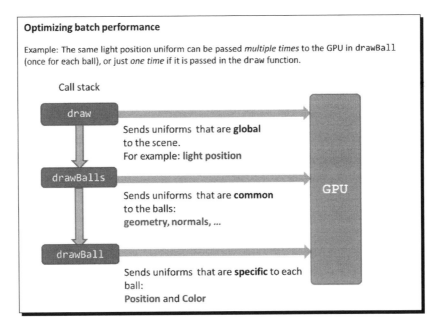

Performing translations in the vertex shader

If you take a look at the code in `ch5_BouncingBalls_Optimized.html`, you may notice that we have taken an extra step and that the Model-View matrix is cached!

The basic idea behind it is to transfer once the original matrix to the GPU (global) and then perform the translation for each ball (local) directly into the vertex shader. This change improves performance considerably because of the parallel nature of the vertex shader.

This is what we do, step-by-step:

1. Create a new uniform that tells the vertex shader if it should perform a translation or not (`uTranslate`).

2. Create a new uniform that contains the ball position for each ball (`uTranslation`).

3. Map these two new uniforms to JavaScript variables (we do this in the `configure` function).

    ```
    prg.uTranslation    = gl.getUniformLocation(prg, "uTranslation");
    gl.uniform3fv(prg.uTranslation, [0,0,0]);


    prg.uTranslate = gl.getUniformLocation(prg, "uTranslate");
    gl.uniform1i(prg.uTranslate, false);
    ```

4. Perform the translation inside the vertex shader. This part is probably the trickiest as it implies a little bit of ESSL programming.

    ```
    //translate vertex if there is a translation uniform
     vec3 vecPosition = aVertexPosition;
     if (uTranslate){
        vecPosition += uTranslation;
     }
    //Transformed vertex position
    vec4 vertex = uMVMatrix * vec4(vecPosition, 1.0);
    ```

    In this code fragment we are defining `vecPosition`, a variable of `vec3` type. This vector is initialized to the vertex position. If the `uTranslate` uniform is active (meaning we are trying to render a bouncing ball) then we update `vecPosition` with the translation. This is implemented using vector addition.

    After this we need to make sure that the transformed vertex carries the translation in case of having one. So the next line looks like the following code:

    ```
    //Transformed vertex position
     vec4 vertex = MV * vec4(vecPosition, 1.0);
    ```

5. In `drawBall` we pass the current ball position as the content for the uniform `uTranslation`:

   ```
   gl.uniform3fv(prg.uTranslation, ball.position);
   ```

6. In `drawBalls` we set the uniform `uTranslate` to `true`:

   ```
   gl.uniform1i(prg.uTranslate, true);
   ```

7. In `draw` we pass the Model-View matrix once for all balls by using the following line of code:

   ```
   transforms.setMatrixUniforms();
   ```

After making these changes we can increase the global variable `NUM_BALLS` from 50 to 300 and see how the application keeps performing reasonably well regardless of the increased scene complexity. The improvement in execution times is shown in the following screenshot:

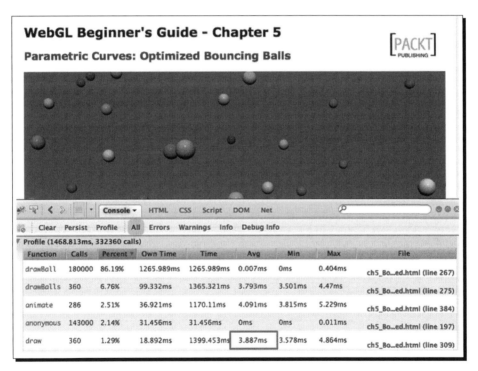

The optimized source code is available at: `/code/ch5_`
`BouncingBalls_Optimized.html`

Interpolation

Interpolation greatly simplifies 3D object's animation. Unlike parametric curves, it is not necessary to define the position of the object as a function of time. When interpolation is used, we only need to define control points or knots. The set of control points describes the path that the object that we want to animate will follow. There are many interpolation methods in the literature; however, it is always a good idea to start from the basics.

Linear interpolation

This method requires that we define the starting and ending points for the location of our object and also the number of interpolating steps. The object will move on the line determined by the starting and ending points.

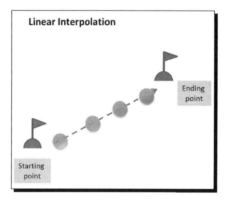

Polynomial interpolation

This method allows us to determine as many control points as we want. The object will move from the starting point to the ending point and it will go through each one of the control points in between.

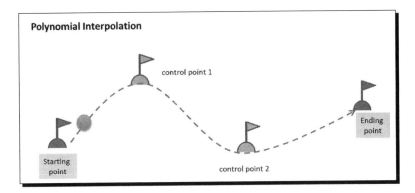

When using polynomials, an increasing number of control points can produce undesired oscillations on the object's path described by this technique. This is known as the **Runge's phenomenon**. In the following figure, you can see the result of moving one of the control points of a polynomial described with 11 control points.

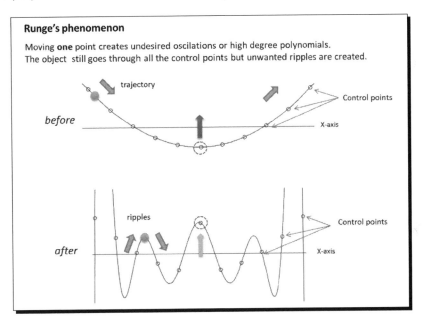

B-Splines

This method is similar to polynomial interpolation with the difference that the control points are outside from the object's path. In other words, the object does not go through the control points as it moves. This method is common in computer graphics in general because the knots allow a much smoother path generation than the polynomial equivalent at the same time that fewer knots are required. B-Splines also respond better to the Runge's phenomenon.

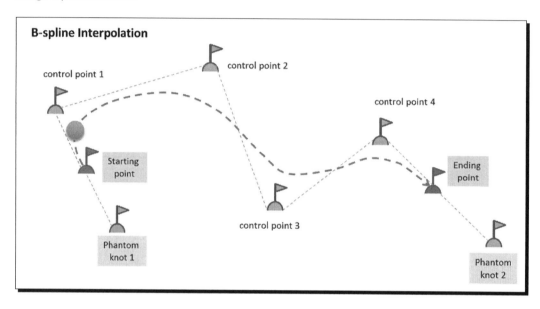

In the following *Time for action* section we are going to see in practice the three different interpolation techniques that have been introduced: linear, polynomial and b-splines interpolation.

Time for action – interpolation

1. Open `ch5_Interpolation.html` using your HTML5 Internet browser.

2. Select **Linear** interpolation if it is not already selected.

3. Move the start and end points using the slider provided.

4. Change the number of interpolation steps. What happens to the animation when you decrease the number of steps?

5. The code for the linear interpolation has been implemented in the `doLinearInterpolation` function.

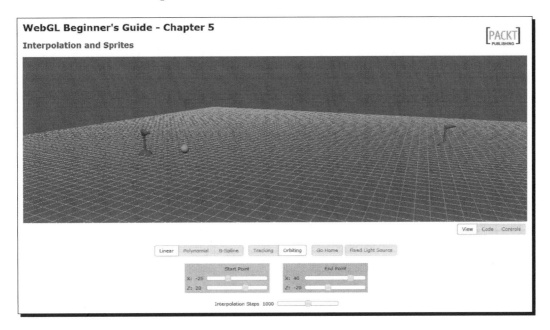

6. Now select **Polynomial** interpolation. In this example we have implemented Lagrange's interpolation method. You can see the source code in the `doLagrangeInterpolation` function.

7. After selecting the polynomial interpolation, you will see that three new control points (flags) appear on screen. Using the sliders provided on the webpage, you can change the location of these control points. You can also change the number of interpolation steps.

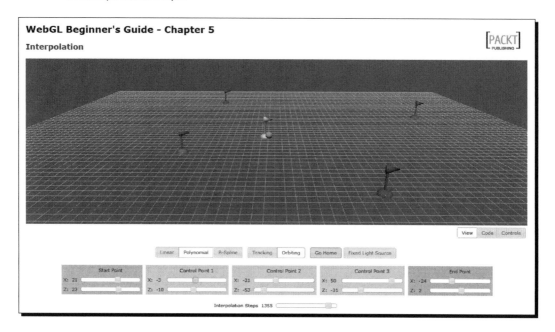

8. You also may have noticed that whenever the ball approaches one of the flags (with the exception of the start and end points) the flag changes color. To do that, we have written the ancillary `close` function. We use this function inside the `draw` routine to determine the color of the flags. If the current position of the ball, determined by `position[sceneTime]` is close to one of the flag positions, the respective flag changes color. When the ball is far from the flag, the flag changes back to its original color.

9. Modify the source code so each flag remains *activated*, this is, with a new color after the ball passes by until the animation loops back to the beginning. This happens when `sceneTime` is equal to `ISTEPS` (see the `animate` function).

10. Now select the **B-Spline** interpolation. Notice how the ball does not reach any of the intermediate flags in the initial configuration. Is there any configuration that you can try so the ball passes through at least two of the flags?

What just happened?

We have learned how to use interpolation to describe the movement of an object in our 3D world. Also, we have created very simple scripts to detect object proximity and alter our scene accordingly (changing flag colors in this example). Reaction to proximity is a key element in game design!

Summary

In this chapter, we have covered the basic concepts behind object animation in WebGL. Specifically we have learned about the difference between local and global transformations. We have seen how matrix stacks allows us saving and retrieving the Model-View matrix and how a stack allows us to implement local transformation.

We learned to use JavaScript timers for animation. The fact that an animation timer is not tied up to the rendering cycle gives a lot of flexibility. Think a moment about it: the time in the scene should be independent of how fast you can render it on your computer. We also distinguished between animation and simulation strategies and learned what problems they solve.

We discussed a couple of methods to optimize animations through a practical example and we have seen what we need to do to implement these optimizations in the code.

Finally, interpolation methods and sprites were introduced and the Runge's phenomenon was explained.

In the next chapter, we will play with colors in a WebGL scene. We will study the interaction between the objects and light colors and we will see how to create translucent objects.

6

Colors, Depth Testing, and Alpha Blending

In this chapter, we will go a little bit deeper in the use of colors in WebGL. We will start by examining how colors are structured and handled in both WebGL and ESSL. Then we will discuss the use of colors in objects, lights and in the scene. After this we will see how WebGL knows how perform object occlusion when one object is in front of another. This is possible thanks to depth testing. In contrast, alpha blending will allows us to combine the colors of objects when one is occluding the other. We will use alpha blending to create translucent objects.

This chapter talks about:

- Using colors in objects
- Assigning colors to light sources
- Working with several light sources in the ESSL program
- The depth test and the z-buffer
- Blending functions and equations
- Creating transparent objects with face culling

Using colors in WebGL

WebGL includes a fourth attribute to the RGB model. This attribute is called **the alpha channel**. The extended model then is known as the **RGBA** model, where A stands for alpha. The alpha channel contains values in the range from 0.0 to 1.0, just like the other three channels (red, green, and blue). The following diagram shows the RGBA color space. On the horizontal axis you can see the different colors that can be obtained by combining the R, G, and B channels. The vertical axis corresponds to the alpha channel.

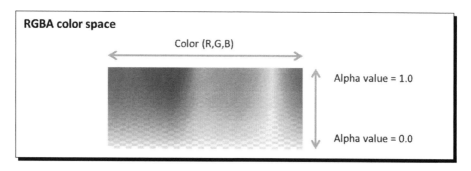

The alpha channel carries extra information about the color. This information affects the way the color is rendered on the screen. For instance, in most cases, the alpha value will refer to the amount of opacity that the color contains. A completely opaque color will have an alpha value of 1.0, whereas a completely transparent color will have an alpha value of 0.0. This is the general case, but as we will see later on, there are some considerations that we need to take into account to obtain translucent colors.

We use colors everywhere in our WebGL 3D scenes:

  ◆ **Objects**: 3D objects can be colored selecting one color for every pixel (fragment) of the object, or by selecting the color that the object will have. This would usually be the *material diffuse* property.

  ◆ **Lights**: Though we have been using white lights so far in the book, there is no reason why we can't have lights whose ambient or diffuse properties contain colors other than white.

◆ **Scene**: The background of our scene has a color that we can change by calling
`gl.clearColor`. Also, as we will see later, there are special operations on objects'
colors in the scene when we have translucent objects.

Use of color in objects

The final color of pixel is assigned in the fragment shader by setting the ESSL special variable
`gl_FragColor`. If all the fragments in the object have the same color we can say that the
object has a constant color. Otherwise, the object has a per-vertex color.

Constant coloring

To obtain a constant color we store the desired color in a uniform that is passed to the
fragment shader. This uniform is usually called the object's **diffuse material property**.
We can also combine object normals and light source information to obtain a Lambert
coefficient. We can use the Lambert coefficient to proportionally change the reflecting
color depending on the angle on which the light hits the object.

As shown in the following diagram, we lose depth perception when we do not use
information about the normals to obtain a Lambert coefficient. Please notice that
we are using a diffusive lighting model.

Usually constant coloring is indicated for objects that are going to become assets in
a 3D game.

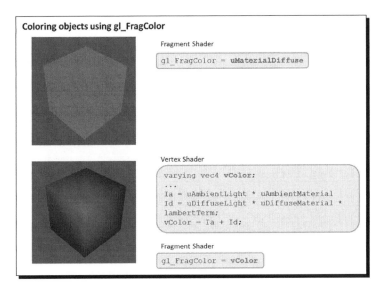

Per-vertex coloring

In medical and engineering visualization applications, it is common to find color maps that are associated to the vertices of the models that we are rendering. These maps assign each vertex a color depending on its scalar value. An example of this idea is the temperature charts where we can see cold temperatures as blue and hot temperatures as red overlaid on a map.

To implement per-vertex coloring, we need to define an attribute that stores the color for the vertex in the vertex shader:

```
attribute vec4 aVertexColor;
```

The next step is to assign the `aVertexColor` attribute to a varying so it can be carried into the fragment shader. Remember that varyings are automatically interpolated. Therefore, each fragment will have a color that is the weighted contribution of the vertices surrounding it.

If we want our color map to be sensitive to lighting conditions we can multiply each vertex color by the diffuse component of the light. The result is then assigned to the varying that will transfer the result to the fragment shader as mentioned before. The following diagram shows two different possibilities for this case. On the left the vertex color is multiplied by the diffuse term of the light source without any weighting due to the light source relative position; on the right, the Lambert coefficient generates the expected shadows giving information about the relative location of the light source.

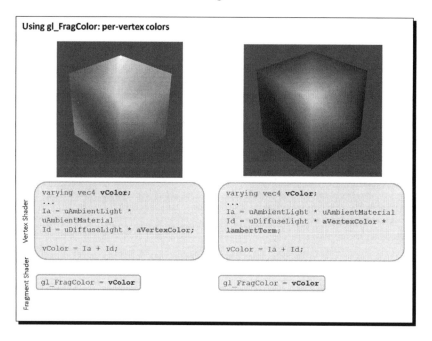

Here we are using a `Vertex Buffer` object that is mapped to the `Vertex Shader` attribute `aVertexColor`. We learned how to map VBOs in the section *Associating Attributes to VBOs* discussed in Chapter 2, *Rendering Geometry*.

Per-fragment coloring

We could also assign a random color to each pixel of the object we are rendering. However, ESSL does not have a pre-built random function. Although there are algorithms that can be used to generate pseudo-random numbers, the purpose and the usefulness of this technique go beyond the scope of this book.

Time for action – coloring the cube

1. Open the file `ch6_Cube.html` using your HTML5 Internet browser. You will see a page like the one shown in the following screenshot:

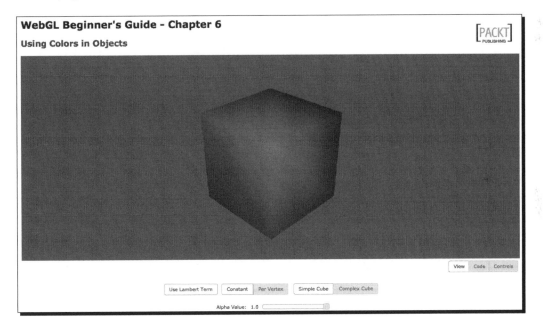

In this exercise, we are going to compare constant versus per-vertex coloring. Let's talk about the page's widgets:

  ❑ **Use Lambert Coefficient**: When selected it will include the Lambert coefficient in the calculation of the final color.

- ❏ **Constant/Per-Vertex**: The two options to color objects explained before.

- ❏ **Simple Cube**: Corresponds to a JSON object where the vertices are defined once.

- ❏ **Complex Cube**: Loads a JSON object where the vertices are repeated with the goal of obtaining multiple normals and multiple colors per vertex. We will explain how this works later.

- ❏ **Alpha Value**: This slider is mapped to the float uniform `uAlpha` in the vertex shader. `uAlpha` sets the alpha value for the vertex color.

2. Disable the use of the Lambert coefficient by clicking on **Use Lambert Coefficient**. Rotate the cube clicking on it with the mouse and dragging it around. As you see, there is loss of depth perception when the Lambert coefficient is not included in the final color calculation. The **Use Lambert Coefficient** button is mapped to the Boolean uniform `uUseLambert`. The code that calculates the Lambert coefficient can be found in the vertex shader included in the page:

```
float lambertTerm = 1.0;

 if (uUseLambert){
  //Transformed normal position
  vec3 normal = vec3(uNMatrix * vec4(aVertexNormal, 1.0));

  //light direction: pointing at the origin
  vec3 lightDirection = normalize(-uLightPosition);

  //weighting factor
  lambertTerm = max(dot(normal,-lightDirection),0.20);
 }
```

If the uniform `uUseLambert` is false, then `lambertTerm` keeps being `1.0` and then it will not affect the final diffuse term which is calculated later on:

```
Id = uLightDiffuse * uMaterialDiffuse * lambertTerm;
```

Otherwise, `Id` will have the Lambert coefficient factored in.

3. Having **Use Lambert Coefficient** disabled, click on the button **Per Vertex**. Rotate the cube to see how ESSL interpolates the vertex colors. The vertex shader key code fragment that allows us to switch from a constant diffuse color to per- vertex colors uses the Boolean uniform `uUseVertexColors` and the `aVertexColor` attribute. This fragment is shown here:

```
if (uUseVertexColor){
  Id = uLightDiffuse * aVertexColor * lambertTerm;
}
```

```
else {
  Id = uLightDiffuse * uMaterialDiffuse * lambertTerm;
}
```

Take a look at the file /models/simpleCube.js. There, the eight vertices of the cube are defined in the vertices array and there is an element in the scalars array for every vertex. As you may expect, each one of these elements correspond to the respective vertex color, as shown in the following diagram:

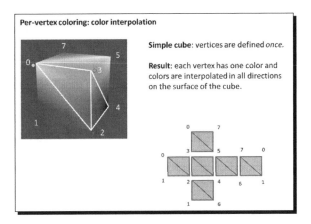

4. Make sure that the **Use Lambert Coefficient** button is not active and then click on the button **Complex Cube**. By repeating vertices in the vertex array in the corresponding JSON file /models/complexCube.js, we can achieve independent face coloring. The following diagram explains how the vertices are organized in complexCube.js. Also note that as the definition of colors occurs by vertex (as we are using the shader attribute), we need to repeat each color four times, because each face has four vertices. This idea is depicted in the following diagram:

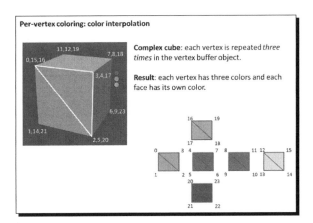

5. Activate the **Use Lambert Coefficient** button and see how the Lambert coefficient affects the color of the object. Try different button configurations and see what happens.

6. Finally, let's quickly explore the effect of changing the alpha channel to a value less than 1.0. For that, click-and-drag the slider to the left that appears at the bottom of the page. What do you see? Please notice that the object does not become transparent but instead it starts losing its color. To obtain transparency, we need to activate blending. We will discuss blending in depth later in this chapter. For now, uncomment these lines in the `configure` function, in the source code:

```
//gl.disable(gl.DEPTH_TEST);
//gl.enable(gl.BLEND);
//gl.blendFunc(gl.SRC_ALPHA, gl.ONE_MINUS_SRC_ALPHA);
```

7. Save the page and reload it in your Internet browser. If you select **Per Vertex, Complex Cube** and reduce the alpha value to 0.25 you will see something like the following screenshot:

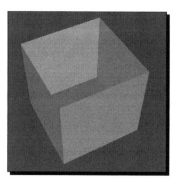

What just happened?

We have studied two different ways for coloring objects: constant coloring and per-vertex coloring. In both cases, the final color for each fragment is assigned by using the fragment shader `gl_FragColor` variable.

We also saw how, by activating the calculation of the Lambert coefficient, we can obtain sensory depth information.

By repeating vertices in our object, we can obtain different coloring effects. For instance, we can color an object by faces instead of doing it by vertices.

Use of color in lights

Colors are light properties. In *Chapter 3*, *Lights*, we saw that the number of light properties depend on the lighting reflection model selected for the scene. For instance, using a Lambertian reflection model we would only need to model one shader uniform: the light diffuse property/color. In contrast, if the Phong reflection model were selected, each light source would need to have three properties: the ambient, diffuse, and specular colors.

The light position is usually also modeled as a uniform when the shader needs to know where the light source is. Therefore, a Phong model with a positional light would have four uniforms: ambient, diffuse, specular, and position.

For the case of directional lights, the fourth uniform is the light direction. Refer to the *More on Lights: positional lights* section discussed in *Chapter 3*, *Lights!*.

We have also seen that each light property is represented by a four-element array in JavaScript and that these arrays are mapped to the vec4 uniforms in the shaders as shown in the following diagram:

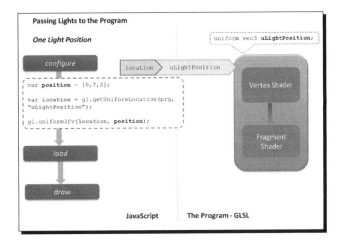

The two functions we use to pass lights to the shaders are:

◆ getUniformLocation—locates the uniform in the program and returns an index we can use to set the value

◆ uniform4fv—since the light components are RGBA, we need to pass a four-element float vector

Using multiple lights and the scalability problem

As you could imagine, the number of uniforms grow rapidly when we want to use more than one light source in our scene—for each one of them, we need to define and map as many uniforms as we need depending on the lighting model of choice. This approach makes the programming effort simple enough—we have exactly one uniform for each light property we want to have, for each light. However, let's think about this for a moment. If we have four properties per light (ambient, diffuse, specular, and location) this means that we have to define four uniforms per each light. If we want to have three lights, we will have to write, use, and map 12 uniforms!

How many uniforms can we use?

The OpenGL Shading Language ES specification delineates the number of uniforms that we are allowed to use. (Section 4.3.4 - Uniforms):

> *There is an implementation dependent limit on the amount of storage for uniforms that can be used for each type of shader and if this is exceeded it will cause a compile-time or link-time error.*

In order to know what the limit is for your WebGL implementation, you can query WebGL using the `gl.getParameter` function with these constants:

```
gl.MAX_VERTEX_UNIFORM_VECTORS
gl.MAX_FRAGMENT_UNIFORM_VECTORS
```

The implementation limit is given by your browser and it depends greatly on your graphics hardware. For instance, my MacBook Pro running Firefox tells me that I can use 1024 uniforms.

Now, the fact that we have enough variable space does not necessarily mean that the problem is solved. We still have to write and map each one of the uniforms and as we will see later in exercise `ch6_Wall_Initial.html`, the shaders become a lot more verbose doing this.

Simplifying the problem

In order to simplify the problem (and code less), we could assume, for instance, that the ambient component is the same for all the lights. This allows reducing the number of uniforms—one uniform less for each light. However, this is not a pretty or an extensible solution for more general cases where we cannot assume that the ambient light is a constant.

Let's see how the shaders in a scene with multiple lights look like. First, let's address some pending updates to our architecture.

Architectural updates

As we move from chapter to chapter and study different WebGL concepts, we should also update our architecture to reflect what we have learned. In this occasion as we are handling a lot of uniforms, we will add support for multiple lights and will improve the way we pass uniforms to the program.

Adding support for light objects

The following diagram shows the changes and additions that we have implemented in the architecture of our exercises. We have updated `Program.js` to simplify how we handle uniforms and we have included a new file: `Ligths.js`. Also, we have modified the `configure` function to use the changes implemented in the `Program` object. We will discuss these improvements next.

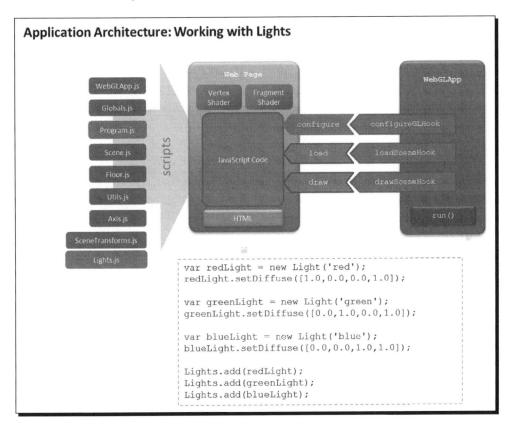

We have created a new JavaScript module `Lights.js` that has two objects:

- `Light`—aggregates lights properties (position, diffuse, specular, and so on) in one single entity.

- `Lights`—contain the lights in our scene. It allows us to retrieve each light by index and by name.

`Lights` also contains the `getArray` method to flatten the arrays of properties by type:

```
getArray: function(type){ //type = 'diffuse' or 'position' or ..
  var a = [];
  for(var i = 0, max = this.list.length; i < max; i+=1){
    a = a.concat(this.list[i][type]); //list: the list of lights
  }
  return a;
}
```

This will be useful when we use uniform arrays later on.

Improving how we pass uniforms to the program

We have also improved the way we pass uniforms to the program. In `WebGLApp.js` we have removed the call to `Program.load()`.

```
function WebGLApp(canvas) {
    this.loadSceneHook = undefined;
    this.configureGLHook = undefined;
    gl = Utils.getGLContext(canvas);
    Program.load();
}
```

And we have deferred this call to the `configure` function in the web page. Remember that `WebGLApp` will call three functions in the web page: `configure`, `load`, and `draw`. These three functions define the life cycle of our application.

The `configure` function is the appropriate place to load the program. We are also going to create a dynamic mapping between JavaScript variables and uniforms. With this in mind, we have updated the `Program.load` method to receive two arrays:

- `attributeList`—an array containing the names of the attributes that we will map between JavaScript and ESSL

- `uniformList`—an array containing the names of the uniforms that we will map between JavaScript and ESSL

The implementation of the function now looks as follows:

```
load : function(attributeList, uniformList) {

   var fragmentShader = Program.getShader(gl, "shader-fs");
   var vertexShader = Program.getShader(gl, "shader-vs");

    prg = gl.createProgram();
    gl.attachShader(prg, vertexShader);
    gl.attachShader(prg, fragmentShader);
    gl.linkProgram(prg);
    if (!gl.getProgramParameter(prg, gl.LINK_STATUS)) {
     alert("Could not initialise shaders");
    }

    gl.useProgram(prg);

   this.setAttributeLocations(attributeList);
   this.setUniformLocations(uniformList);


    }
```

The last two lines correspond to the two new functions setAttributeLocations and setUniformLocations:

```
setAttributeLocations: function (attrList){

   for(var i=0, max = attrList.length; i <max; i+=1){
     this[attrList[i]] = gl.getAttribLocation(prg, attrList[i]);
   }
},

setUniformLocations: function (uniformList){

for(var i=0, max = uniformList.length; i < max; i +=1){
    this[uniformList[i]] = gl.getUniformLocation(prg,
                           uniformList[i]);
   }
}
```

As you can see, these functions read the attribute and uniform lists, respectively, and after obtaining the location for each element of the list, attach the location as a property of the object Program.

This way, if we include the uniform name `uLightPosition` in the list `uniformList` that we pass to `Program.load`, then we will have a property `Program.uLightPosition` that will contain the location of the respective uniform! Neat, isn't it?

Once we load the program in the `configure` function, we can also initialize the values of the uniforms that we want right there by writing something as follows:

```
gl.uniform3fv(Program.uLightPosition, value);
```

Time for action – adding a blue light to a scene

Now we are ready to take a look at the first example of this chapter. We will work on a scene with **per-fragment** lighting that has three light sources.

Each light has a position and a diffuse color property. This means we have two uniforms per light.

1. Also for simplicity, we have assumed here that the ambient color is the same for the three light sources. For the sake of simplicity, we have removed the specular property. Open the file `ch6_Wall_Initial.html` using your HTML5 web browser.

2. You will see a scene such as the one displayed in the following screenshot where there are two lights (red and green) illuminating a black wall:

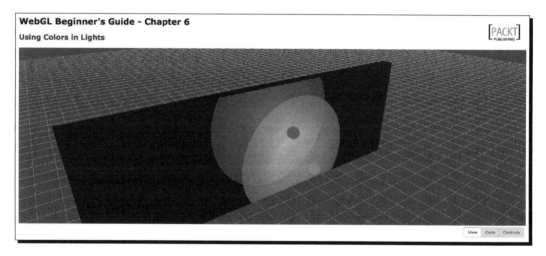

3. Open the file `ch6_Wall_Initial.html` using your preferred text editor. We will update the vertex shader, the fragment shader, the JavaScript code, and the HTML code to add the blue light.

4. **Updating the vertex shader**: Go to the vertex shader. You can see these two uniforms:

```
uniform vec3 uPositionRedLight;
uniform vec3 uPositionGreenLight;
```

Let's add the third uniform here:

```
uniform vec3 uPositionBlueLight;
```

5. We also need to define a varying to carry the interpolated light ray direction to the fragment shader. Remember here that we are using per-fragment lighting.

Check where the varyings are defined:

```
varying vec3 vRedRay;
varying vec3 vGreenRay;
```

And add the third varying there:

```
varying vec3 vBlueRay;
```

6. Now let's take a look at the body of the vertex shader. We need to update each one of the light locations according to our position in the scene. We achieve this by writing:

```
vec4 bluePosition = uMVMatrix * vec4(uPositionBlueLight, 1.0);
```

As you can see there, the positions for the other two lights are being calculated too.

7. Now let's calculate the light ray for the updated position from our blue light to the current vertex. We do that by writing the following code:

```
vBlueRay = vertex.xyz-bluePosition.xyz;
```

That is all we need to modify in the vertex shader.

8. **Updating the fragment shader:** So far, we have included a new light position and we have calculated the light rays in the vertex shader. These rays will be interpolated by the fragment shader.

Now let's work out how the colors on the wall will change by including our new blue source of light. Scroll down to the fragment shader and let's add a new uniform—the blue diffuse property. Look for these uniforms declared right before the main function:

```
uniform vec4 uDiffuseRedLight;
uniform vec4 uDiffuseGreenLight;
```

Then insert the following line of code:

```
uniform vec4 uDiffuseBlueLight;
```

To calculate the contribution of the blue light to the final color we need to obtain the light ray we defined previously in the vertex shader. So this varying is available in the fragment shader, you need to also declare it before the main function. Look for:

```
varying vec3 vRedRay;
varying vec3 vGreenRay;
```

Then insert the following code right below:

```
varing vec3 vBlueRay;
```

9. It is assumed that the ambient component is the same for all the lights. This is reflected in the code by having only one `uLightAmbient` variable. The ambient term `Ia` is obtained as the product of `uLightAmbient` and the wall's material ambient property:

```
//Ambient Term
vec4 Ia = uLightAmbient * uMaterialAmbient;
```

If `uLightAmbient` is set to `(1,1,1,1)` and `uMaterialAmbient` is set to `(0.1,0.1,0.1,1.0)` then the resulting ambient term `Ia` will be really small. This means that the contribution of the ambient light will be low in this scene.

In contrast, the diffuse component will be different for every light.

Let's add the effect of the blue diffuse term. In the fragment shader main function, look for the following code:

```
//Diffuse Term
vec4 Id1 = vec4(0.0,0.0,0.0,1.0);
vec4 Id2 = vec4(0.0,0.0,0.0,1.0);
```

Then add the following line immediately below:

```
vec Id3 = vec4(0.0,0.0,0.0,1.0);
```

Then scroll down to:

```
//Lambert's cosine law
float lambertTermOne   = dot(N,-normalize(vRedRay));
float lambertTermTwo   = dot(N,-normalize(vGreenRay));
```

And add the following line of code right below:

```
float lambertTermThree  = dot(N,-normalize(vBlueRay));
```

Now scroll to:

```
if(lambertTermTwo > uCutOff){
   Id2 = uDiffuseGreenLight * uMaterialDiffuse * lambertTermTwo;
}
```

And insert the following code after it:

```
if(lambertTermThree > uCutOff){
  Id3 = uDiffuseBlueLight * uMaterialDiffuse * lambertTermTwo;
}
```

Finally update `finalColor` so it includes `Id3`:

```
vec4 finalColor = Ia + Id1 + Id2 +Id3;
```

That's all we need to do in the fragment shader. Let's move on to our JavaScript code.

10. **Updating the configure function:** Up to this point, we have written the code that is needed to handle one more light inside our shaders. Let's see how we create the blue light from the JavaScript side and how we map it to the shaders. Scroll down to the `configure` function and look for the following code:

```
var green = new Light('green');
green.setPosition([2.5,3,3]);
green.setDiffuse([0.0,1.0,0.0,1.0]);
```

11. Then insert the following code:

```
var blue = new Light('blue');
blue.setPosition([-2.5,3,3]);
blue.setDiffuse([0.0,0.0,1.0,1.0]);
```

Next, Scroll down to:

```
Lights.add(red);
Lights.add(green);
```

Then add the blue light:

```
Lights.add(blue);
```

12. Scroll down to the point where the attribute list is defined. As mentioned earlier in this chapter, this new mechanism makes it easier to obtain locations for the uniforms. Add the two new uniforms that we are using for the blue light. The list should look like the following code:

```
uniformList = [  "uPMatrix",
          "uMVMatrix",
          "uNMatrix",
          "uMaterialDiffuse",
          "uMaterialAmbient",
          "uLightAmbient",
          "uDiffuseRedLight",
          "uDiffuseGreenLight",
```

```
"uDiffuseBlueLight",
    "uPositionRedLight",
    "uPositionGreenLight",
"uPositionBlueLight",
    "uWireframe",
    "uLightSource",
    "uCutOff"
    ];
```

13. Let's pass the position and diffuse values of our newly defined light to the program. After the line that loads the program (what line is that?), insert the following code:

```
gl.uniform3fv(Program.uPositionBlueLight, blue.position);
gl.uniform4fv(Program.uDiffuseBlueLight,  blue.diffuse);
```

That's all we need to do in the `configure` function.

> Coding lights code using one uniform per light property makes the code really verbose. Please bear with me; we will see later on in the exercise `ch6_Wall_LightArrays.html` that the coding efforts are reduced by using uniform arrays. If you are really eager, you can go now and check the code in that exercise, and see how uniform arrays are used.

14. Updating the load function: Now let's update the `load` function. We need a new sphere to represent the blue light, the same way we have two spheres in the scene: one for the red light and the other for the green light. Append the following line:

```
Scene.loadObject('models/geometry/smallsph.json','light3');
```

15. Updating the draw function: As we saw in the `load` function, we are loading the same geometry (sphere) three times. In order to differentiate the sphere that represents the light source we are using local transforms for the sphere (initially centered at the origin).

Then add the following code:

```
if (object.alias == 'light2'){
mat4.translate(transforms.mvMatrix,gl.getUniform(prg,
Program.uPositionGreenLight));
object.diffuse = gl.getUniform(prg, Program.uDiffuseGreenLight);
gl.uniform1i(Program.uLightSource,true);
}
```

Next, add the following code:

```
if (object.alias == 'light3'){
mat4.translate(transforms.mvMatrix,gl.getUniform(prg,
Program.uPositionBlueLight));
  object.diffuse = gl.getUniform(prg, Program.uDiffuseBlueLight);
  gl.uniform1i(Program.uLightSource,true);
}
```

16. That is it. Now, save the page with a different name and try it on your HTML5 browser.

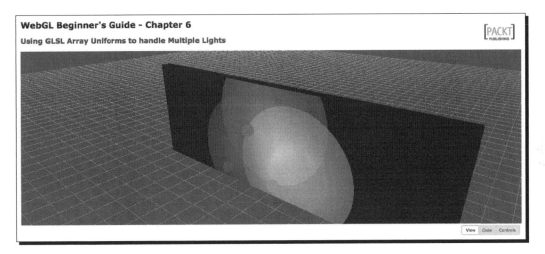

17. If you do not obtain the expected result, please go back and check the steps. You will find the completed exercise in the file `ch6_Wall_Final.html`.

What just happened?

We have modified our sample scene by adding one more light: a blue light. We have updated the following:

- The vertex shader
- The fragment shader
- The `configure` function
- The `load` function
- The `draw` function

Handling light properties one uniform at a time is not very efficient as you can see. We will study a more effective way to handle lights in a WebGL scene later in this chapter.

Have a go hero – adding interactivity with JQuery UI

We are going to add some HTML and JQuery UI code to interactively change the position of the blue light that we just added.

We will use three **JQuery UI Sliders**, one for each one of the blue light coordinates.

 You can find more information about JQuery UI widgets here:
`http://jqueryui.com`

1. Create three sliders: one for the x coordinate, one for the y coordinate, and a third one for the z coordinate for the blue light. The function that you need to call on the `change` and `slide` events for these sliders is `updateLightPosition(3)`.

2. For this to work, you need to update the `updateLightPosition` function and add the following case:

    ```
    case 3: gl.uniform3fv(Program.uPositionBlueLight, [x,y,z]); break;
    ```

3. The final GUI should include the new blue light sliders which should look as shown in the following diagram:

4. Use the sliders present in the page to guide your work.

Using uniform arrays to handle multiple lights

As stated before, handling light properties with individual uniforms make the code verbose and also difficult to maintain. Hopefully, ESSL provides several mechanisms that we can use to solve the problem of handling multiple lights. One of them is **uniform arrays**.

This technique allows us to handle multiple lights by introducing light arrays in the shaders. This way we calculate light contributions by iterating through the light arrays in the shaders. We still need to define each light in JavaScript but the mapping to ESSL becomes simpler as we are not defining one uniform per light property. Let's see how this technique works.

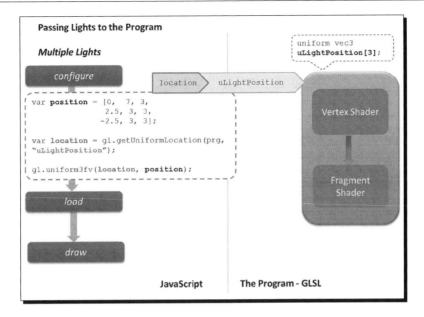

We just need to do two simple changes in our code.

Uniform array declaration

First, we need to declare the light uniforms as arrays inside of our ESSL shaders. For instance, for the light position in a scene with three lights we would write something like:

```
uniform vec3 uPositionLight[3];
```

It is important to realize here that ESSL does not support dynamic initialization of uniform arrays. If you wrote something like:

```
uniform int uNumLights;
uniform vec3 uPositionLight[uNumLights];   //will not work
```

the shader will not compile and you will obtain an error as follows:

```
ERROR: 0:12: ":constant expression required
ERROR: 0:12: ":array size must be a constant integer expression"
```

However, this construct is valid:

```
const int uNumLights = 3;
uniform vec3 uPositionLight[uNumLights];   //will work
```

We declare one uniform array per light property, regardless of how many lights we are going to have. So, if we want to pass information about diffuse and specular components of five lights, for example, we need to declare two uniform arrays as follows:

```
uniform vec4 uDiffuseLight[5];
uniform vec4 uSpecularLight[5];
```

JavaScript array mapping

Next, we will need to map the JavaScript variables where we have the light property information to the program. For example, if we wanted to map these three light positions:

```
var LightPos1 = [0.0, 7.0, 3.0];
var LightPosition2 = [2.5, 3.0, 3.0];
var LightPosition3 = [-2.5, 3.0, 3.0];
```

Then, we need to retrieve the uniform array location (just like in any other case):

```
var location = gl.getUniformLocation(prg, "uPositionLight");
```

Here is the difference, we map these positions as a concatenated flat array:

```
gl.uniform3fv(location, [0.0,7.0,3.0,2.5,3.0,3.0,-2.5,3.0,3.0]);
```

There are two things you should notice here:

- The name of the uniform is passed to `getUniformLocation` the same way it was passed before. That is, the fact that `uPositionLight` is now an array does not change a thing when you locate the uniform with `getUniformLocation`.

- The JavaScript array that we are passing to the uniform is a flat array. If you write something as follows the mapping will not work:

  ```
  gl.uniform3fv(location, [[0.0,7.0,3.0],[2.5,3.0,3.0],[-2.5,3.0,3.0]]);
  ```

  So, if you have one variable per light you should make sure to concatenate them appropriately before passing them to the shader.

Time for action – adding a white light to a scene

1. Open the file `ch6_Wall_LightArrays.html` in your HTML5 browser. This scene looks exactly as `ch6_Wall_Final.html`, however the code required to write this scene is much less as we are using uniform arrays. Let's see how the use of uniform arrays change our code.

2. Let's update the vertex shader first. Open the file ch6_Wall_LightArrays.html using your favorite source code editor. Let's take a look at the vertex shader. Note the use of the constant integer expression const int NUM_LIGHTS = 3; to declare the number of lights that the shader will handle.

3. Also, you can see there that a uniform array is being used to operate on light positions.

Note that we are using a varying array to pass the light rays (for each light) to the fragment shader.

```
//Calculate light ray per each light
 for(int i=0; i < NUM_LIGHTS; i++){
   vec 4 lightPosition = uMVMatrix * vec4(uLightPosition[i], 1.0);
   vLightRay[i] = vertex.xyz - lightPosition[i].xyz;
 }
```

This fragment of code calculates one varying light ray per light. If you remember, the same code in the file ch6_Wall_Final.html looks like the following code:

```
//Transformed light position
 vec4 redPosition = uMVMatrix * vec4(uPositionRedLight,1.0);
 vec4 greenPosition = uMVMatrix * vec4(uPositionGreenLight,1.0);
 vec4 bluePosition = uMVMatrix * vec4(uPositionBlueLight, 1.0);

 //Light position
 vRedRay   = vertex.xyz-redPosition.xyz;
 vGreenRay = vertex.xyz-greenPosition.xyz;
 vBlueRay  = vertex.xyz-bluePosition.xyz;
```

At this point the advantage of using uniform arrays (and array varyings) to write shading programs should start being evident.

4. Similarly, the fragment shader also uses uniform arrays. In this case, the fragment shader iterates through the light diffuse properties to calculate the contribution of each one to the final color on the wall:

```
for(int i = 0; i < NUM_LIGHTS; i++){    //For each light

  L = normalize(vLightRay[i]);       //Calculate reflexion
  lambertTerm = dot(N, -L);

  if (lambertTerm > uCutOff){
      finalColor += uLightDiffuse[i] * uMaterialDiffuse
*lambertTerm;
      //Add diffuse component, one per light
  }
}
```

5. For the sake of brevity we will not see the corresponding verbose code from the ch6_Wall_Final.html exercise.

6. In the configure function, the size of the JavaScript array that contains the uniform names has decreased considerably because now we have just one element per property regardless of the number of lights:

```
var uniformList = [
            "uPMatrix",
            "uMVMatrix",
            "uNMatrix",
            "uMaterialDiffuse",
            "uMaterialAmbient",
            "uLightAmbient",
            "uLightDiffuse",
            "uPositionLight",
            "uWireframe",
            "uLightSource",
            "uCutOff"
            ];
```

7. Also, the mapping between JavaScript Light objects and uniform arrays is simpler because of the getArray method of the Lights class. As we described in the section *Architectural Updates*, the getArray method concatenates in one flat array the property that we want for all the lights.

8. The load and draw functions look exactly the same. If we wanted to add a new light, we will still need to load a new sphere in the load function (to represent the light source in our scene) and we still need to translate this sphere to the appropriate location in the draw function.

9. Let's see how much effort we need to add a new light. Go to the configure function and create a new light object like this:

```
var whiteLight = new Light('white');
whiteLight.setPosition([0,10,2]);
whiteLight.setDiffuse([1.0,1.0,1.0,1.0]);
```

10. Add `whiteLight` to the `Lights` object as follows:

```
Lights.add(whiteLight);
```

11. Now move to the `load` function and append this line:

```
Scene.loadObject('models/geometry/smallsph.json','light4');
```

12. And just like in the previous *Time For Action* section, add this to the `draw` function:

```
if (object.alias == 'light4'){
  mat4.translate(transforms.mvMatrix,Lights.get('white').
position);
  object.diffuse = Lights.get('white').diffuse;
  gl.uniform1i(Program.uLightSource,true);
}
```

13. Save the webpage with a different name and open it using your HTML5 browser. We have also included the completed exercise in `ch6_Wall_LightArrays_White.html`. The following diagram shows the final result:

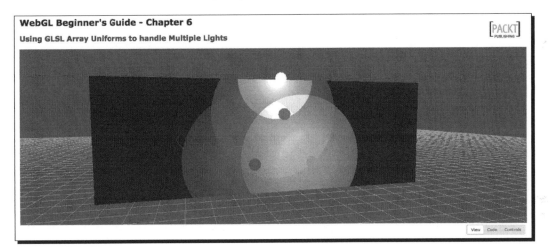

That is all you need to do! Evidently, if you want to control the white light properties through JQuery UI you would need to write the corresponding code, the same way we did it for the previous hero section. And talking about heroes.

Time for action – directional point lights

In *Chapter 3, Lights!*, we compared point and directional lights:

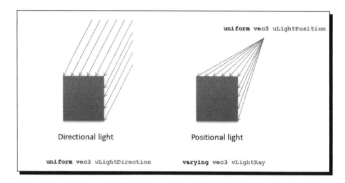

In this section, we will combine directional and positional lights. We are going to create a third type of light: a **directional point light**. This light has both position and direction properties. We are ready to do this as our shaders can easily handle lights with multiple properties.

The trick to create these lights consist into subtract the light direction vector from the normal for each vertex. The resulting vector will originate a different Lambert coefficient that will reflect into the cone generated by the light source.

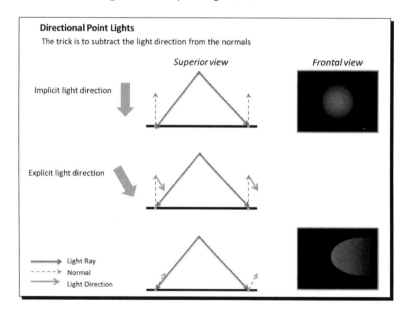

1. Open `ch6_Wall_Directional.html` in your HTML5 Internet web browser. As you can see there, the three light sources have now a direction. Let's take a look at the code.

2. Open `ch6_Wall_Directional.html` in your source code editor.

3. To create a light cone we need to obtain a Lambert coefficient per fragment. Just like in previous exercises, we obtain these coefficients in the fragment shader by calculating the dot product between the inverted light ray and the normal that has been interpolated. So far, we have been using one varying to do this: `vNormal`.

4. Only one varying has sufficed so far, as we have not had to update the normals, no matter how many lights we have in the scene. However to create directional point lights we do have to update the normals: the direction of each light will create a different normal. Therefore, we replace `vNormal` with a **varying array**:

```
varying vec3 vNormal[numLights];
```

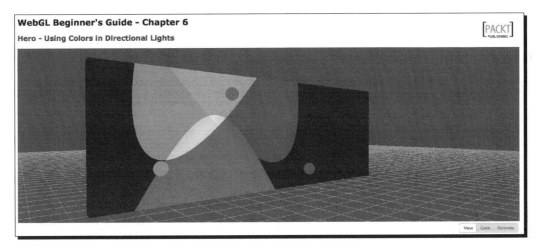

5. The line that subtracts the light direction from the normal occurs inside the `for` loop. This is because we do this for every light in the scene, as every light has its own light direction:

```
//Calculate normals and light rays
for(int i = 0; i < numLights; i++){
vec4 positionLight = uMVMatrix * vec4(uLightPosition[i],1.0);
vec3 directionLight = vec3(uNMatrix * vec4(uLightDirection[i],
1.0));
vNormal[i] = normal - directionLight;
vLightRay[i] = vertex.xyz-positionLight.xyz;
 }
```

Also, here the light direction is transformed by the Normal matrix while the light position is transformed by the Model-View matrix.

6. In the fragment shader, we calculate the Lambert coefficients: one per light and per fragment. The key difference is this line in the fragment shader:

```
N = normalize(vNormal[i]);
```

Here we obtain the interpolated updated normal per light.

7. Let's create a cut-off by restricting the allowed Lambert coefficients. There are at least two different ways to obtain a light cone in the fragment shader. The first one consists of restricting the Lambert coefficient to be higher than the uniform uCutOff (cut-off value). Let's us take a look at the fragment shader:

```
if (lambertTerm > uCutOff){
    finalColor += uLightDiffuse[i] * uMaterialDiffuse
}
```

Remember that the Lambert coefficient is the cosine of the angle between the reflected light and the surface normal. If the light ray is perpendicular to the surface we obtain the highest Lambert coefficient, and as we move away from the center, the Lambert coefficients changes following the cosine function until the light rays are completely parallel to the surface creating a cosine of 90 degrees between the normal and the light ray. This produces a Lambert coefficient of zero.

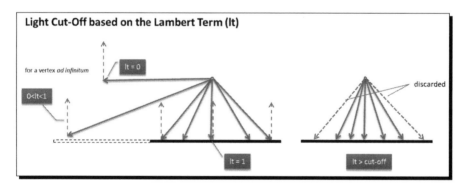

8. Open ch6_Wall_Directional.html in your HTML5 browser if you have not done so yet. Use the cut-off slider on the page and notice how this affects the light cone making it wider or narrower. After playing with the slider, you can notice that these lights do not look very realistic. The reason is that the final color is the same no matter what Lambert coefficient you obtained: as long as the Lambert coefficient is higher than the set cut-off value, you will obtain the full diffuse contribution from the three light sources.

9. To change it, open the web page using your source code editor, go to the fragment shader and multiply the Lambert coefficient in the line that calculates the final color:

```
finalColor += uLightDiffuse[i] * uMaterialDiffuse * lambertTerm;
```

10. Save the web page with a different name (so you can keep the original) and then go ahead and load it on your web browser. You will notice that the light colors appear attenuated as you depart from the center of each light reflection on the wall. This looks better but there is an even better way to create light cut-offs.

11. Now let's create a cut-off by using an **exponential attenuation factor**. In the fragment shader replace the following code:

```
if (lambertTerm > uCutOff){
       finalColor += uLightDiffuse[i] * uMaterialDiffuse;
}
```

With:

```
finalColor += uLightDiffuse[i] * uMaterialDiffuse *
pow(lambertTerm, 10.0 * uCutOff);
```

Yes, we have gotten rid of the `if` section and we have only left its contents. This time the attenuation factor is `pow(lambertTerm, 10*uCutOff)`.

This modification works because this factor attenuates the final color exponentially. If the Lambert coefficient is close to zero, the final color will be heavily attenuated.

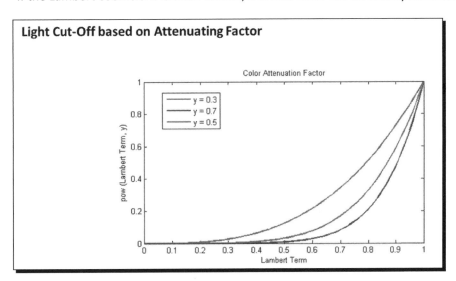

12. Save the web page with a different name and load it in your browser. The improvement is dramatic!

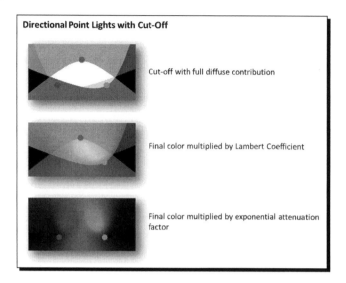

Directional Point Lights with Cut-Off

Cut-off with full diffuse contribution

Final color multiplied by Lambert Coefficient

Final color multiplied by exponential attenuation factor

We have included the completed exercises here:

- ◆ Ch6_Wall_Directional_Proportional.html
- ◆ Ch6_Wall_Directional_Exponential.html

What just happened?

We have learned how to implement directional point lights. We have also discussed attenuation factors that improve lighting effects.

Use of color in the scene

It is time to discuss transparency and alpha blending. We mentioned before that the alpha channel can carry information about the opacity of the color with which the object is being painted. However, as we saw in the cube example, it is not possible to obtain a translucent object unless alpha blending is activated. Things get a bit more complicated when we have several objects in the scene. We will see here what to do in order to have a consistent scene when we have translucent and opaque objects.

Transparency

The first approach to obtain transparent objects is to use **polygon stippling**. This technique consists of discarding some fragments so you can see through the object. Think of it as punching little holes throughout the surface of your object.

OpenGL supports polygon stippling through the `glPolygonStipple` function. This function is not available in WebGL. You could try to replicate this functionality by dropping some fragments in the fragment shader using the ESSL `discard` command.

More commonly, we can use the alpha channel information to obtain translucent objects. However, as we saw in the cube example, modifying the alpha values does not produce transparency automatically.

Creating transparencies corresponds to alter the fragments that we have already written to the frame buffer. Think for instance of a scene where there is one translucent object in front of an opaque object (from our camera view). For the scene to be rendered correctly we need to be able to see the opaque object through the translucent object. Therefore, the fragments that overlap between the far and the near objects need to be combined somehow to create the transparency effect.

Similarly, when there is only one translucent object in the scene, the same idea applies. The only difference is that, in this case, the far fragments correspond to the back face of the object and the near fragments correspond to the front face of the object. In this case, to produce the transparency effect, the far and near fragments need to be combined.

To implement transparencies, we need to learn about two important WebGL concepts: depth testing and alpha blending.

Updated rendering pipeline

Depth testing and alpha blending are two optional stages for the fragments once they have been processed by the fragment shader. If the depth test is not activated, all the fragments are automatically available for alpha blending. If the depth test is enabled, those fragments that fail the test will be automatically discarded by the pipeline and will no longer be available for any other operation. This means that discarded fragments will not be rendered. This behavior is similar to using the ESSL discard command.

The following diagram shows the order in which depth testing and alpha blending are performed:

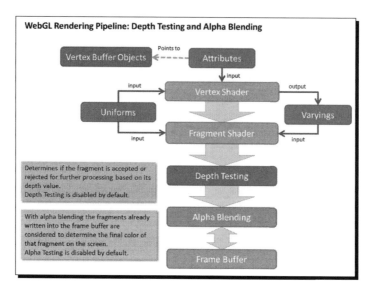

Now let's see what depth testing is about and why it is relevant for alpha blending.

Depth testing

Each fragment that has been processed by the fragment shader carries an associated depth value. Though fragments are two-dimensional as they are going to be displayed on the screen, the depth value keeps the information of how distant the fragment is from the camera (screen). Depth values are stored in a special WebGL buffer named **depth buffer** or **z-buffer**. The z comes from the fact that x and y values correspond to the screen coordinates of the fragment while the z value measures distance perpendicular to the screen.

After the fragment has been calculated by the fragment shader, it is eligible for depth testing. This only occurs if the depth test is enabled. Assuming that gl is the JavaScript variable that contains our WebGL context, we can enable depth testing by writing:

```
gl.enable(gl.DEPTH_TEST)
```

The depth test takes into consideration the depth value of a fragment and it compares it to the depth value for the same fragment coordinates already stored in the depth buffer. The depth test determines whether or not that fragment is accepted for further processing in the rendering pipeline.

Only the fragments that pass the depth test will be processed. Otherwise, any fragment that does not pass the depth test will be discarded.

In normal circumstances when the depth test is enabled, only those fragments with a lower depth value than the corresponding fragments present in the depth buffer will be accepted.

Depth testing is a commutative operation with respect to the rendering order. This means that no matter which object gets rendered first, as long as depth testing is enabled, we will always have a consistent scene.

Let's see this with an example. In the following diagram, there is a cone and a sphere. The depth test is disabled using the following code:

```
gl.disable(gl.DEPTH_TEST)
```

The sphere is rendered first. As it is expected, the cone fragments that overlap the cone are not discarded when the cone is rendered. This occurs because there is no depth test between the overlapping fragments.

Now let's enable the depth test and render the same scene. The sphere is rendered first. Since all the cone fragments that overlap the sphere have a higher depth value (they are farer from the camera) these fragments fail the depth test and are discarded creating a consistent scene.

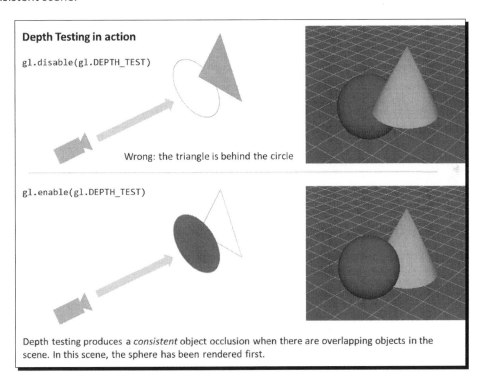

Depth Testing in action

`gl.disable(gl.DEPTH_TEST)`

Wrong: the triangle is behind the circle

`gl.enable(gl.DEPTH_TEST)`

Depth testing produces a *consistent* object occlusion when there are overlapping objects in the scene. In this scene, the sphere has been rendered first.

Depth function

In some applications, we could be interested in changing the default function of the depth-testing mechanism which discards fragments with a higher depth value than those fragments in the depth buffer. For that purpose WebGL provides the `gl.depthFunc(function)` function.

This function has only one parameter, the `function` to use:

Parameter	Description
gl.NEVER	The depth test always fails
gl.LESS	Only fragments with a depth lower than current fragments on the depth buffer will pass the test
gL.LEQUAL	Fragments with a depth less than or equal to corresponding current fragments in the depth buffer will pass the test
gl.EQUAL	Only fragments with the same depth as current fragments on the depth buffer will pass the test
gl.NOTEQUAL	Only fragments that do not have the same depth value as fragments on the depth buffer will pass the test
gl.GEQUAL	Fragments with greater or equal depth value will pass the test
gl.GREATER	Only fragments with a greater depth value will pass the test
gl.ALWAYS	The depth test always passes

 The depth test is disabled by default in WebGL. When enabled, if no depth function is set, the `gl.LESS` function is selected by default.

Alpha blending

A fragment is eligible for alpha blending if it has passed the depth test. However, when depth testing is disabled, all fragments are eligible for alpha blending.

Alpha blending is enabled using the following line of code:

```
gl.enable(gl.BLEND);
```

For each eligible fragment the alpha blending operation reads the color present in the frame buffer for those fragment coordinates and creates a new color that is the result of a linear interpolation between the color previously calculated in the fragment shader (gl_FragColor) and the color already present in the frame buffer.

 Alpha blending is disabled by default in WebGL.

Blending function

With blending enabled, the next step is to define a blending function. This function will determine how the fragment colors coming from the object we are rendering (source) will be combined with the fragment colors already present in the frame buffer (destination).

We combine source and destination as follows:

```
Color Output = S * sW + D * dW
```

Here,

- S: source color
- D: destination color
- sW: source scaling factor
- dW: destination scaling factor
- S.rgb: rgb components of the source color
- S.a: alpha component of the source color
- D.rgb: rgb components of the destination color
- D.a: alpha component of the destination color

It is very important to notice here that the rendering order will determine what the source and the destination fragments are in the previous equations. Following the example from the previous section, if the sphere is rendered first, then it will become the destination of the blending operation because the sphere fragments will be already stored in the frame buffer when the cone is rendered. In other words, alpha blending is a non-commutative operation with respect to the rendering order.

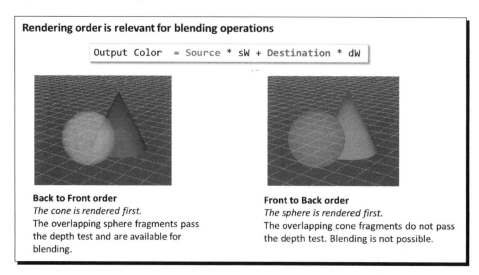

Rendering order is relevant for blending operations

```
Output Color  = Source * sW + Destination * dW
```

Back to Front order
The cone is rendered first.
The overlapping sphere fragments pass the depth test and are available for blending.

Front to Back order
The sphere is rendered first.
The overlapping cone fragments do not pass the depth test. Blending is not possible.

Separate blending functions

It is also possible to determine how the RGB channels are going to be combined independently from the alpha channels. For that, we use the `gl.blendFuncSeparate` function.

We define two independent functions this way:

```
Color output = S.rgb * sW.rgb + D.rgb * dW.rgb
Alpha output = S.a * sW.a + D.a * dW.a
```

Here,

- `sW.rgb`: source scaling factor (only rgb)
- `dW.rgb`: destination scaling factor (only rgb)
- `sW.a`: source scaling factor for the source alpha value
- `dW.a`: destination scaling factor for the destination alpha value

Then we could have something as follows:

```
Color output = S.rgb * S.a + D.rbg * (1 - S.a)
Alpha output = S.a * 1 + D.a * 0
```

This would be translated into code as:

```
gl.blendFuncSeparate(gl.SRC_ALPHA, gl.ONE_MINUS_SRC_ALPHA, gl.ONE,
gl.ZERO)
```

This particular configuration is equivalent to our previous case where we did not separate the functions. The parameters for the `gl.blendFuncSeparate` function are the same as that can be passed to `gl.blendFunc`. As stated before, you will find the complete list later in this section.

Blend equation

We could have the case where we do not want to interpolate the source and destination fragment colors by scaling them and adding them as shown before. It could be the case where we want to subtract one from the other. In that case, WebGL provides the `gl.blendEquation` function. This function receives one parameter that determines the operation on the scaled source and destination fragment colors.

`gl.blendEquation(gl.FUNC_ADD)` will correspond to:

```
Color output = S * sW + D *dW
```

While `gl.blendEquation(gl.FUNC_SUBTRACT)` corresponds to:

```
Color output = S * sW - D *dW
```

There is a third option: `gl.blendEquation(gl.FUNC_REVERSE_SUBTRACT)` that corresponds to:

```
Color output = D* dw - S*sW
```

As it is expected, it is also possible to define the blending equation separately for the RGB channels and for the alpha channel. For that, we use the `gl.blendEquationSeparate` function.

Blend color

WebGL provides the scaling factors `gl.CONSTANT_COLOR` and `gl.ONE_MINUS_CONSTANT_COLOR`. These scaling factors can be used with `gl.blendFunc` and with `gl.blendFuncSeparate`. However, we need to establish beforehand what the blend color is going to be. We do so by invoking `gl.blendColor`.

WebGL alpha blending API

The following table summarizes the WebGL functions that are relevant to performing alpha blending operations:

WebGL Function	Description
`gl.enable|disable (gl.BLEND)`	Enable/disable blending
`gl.blendFunc (sW, dW)`	Specify pixel arithmetic. Accepted values for `sW` and `dW` are:
	`ZERO`
	`ONE`
	`SRC_COLOR`
	`DST_COLOR`
	`SRC_ALPHA`
	`DST_ALPHA`
	`CONSTANT_COLOR`
	`CONSTANT_ALPHA`
	`ONE_MINUS_SRC_ALPHA`
	`ONE_MINUS_DST_ALPHA`
	`ONE_MINUS_SRC_COLOR`
	`ONE_MINUS_DST_COLOR`
	`ONE_MINUS_CONSTANT_COLOR`
	`ONE_MINUS_CONSTANT_ALPHA`
	In addition, `sW` can also be `SRC_ALPHA_SATURATE`
`gl.blendFuncSeparate(sW_rgb, dW_rgb, sW_a, dW_a)`	Specify pixel arithmetic for RGB and alpha components separately

WebGL Function	Description

`gl.blendEquation(mode)`	Specify the equation used for both the RGB blend equation and the alpha blend equation. Accepted values for `mode` are:
	
	`gl.FUNC_ADD`
	
	`gl.FUNC_SUBTRACT`
	
	`gl.FUNC_REVERSE_SUBTRACT`

`gl.blendEquationSeparate(modeRGB, modeAlpha)`	Set the RGB blend equation and the alpha blend equation separately
`gl.blendColor ( red, green, blue, alpha)`	Set the blend color

`gl.getParameter(pname)`	Just like with other WebGL variables, it is possible to query blending parameters using `gl.getParameter`.
	
	Relevant parameters are:
	
	`gl.BLEND`
	
	`gl.BLEND_COLOR`
	
	`gl.BLEND_DST_RGB`
	
	`gl.BLEND_SRC_RGB`
	
	`gl.BLEND_DST_ALPHA`
	
	`gl.BLEND_SRC_ALPHA`
	
	`gl.BLEND_EQUATION_RGB`
	
	`gl.BLEND_EQUATION_ALPHA`

Alpha blending modes

Depending on the parameter selection for `sW` and `dW` we can create different blending modes. In this section we are going to see how to create additive, subtractive, multiplicative, and interpolative blending modes. All blending modes depart from the already known formula:

```
Color output = S * (sW) + D * dW
```

Additive blending

Additive blending simply adds the colors of the source and destination fragments, creating a lighter image. We obtain additive blending by writing:

```
gl.blendFunc(gl.ONE, gl.ONE);
```

This assigns the weights for source and destination fragments sW and dW to 1. The color output will be:

```
Color output = S * 1 + D * 1
```

```
Color output = S + D
```

Since each color channel is in the [0, 1] range, this blending will clamp all values over 1. When all channels are 1 this results in a white color.

Subtractive blending

Similarly, we can obtain subtractive blending by writing:

```
gl.blendEquation(gl.FUNC_SUBTRACT);
gl.blendFunc(gl.ONE, gl.ONE);
```

This will change the blending equation to:

```
Color output = S * (1) - D * (1)
Color output = S - D
```

Any negative values will be simply shown as zero. When all channels are negative this results in black color.

Multiplicative blending

We obtain multiplicative blending by writing:

```
gl.blendFunc(gl.DST_COLOR, gl.ZERO);
```

This will be reflected in the blending equation as:

```
Color output = S * (D) + D * (0)
Color output = S * D
```

The result will be always a darker blending.

Interpolative blending

If we set sW to S.a and dW to 1-S.a then:

```
Color output = S * S.a + D *(1-S.a)
```

This will create a linear interpolation between the source and destination color using the source alpha color $S.a$ as the scaling factor. In code, this is translated as:

```
gl.blendFunc(gl.SRC_ALPHA, gl.ONE_MINUS_SRC_ALPHA);
```

Interpolative blending allows us to create a transparency effect as long as the destination fragments have passed the depth test. This implies that the objects need to be rendered from back to front.

In the next section you will play with different blending modes on a simple scene constituted by a cone and a sphere.

Time for action – blending workbench

1. Open the file `ch6_Blending.html` in your HTML5 Internet browser. You will see an interface like the one shown in the following screenshot:

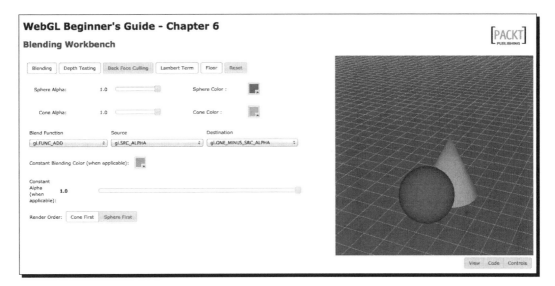

2. This interface has most of the parameters that allow you to configure alpha blending. The settings by default are source: `gl.SRC_ALPHA` and destination: `gl.ONE_MINUS_SRC_ALPHA`. These are the parameters for interpolative blending. Which slider do you need to use in order to change the scaling factor for interpolative blending? Why?

3. Change the sphere alpha slider to `0.5`. You will see some shadow-like artifacts on the surface of the sphere. This occurs because the sphere back face is now visible. To get rid of the back face click on **Back Face Culling**.

4. Click on the **Reset** button.

5. Disable the **Lambert Term** and **Floor** buttons.

6. Enable the **Back Face Culling** button.

7. Let's implement multiplicative blending. What values do source and destination need to have?

8. Click-and-drag on the canvas. Check that the multiplicative blending create dark regions where the objects overlap.

9. Change the blending function to `gl.FUNC_SUBTRACT` using the provided drop-down menu.

10. Change **Source** to `gl.ONE` and **Destination** to `gl.ONE`.

11. What blending mode is this? Click-and-drag on the canvas to check the appearance of the overlapped regions.

12. Go ahead and try different parameter configurations. Remember you can also change the blending function. If you decide to use a constant color or constant alpha, please use the color widget and the respective slider to modify the values of these parameters.

What just happened?

You have seen how the additive, multiplicative, subtractive, and interpolative blending modes work through a simple exercise.

You have seen that the combination `gl.SRC_ALPHA` and `gl.ONE_MINUS_SRC_ALPHA` produces transparency.

Creating transparent objects

We have seen that in order to create transparencies we need to:

1. Enable alpha blending and select the interpolative blending function.
2. Render the objects back-to-front.

How do we create transparent objects when there is nothing to blend them against? In other words, if there is only one object, how do we make it transparent?

One alternative to do this is to use **face culling**.

Face culling allows rendering the back face or the front face of an object only. You saw this in the previous *Time For Action* section when we only rendered the front face by enabling the **Back Face Culling** button.

Let's use the color cube that we used earlier in the chapter. We are going to make it transparent. For that effect, we will:

1. Enable alpha blending and use the interpolative blending mode.
2. Enable face culling.
3. Render the back face (by culling the front face).
4. Render the front face (by culling the back face).

Similar to other options in the pipeline, culling is disabled by default. We enable it by calling:

```
gl.enable(gl.FACE_CULLING);
```

To render only the back face of an object we call `gl.cullFace(gl.FRONT)` before we call `drawArrays` or `drawElements`.

Similarly, to render only the front face, we use `gl.cullFace(gl.BACK)` before the draw call.

The following diagram summarizes the steps to create a transparent object with alpha blending and face culling.

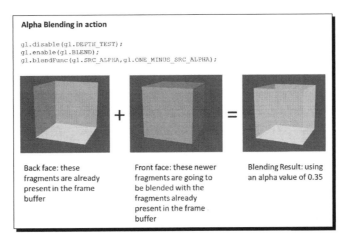

Time for action – culling

1. Open the `ch6_Culling.html` file using your HTML5 Internet browser.

2. You will see that the interface is similar to the blending workbench exercise. However, on the top row you will see these three options:

   ❑ **Alpha Blending**: enables or disables alpha blending

   ❑ **Render Front Face**: if active, renders the front face

   ❑ **Render Back Face**: if active, renders the back face

   Remember that for blending to work objects need to be rendered back-to-front. Therefore, the back face of the cube is rendered first.

   This is reflected in the `draw` function:

```
if(showBackFace){
    gl.cullFace(gl.FRONT);   //renders the back face
    gl.drawElements(gl.TRIANGLES, object.indices.length,
                gl.UNSIGNED_SHORT,0);
}
if (showFrontFace){
    gl.cullFace(gl.BACK);   //renders the front face
    gl.drawElements(gl.TRIANGLES, object.indices.length,
                gl.UNSIGNED_SHORT,0);
}
```

   Going back to the web page, notice how the interpolative blending function produces the expected transparency effect. Move the alpha value slider that appears below the button options to adjust the scaling factor for interpolative blending.

3. Review to the interpolative blending function. In this case, the destination is the back face (rendered first) and the source is the front face. If the alpha `source = 1` what would you obtain according to the function? Go ahead and test the result by moving the alpha slider to zero.

4. Let's visualize the back face only. For that, disable the **Render Front Face** button by clicking on it. Increase the alpha value using the alpha value slider that appears right below the button options. Your screen should look like this:

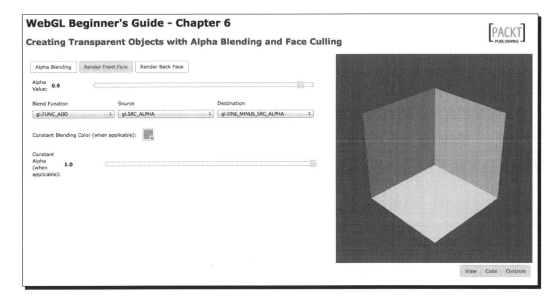

5. Click-and-drag the cube on the canvas. Notice how the back face is calculated every time you move the camera around.

6. Click on the **Render Front Face** again to activate it. Change the blending function so you can obtain subtractive blending.

7. Try different blending configurations using the controls provided in this exercise.

What just happened?

We have seen how to create transparent objects using alpha blending interpolative mode and face culling.

Now let's see how to implement transparencies when there are two objects on the screen. In this case we have a wall that we want to make transparent. Behind it there is a cone.

Time for action – creating a transparent wall

1. Open `ch6_Transparency_Initial.html` in your HTML5 web browser. We have two completely opaque objects: a cone behind a wall. Click-and-drag on the canvas to move the camera behind the wall and see the cone as shown in the following screenshot:

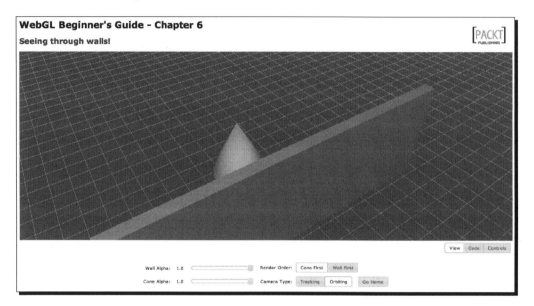

2. Change the wall alpha value by using the provided slider.

3. As you can see, modifying the alpha value does not produce any transparency. The reason for this is that the alpha blending is not being enabled. Let's edit the source code and include alpha blending. Open the file `ch6_Transparency_Initial.html` using your preferred source code editor. Scroll to the `configure` function and below these lines:

```
gl.enable(gl.DEPTH_TEST);
gl.depthFunc(gl.LEQUAL);
```

Add:

```
gl.enable(gl.BLEND);
gl.blendFunc(gl.SRC_ALPHA,gl.ONE_MINUS_SRC_ALPHA);
```

4. Save your changes as `ch6_Transparency_Final.html` and load this page on your web browser.

5. As expected, the wall changes its transparency as you modify its alpha value using the respective slider.

6. **A note on rendering order:** Remember that in order for transparency to be effective the objects need to be rendered back to front. Let's take a look at the source code. Open `ch6_Transparency_Final.html` in your source code editor.

   The cone is the farthest object in the scene. Hence, it is loaded first. You can check that by looking at the `load` function:

   ```
   Scene.loadObject('models/geometry/cone.json','cone');
   Scene.loadObject('models/geometry/wall.json','wall',{diffu
   se:[0.5,0.5,0.2,1.0], ambient:[0.2,0.2,0.2,1.0]});
   ```

   Therefore it occupies a lower index in the `Scene.objects` list. In the `draw` function, the objects are rendered in the order in which they appear in the `Scene.objects` list like this:

   ```
   for (var i = 0, max=Scene.objects.length; i < max; i++){
       var object = Scene.objects[i];
       ...
   ```

7. What happens if we rotate the scene so the cone is closer to the camera and the wall is farer away? Open `ch6_Transparency_Final.html` and rotate the scene such that the cone appears in front of the wall. Now decrease the alpha value of the cone while the alpha value of the wall remains at 1.0.

8. As you can see, the blending is inconsistent. This does not have to do with alpha blending because in `ch6_Transparency_Final.html` the blending is enabled (you just enabled it on step 3). It has to do with the **rendering order**. Click on the **Wall First button**. The scene should appear consistent now.

   The **Cone First** and **Wall First** buttons use a couple of new functions that we have included in the `Scene` object to change the rendering order. These functions are `renderSooner` and `renderFirst`.

   In total, we have added these functions to the `Scene` object to deal with rendering order:

   ❑ `renderSooner(objectName)` —moves the object with name `objectName` one position before in the `Scene.objects` list.

   ❑ `renderLater(objectName)` —moves the object with name `objectName` one position after in the `Scene.objects` list.

   ❑ `renderFirst(objectName)` —moves the object with name `objectName` to the first position of the list (index 0).

   ❑ `renderLast(objectName)` —moves the object with name `objectName` to the last position of the list.

❑   `renderOrder()`—lists the objects in the `Scene.objects` list in the order in which they are rendered. This is the same order in which they are stored in the list. For any two given objects, the object with the lower index will be rendered first.

You can use these functions from the JavaScript console in your browser and see what effect these have on the scene.

What just happened?

We have taken a simple scene where we have implemented alpha blending. After that we have analyzed the importance of the rendering order in creating consistent transparencies. Finally, we have presented the new methods of the `Scene` object that control the rendering order.

Summary

In this chapter, we have seen how to use colors on objects, lights, and on the scene in general. Specifically, we have learned that an object can be colored per vertex, per fragment, or it can have a constant color.

The color of light sources in the scene depends on implemented lighting model. Not all lights need to be always white. We have also seen how uniform arrays simplify working with multiple lights in ESSL and in JavaScript WebGL. Also we have created point directional lights.

The alpha value does not necessarily make an object translucent. Interpolative blending is necessary to create translucent objects. Also, the objects need to be rendered back-to-front.

Additionally, face culling can help to produce better results when there are multiple translucent objects present in the scene.

In *Chapter 7, Textures*, we will study how to paint images over our objects. For that we will use WebGL textures.

7
Textures

So far, we've added details to our scene with geometry, vertex colors, and lighting; but often that won't be enough to achieve the look that we want. Wouldn't it be great if we could "paint" additional details onto our scene without needing additional geometry? We can, through a technique called texture mapping. In this chapter, we'll examine how we can use textures to make our scene more detailed.

In this chapter, we'll learn the following:

- ◆ How to create a texture
- ◆ How to use a texture when rendering
- ◆ Filter and wrapping modes and how they affect the texture's use
- ◆ Multi-texturing
- ◆ Cube mapping

Let's get started!

What is texture mapping?

Texture mapping is, at its most basic, a method for adding detail to the geometry being rendered by displaying an image on the surface. Consider the following image:

Using only the techniques that we've learned so far, this relatively simple scene would be very difficult to build and unnecessarily complex. The WebGL logo would have to be carefully constructed out of many little triangles with appropriate colors. Certainly such an approach is possible, but the additional geometry needed would make it quickly impractical for use in even a marginally complex scene.

Luckily for us, texture mapping makes the above scene incredibly simple. All that's required is an image of the WebGL logo in an appropriate file format, an additional vertex attribute on the mesh, and a few additions to our shader code.

Creating and uploading a texture

First off, for various reasons your browser will naturally load textures "upside down" from how textures are traditionally used in desktop OpenGL. As a result, many WebGL applications specify that the textures should be loaded with the Y coordinate flipped. This is done with a single call from somewhere near the beginning of the code.

```
gl.pixelStorei(gl.UNPACK_FLIP_Y_WEBGL, true);
```

Whether or not you use this mode is up to you, but we will be using it throughout this chapter.

The process of creating a texture is very similar to that of creating a vertex or an index buffer. We start by creating the texture object as follows:

```
var texture = gl.createTexture();
```

Textures, like buffers, must be bound before we can manipulate it in any way.

```
gl.bindTexture(gl.TEXTURE_2D, texture);
```

The first parameter indicates the type of texture we're binding, or the texture target. For now, we'll focus on 2D textures, indicated with `gl.TEXTURE_2D` in the previous code snippet. More targets will be introduced in the *Cube maps* section.

Once we have bound the texture, we can provide it with image data. The simplest way to do that is to pass a DOM image into the `texImage2D` function as shown in the following code snippet:

```
var image = document.getElementById("textureImage");
gl.texImage2D(gl.TEXTURE_2D, 0, gl.RGBA, gl.RGBA, gl.UNSIGNED_BYTE,
image);
```

You can see in this example that we have selected an image element from our page with the ID of `"textureImage"` to act as the source for our texture. This is known as **Uploading** the texture, since the image will be stored for fast access during rendering, often in the GPU's video memory. The source can be in any image format that can be displayed on a web page, such as JPEG, PNG, GIF, or BMP files.

The image source for the texture is passed in as the last parameter of the `texImage2D` call. When `texImage2D` is called with an image in this way, WebGL will automatically determine the dimensions of the texture from the image you provide. The rest of the parameters instruct WebGL about the type of information the image contains and how to store it. Most of the time, the only value you will need to worry about changing is the third and fourth parameter, which can also be `gl.RGB` to indicate that your texture has no alpha (transparency) channel.

In addition to the image, we also need to instruct WebGL how to filter the texture when rendering. We'll get into what filtering means and what the different filtering modes do in a bit. In the meantime let's use the simplest one to get us started:

```
gl.texParameteri(gl.TEXTURE_2D, gl.TEXTURE_MAG_FILTER, gl.NEAREST);
gl.texParameteri(gl.TEXTURE_2D, gl.TEXTURE_MIN_FILTER, gl.NEAREST);
```

Finally, just as with buffers, it's a good practice to unbind a texture when you are finished using it, which is accomplished by binding `null` as the active texture:

```
gl.bindTexture(gl.TEXTURE_2D, null);
```

Of course, in many cases you won't want to have all of the textures for your scene embedded on your web page, so it's often more convenient to create the image element on the fly and have it dynamically load the image needed. Putting all of this together gives us a simple function that will load any image URL that we provide as a texture.

```
var texture = gl.createTexture();
var image = new Image();
image.onload = function(){
    gl.bindTexture(gl.TEXTURE_2D, texture);
```

```
    gl.texImage2D(gl.TEXTURE_2D, 0, gl.RGBA, gl.RGBA, gl.UNSIGNED_
BYTE, image);
    gl.texParameteri(gl.TEXTURE_2D, gl.TEXTURE_MAG_FILTER,
gl.NEAREST);
    gl.texParameteri(gl.TEXTURE_2D, gl.TEXTURE_MIN_FILTER,
gl.NEAREST);
    gl.bindTexture(gl.TEXTURE_2D, null);
}
image.src = "textureFile.png";
```

 There is a slight 'gotcha' when loading images in this way. The image loading is asynchronous, which means that your program won't stop and wait for the image to finish loading before continuing execution. So what happens if you try to use a texture before it's been populated with image data? Your scene will still render, but any texture values you sample will be black.

In summary, creating textures follows the same pattern as using buffers. For every texture we create, we want to do the following:

- Create a new texture
- Bind it to make it the current texture
- Pass the texture contents, typically from an image
- Set the filter mode or other texture parameters
- Unbind the texture

If we reach a point where we no longer need a texture, we can remove it and free up the associated memory using `deleteTexture`:

```
gl.deleteTexture(texture);
```

After this the texture is no longer valid. Attempts to use it will react as though `null` has been passed.

Using texture coordinates

So now that we have our texture ready to go, we need to apply it to our mesh somehow. The most basic question that arises then is what part of the texture to show on which part of the mesh. We do this through another vertex attribute named **texture coordinates**.

Texture coordinates are two-element float vectors that describe a location on the texture that coincides with that vertex. You might think that it would be most natural to have this vector be an actual pixel location on the image, but instead, WebGL forces all the texture coordinates into a 0 to 1 range, where [0, 0] represents the top left-hand side corner of the texture and [1, 1] represents the bottom right-hand side corner, as is shown in the following image:

This means that to map a vertex to the center of any texture, you would give it a texture coordinate of [0.5, 0.5]. This coordinate system holds true even for rectangular textures.

At first this may seem strange. After all, it's easier to determine what the pixel coordinates of a particular point are than what percentage of an image's height and width that point is at, but there is a benefit to the coordinate system that WebGL uses.

Let's say you create a WebGL application with some very high resolution textures. At some point after releasing your application, you get feedback from users saying that the textures are taking too long to load, or that the large textures are causing their device to render slowly. As a result, you decide to offer a lower resolution texture option for these users.

If your texture coordinates were defined in terms of pixels, you would now have to modify every mesh used by your application to ensure that the texture coordinates match up to the new, smaller textures correctly. However, when using WebGL's 0 to 1 coordinate range, the smaller textures can use the exact same coordinates as the larger ones and still display correctly!

Figuring out what the texture coordinates for your mesh should be, especially if the mesh is complex, can be one of the trickier parts of creating 3D resources, but fortunately most 3D modeling tools come with excellent utilities for laying out texture coordinates. This process is called **Unwrapping**.

Just like the vertex position components are commonly represented with the characters X, Y, and Z, texture coordinates also have a common symbolic representation. Unfortunately, it's not consistent across all 3D software applications. OpenGL (and therefore WebGL) refers to the coordinates as S and T for the X and Y components respectively. However, DirectX and many popular modeling packages refer to them as U and V. As a result, you'll often see people referring to texture coordinates as "UVs" and Unwrapping as "UV Mapping".

We will use ST for the remainder of the book to be consistent with WebGL's usage.

Using textures in a shader

Texture coordinates are exposed to the shader code in the same way that we have any other vertex attribute; no surprises here. We'll want to include a two-element vector attribute in our vertex shader that will map to our texture coordinates:

```
attribute vec2 aVertexTextureCoords;
```

Additionally, we will also want to add a new uniform to the fragment shader that uses a type we haven't seen before: sampler2D. The sampler2D uniform is what allows us to access the texture data in the shader.

```
uniform sampler2D uSampler;
```

In the past, when we've used uniforms, we have always set them to the value that we want them to be in the shader, such as a light color. **Samplers** work a little differently, however. The following shows how to associate a texture with a specific sampler uniform:

```
gl.activeTexture(gl.TEXTURE0);
gl.bindTexture(gl.TEXTURE_2D, texture);
gl.uniform1i(Program.uSampler, 0);
```

So what's going on here? First off, we are changing the active texture index with gl.activeTexture. WebGL supports using multiple textures at once (which we'll talk about later on in this chapter), so it's a good practice to specify which texture index we're working with, even though it won't change for the duration of this program. Next, we bind the texture we wish to use, which associates it with the currently active texture TEXTURE0. Finally, we tell the sampler uniform which texture it should be associated with, not with the texture itself, but with the texture unit provided via gl.uniform1i. Here we give it 0 to indicate that the sampler should use TEXTURE0.

That's quite a bit of setup, but now we are finally ready to use our texture in the fragment shader! The simplest way to use a texture is to return its value as the fragment color as shown here:

```
gl_FragColor = texture2D(uSampler, vTextureCoord);
```

`texture2D` takes in the sampler uniform we wish to query and the coordinates to lookup, and returns the color of the texture image at those coordinates as a `vec4`. Even if the image has no alpha channel, a `vec4` will still be returned with the alpha component always set to 1.

Time for action – texturing the cube

Open the file `ch7_Textured_Cube.html` in your favorite HTML editor. This contains the simple lit cube example from the previous chapter. If you open it in an HTML5 browser, you should see a scene that looks like the following screenshot:

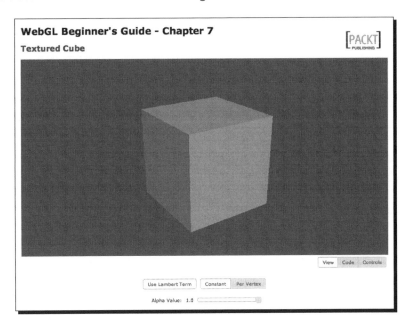

In this example we will add a texture map to this cube as shown here:

1. First, let's load the texture image. At the top of the script block, add a new variable to hold the texture:

    ```
    var texture = null;
    ```

2. Then, at the bottom of the `configure` function, add the following code, which creates the texture object, loads an image, and sets the image as the texture data. In this case, we'll use a PNG image with the WebGL logo on it as our texture.

    ```
    //Init texture
    texture = gl.createTexture();

    var image = new Image();
    image.onload = function(){
    ```

```
     gl.bindTexture(gl.TEXTURE_2D, texture);
     gl.texImage2D(gl.TEXTURE_2D, 0, gl.RGBA, gl.RGBA, gl.UNSIGNED_
BYTE, image);
     gl.texParameteri(gl.TEXTURE_2D, gl.TEXTURE_MAG_FILTER,
gl.NEAREST);
     gl.texParameteri(gl.TEXTURE_2D, gl.TEXTURE_MIN_FILTER,
gl.NEAREST);
     gl.bindTexture(gl.TEXTURE_2D, null);
}
image.src = 'textures/webgl.png';
```

3. Next, in the draw function after the vertexColors binding block, add the following code to expose the texture coordinate attribute to the shader:

```
if (object.texture_coords){
     gl.enableVertexAttribArray(Program.aVertexTextureCoords);
     gl.bindBuffer(gl.ARRAY_BUFFER, object.tbo);
     gl.vertexAttribPointer(Program.aVertexTextureCoords, 2,
gl.FLOAT, false, 0, 0);
}
```

4. Within that same if block, add the following code to bind the texture to the shader sampler uniform:

```
gl.activeTexture(gl.TEXTURE0);
gl.bindTexture(gl.TEXTURE_2D, texture);
gl.uniform1i(Program.uSampler, 0);
```

5. Now we need to add the texture-specific code to the shader. In the vertex shader, add the following attribute and varying to the variable declarations:

```
attribute vec2 aVertexTextureCoords;
varying vec2 vTextureCoords;
```

6. And at the end of the vertex shader's main function, make sure to copy the texture coordinate attribute into the varying so that the fragment shader can access it:

```
vTextureCoord = aVertexTextureCoords;
```

7. The fragment shader also needs two new variable declarations: The sampler uniform and the varying from the vertex shader.

```
uniform sampler2D uSampler;
varying vec2 vTextureCoord;
```

8. We must also remember to add `aVertexTextureCoords` to the `attributeList` and `uSampler` to the `uniformList` in the `configure` function so that the new variables can be accessed from our JavaScript binding code.

9. To access the texture color, we call `texture2D` with the sampler and the texture coordinates. As we want the textured surface to retain the lighting that was calculated, we'll multiply the lighting color and the texture color together, giving us the following line to calculate the fragment color:

```
gl_FragColor = vColor * texture2D(uSampler, vTextureCoord);
```

10. If everything has gone according to the plan, opening the file now in an HTML5 browser should yield a scene like this one:

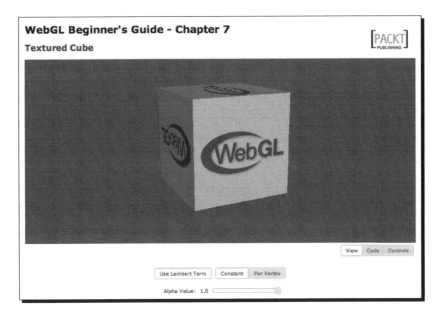

 If you're having trouble with a particular step and would like a reference, the completed code is available in `ch7_Textured_Cube_Finished.html`.

What just happened?

We've just loaded a texture from a file, uploaded it to the GPU, rendered it on the cube geometry, and blended with the lighting information that was already being calculated.

The remaining examples in this chapter will omit calculation of lighting for simplicity and clarity, but all of the examples could have lighting applied to them if desired.

Have a go hero – try a different texture

Go grab one of your own images and see if you can get it to display as the texture instead. What happens if you provide a rectangular image rather than a square one?

Texture filter modes

So far, we've seen how textures can be used to sample image data in a fragment shader, but we've only used them in a limited context. Some interesting issues arise when you start to look at texture use in more robust situations.

For example, if you were to zoom in on the cube from the previous demo, you would see that the texture begins to alias pretty severely.

As we zoom in, you can see jagged edges develop around the WebGL logo. Similar problems become apparent when the texture is very small on the screen. Isolated to a single object, such artifacts are easy to overlook, but they can become very distracting in complex scenes.

So why do we see these artifacts in the first place?

Recall from the previous chapter how vertex colors are interpolated, so that the fragment shader is provided a smooth gradient of color. Texture coordinates are interpolated in exactly the same way, with the resulting coordinates being provided to the fragment shader and used to sample color values from the texture. In a perfect situation, the texture would display at a 1:1 ratio on screen, meaning each pixel of the texture (known as **texels**) would take up exactly one pixel on screen. In this scenario, there would be no artifacts.

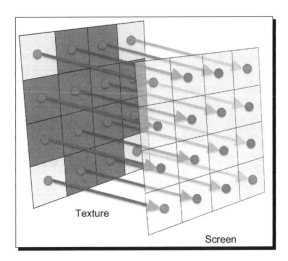

The reality of 3D applications, however, is that the textures are almost never displayed at their native resolution. We refer to these scenarios as **magnification** and **minification**, depending on whether the texture has a lower or higher resolution than the screen space it occupies.

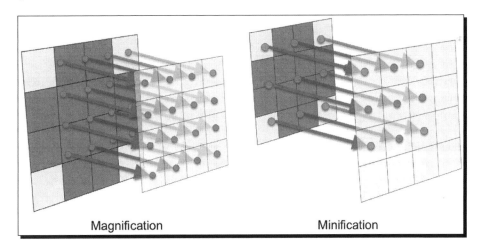

When a texture is magnified or minified, there can be some ambiguity about what color the texture sampler should return. For example, consider the following diagram of sample points against a slightly magnified texture:

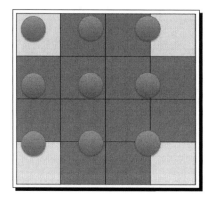

It's pretty obvious what color you would want the top left-hand side or middle sample points to return, but what about those that sit between texels? What color should they return? The answer is determined by your filter mode. Texture filtering gives us a way to control how textures are sampled and achieve the look that we want.

Setting a texture's filter mode is very straightforward, and we've already seen an example of how it works when talking about creating textures.

```
gl.texParameteri(gl.TEXTURE_2D, gl.TEXTURE_MAG_FILTER, gl.NEAREST);
gl.texParameteri(gl.TEXTURE_2D, gl.TEXTURE_MIN_FILTER, gl.NEAREST);
```

As with most WebGL calls, `texParameteri` operates on the currently bound texture, and must be set for every texture you create. This also means that different textures can have different filters, which can be useful when trying to achieve specific effects.

In this example we are setting both the magnification filter (`TEXTURE_MAG_FILTER`) and the minification filter (`TEXTURE_MIN_FILTER`) to `NEAREST`. There are several modes that can be passed for the third parameter, and the best way to understand the visual impact that they have on a scene is to see the various filter modes in action.

Let's look at a demonstration of the filters in your browser while we discuss different parameters.

Time for action – trying different filter modes

1. Open the file ch7_Texture_Filters.html using your HTML5 Internet browser:

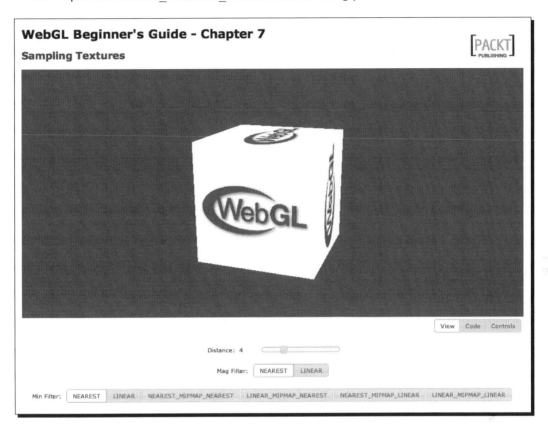

2. The controls along the bottom include a slider to adjust the distance of the box from the viewer, and the buttons modify the magnification and minification filters.

3. Experiment with different modes to observe the effect they have on the texture. Magnification filters take effect when the cube is closer, minification filters when it is further away. Be sure to rotate the cube as well and observe what the texture looks like when viewed at an angle with each mode.

What just happened?

Let's look at each of the filter modes in depth, and discuss how they work.

NEAREST

Textures using the NEAREST filter always return the color of the texel whose center is nearest to the sample point. Using this mode textures will look blocky and pixilated when viewed up close, which can be useful for creating "retro" graphics. NEAREST can be used for both MIN and MAG filters.

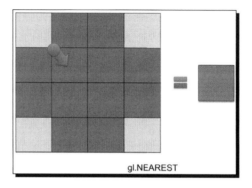

gl.NEAREST

LINEAR

The LINEAR filter returns the weighted average of the four pixels whose centers are nearest to the sample point. This provides a smooth blending of texel colors when looking at textures close up, and generally is a much more desirable effect. This does mean that the graphics hardware has to read four times as many pixels per fragment, so naturally it's slower than NEAREST, but modern graphics hardware is so fast that this is almost never an issue. LINEAR can be used for both MIN and MAG filters. This filtering mode is also known as **bilinear filtering**.

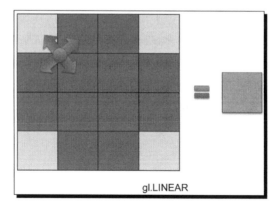

gl.LINEAR

Looking back at the close-up example image we showed earlier in the chapter, had we used LINEAR filtering it would have looked like this:

Mipmapping

Before we can discuss the remaining filter modes that are only applicable to TEXTURE_MIN_FILTER, we need to introduce a new concept: **mipmapping**.

A problem arises when sampling minified textures; even when using LINEAR filtering where the sample points can be so far apart that we can completely miss some details of the texture. As the view shifts, the texture fragments that we miss changes and the result is a shimmering effect. You can see this in action by setting the MIN filter in the demo to NEAREST or LINEAR, zooming out, and rotating the cube.

To avoid this, graphics cards can utilize a **mipmap chain**.

Mipmaps are scaled-down copies of a texture, with each copy being exactly half the size of the previous one. If you were to show a texture and all of it's mipmaps in a row, it would look like this:

The advantage is that when rendering, the graphics hardware can choose the copy of the texture that most closely matches the size of the texture on screen and sample from it instead, which reduces the number of skipped texels and the jittery artifacts that accompany it. However, mipmapping is only used if you use the appropriate texture filters. The following TEXTURE_MIN_FILTER modes will utilize mipmaps in some fashion or the other.

NEAREST_MIPMAP_NEAREST

This filter will select the mipmap that most closely matches the size of the texture on screen and sample from it using the NEAREST algorithm.

LINEAR_MIPMAP_NEAREST

This filter selects the mipmap that most closely matches the size of the texture on screen and sample from it using the LINEAR algorithm.

NEAREST_MIPMAP_LINEAR

This filter selects two mipmaps that most closely matches the size of the texture on screen and samples from both of them using the NEAREST algorithm. The color returned is a weighted average of those two samples.

LINEAR_MIPMAP_LINEAR

This filter selects two mipmaps that most closely matches the size of the texture on screen and samples from both of them using the LINEAR algorithm. The color returned is a weighted average of those two samples. This mode is also known as **trilinear filtering**.

Of the *_MIPMAP_* filter modes, NEAREST_MIPMAP_NEAREST is the fastest and of lowest quality while LINEAR_MIPMAP_LINEAR will provide the best quality at the lowest performance, with the other two modes sitting somewhere in between on the quality/speed scale. In most cases, however, the performance tradeoff will be minor enough so that you should always favor LINEAR_MIPMAP_LINEAR.

Generating mipmaps

WebGL doesn't automatically create mipmaps for every texture; so if we want to use one of the *_MIPMAP_* filter modes, we have to create the mipmaps for the texture first. Fortunately, all this takes is a single function call:

```
gl.generateMipmap(gl.TEXTURE_2D);
```

generateMipmap must be called after the texture has been populated with texImage2D and will automatically create a full mipmap chain for the image.

Alternately, if you want to provide the mipmaps manually you can always specify that you are providing a mipmap level rather than the source texture when calling texImage2D by passing a number other than 0 as the second parameter.

```
gl.texImage2D(gl.TEXTURE_2D, 1, gl.RGBA, gl.RGBA, gl.UNSIGNED_BYTE,
mipmapImage);
```

Here we're manually creating the first mipmap level, which is half the height and width of the normal texture. The second level would be quarter the dimensions of the normal texture, and so on.

This can be useful in some advanced effects, or when using compressed textures which cannot be used with `generateMipmap`.

In order to use mipmaps with a texture it needs to satisfy some dimension restrictions. Namely, the texture width and height must both be **Powers Of Two (POT)**. That is, the width and height can be `pow(2,n)` pixels, where n is any integer. Examples are 16px, 32px, 64px, 128px, 256px, 512px, 1024px, and so on. Also, note that the width and height do not have to be the same as long as both are powers of two. For example, a 512x128 texture can still be mipmapped.

Why the restriction to power of two textures? Recall that the mipmap chain is made of textures whose sizes are half of the previous level. When the dimensions are powers of two this will always produce integer numbers, which means that the number of pixels never needs to be rounded off and hence produces clean and fast scaling algorithms.

Non Power Of Two (NPOT) textures can still be used with WebGL, but are restricted to only using `NEAREST` and `LINEAR` filters.

 For all the texture code samples after this point, we'll be using a simple texture class that cleanly wraps up the texture's download, creation, and setup. Any textures created with the class will automatically have mipmaps generated for them and be set to use `LINEAR` for the magnification filter and `LINEAR_MIPMAP_LINEAR` for the minification filter.

Texture wrapping

In the previous section, we used `texParameteri` to set the filter mode for textures, but as you might expect from the generic function name, that's not all that it can do. Another texture behavior that we can manipulate is the **texture wrapping** mode.

Texture wrapping describes the behavior of the sampler when the texture coordinates fall outside the range of 0-1.

The wrapping mode can be set independently for both the S and T coordinates, so changing the wrapping mode typically takes two calls:

```
gl.texParameteri(gl.TEXTURE_2D, gl.TEXTURE_WRAP_S, gl.CLAMP_TO_EDGE);
gl.texParameteri(gl.TEXTURE_2D, gl.TEXTURE_WRAP_T, gl.CLAMP_TO_EDGE);
```

Here we're setting both the S and T wrapping modes for the currently bound texture to CLAMP_TO_EDGE, the effects of which we will see in a moment.

As with texture filters, it's easiest to demonstrate the effects of the different wrapping modes via an example and then discuss the results. Let's open up your browser again for another demonstration.

Time for action – trying different wrap modes

1. Open the file ch7_Texture_Wrapping.html using your HTML5 Internet browser.

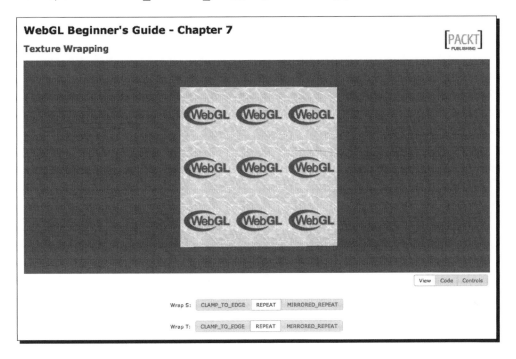

2. The cube shown has texture coordinates that range from -1 to 2, which forces the texture wrapping mode to be used for everything but the center tile of the texture.

3. Experiment with the controls along the bottom to see the effect that the different wrap modes have on the texture.

What just happened?

Let's look at each of the wrap modes and discuss how they work.

CLAMP_TO_EDGE

This wrap mode rounds any texture coordinates greater than 1 down to 1 and lower than 0 up to 0, "clamping" the values to the 0-1 range. Visually, this has the effect of repeating the border pixels of the texture indefinitely once the coordinates go out of the 0-1 range. Note that this is the only wrapping mode that is compatible with NPOT textures.

REPEAT

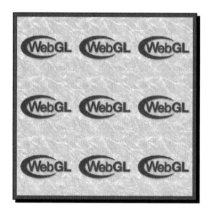

This is the default wrap mode, and the one that you'll probably use most often. In mathematical terms this wrap mode simply ignores the integer part of the texture coordinate. This creates the visual effect of the texture repeating as you go outside the 0-1 range. This can be a useful effect for displaying surfaces that have a natural repeating pattern to them, such as a tile floor or brick wall.

MIRRORED_REPEAT

The algorithm for this mode is a little more complicated. If the coordinate's integer portion is even, the texture coordinates will be the same as with REPEAT. If the integer portion of the coordinate is odd, however, the resulting coordinate is 1 minus the fractional portion of the coordinate. This results in a texture that "flip-flops" as it repeats, with every other repetition being a mirror image.

As was mentioned earlier, these modes can be mixed and matched if needed. For example, consider the following code snippet:

```
gl.texParameteri(gl.TEXTURE_2D, gl.TEXTURE_WRAP_S, gl.REPEAT);
gl.texParameteri(gl.TEXTURE_2D, gl.TEXTURE_WRAP_T, gl.CLAMP_TO_EDGE);
```

It would produce the following effect on the texture from the sample:

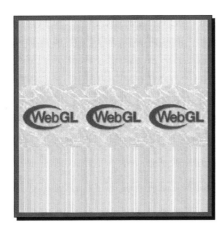

Wondering why the shader uniforms are called "samplers" instead of "textures"? A texture is just the image data stored on the GPU, while a sampler contains all the information about how to look up texture information, including filter and wrap modes.

Using multiple textures

Up to this point, we've been doing all of our rendering using a single texture at a time. As you've seen this can be a useful tool. But there are times where we may want to have multiple textures that contribute to a fragment to create more complex effects. For these cases, we can use the WebGL's ability to access multiple textures in a single draw call, otherwise known as **multitexturing**.

We've already brushed up against multitexturing earlier in a chapter, so let's go back and look at it again. When talking about exposing a texture to a shader as a sampler uniform we used the following code:

```
gl.activeTexture(gl.TEXTURE0);
gl.bindTexture(gl.TEXTURE_2D, texture);
```

The first line, `gl.activeTexture`, is the key to utilizing multitexturing. We use it to tell the WebGL state machine which texture we are going to be manipulating with, in subsequent texture functions. In this case, we passed `gl.TEXTURE0`, which means that any following texture calls (such as `gl.bindTexture`) will alter the state of the first texture unit. If we wanted to attach a different texture to the second texture unit, we would use `gl.TEXTURE1` instead.

Different devices will support different numbers of texture units, but WebGL specifies that compatible hardware must always support at least two texture units. We can find out how many texture units the current device supports with the following function call:

```
gl.getParameter(gl.MAX_COMBINED_TEXTURE_IMAGE_UNITS);
```

WebGL provides explicit enumerations for `gl.TEXTURE0` thorough `gl.TEXTURE31`, which is likely more than your hardware is capable of using. Sometimes it is convenient to specify the texture unit programmatically, or you may find a need to refer a texture unit above 31. To that end, you can always substitute `gl.TEXTURE0 + i` for `gl.TEXTUREi`. For example:

```
gl.TEXTURE0 + 2 === gl.TEXTURE2;
```

Accessing multiple textures in a shader is as simple as declaring multiple samplers.

```
uniform sampler2D uSampler;
uniform sampler2D uOtherSampler;
```

When setting up your draw call, you tell the shader which texture is associated with which sampler by providing the texture unit to `gl.uniform1i`. The code to bind two textures to the samplers above would look something like this:

```
// Bind the first texture
gl.activeTexture(gl.TEXTURE0);
gl.bindTexture(gl.TEXTURE_2D, texture);
gl.uniform1i(Program.uSampler, 0);

// Bind the second texture
gl.activeTexture(gl.TEXTURE1);
gl.bindTexture(gl.TEXTURE_2D, otherTexture);
gl.uniform1i(Program. uOtherSampler, 1);
```

So now we have two textures available to our fragment shader. The question is what do we want to do with them?

As an example we're going to implement a simple multitexture effect that layers another texture on top of a simple textured cube to simulate static lighting.

Time for action – using multitexturing

1. Open the file `ch7_Multitexture.html` with your choice of HTML editor.

2. At the top of the script block, add another texture variable:

   ```
   var texture2 = null;
   ```

3. At the bottom of the `configure` function, add the code to load the second texture. As mentioned earlier, we're using a class to make this process easier, so the new code is as follows:

   ```
   texture2 = new Texture();
   texture2.setImage('textures/light.png');
   ```

4. The texture we're using is a white radial gradient that simulates a spot light:

5. In the `draw` function, directly below the code that binds the first texture, add the following to expose the new texture to the shader:

```
gl.activeTexture(gl.TEXTURE1);
gl.bindTexture(gl.TEXTURE_2D, texture2.tex);
gl.uniform1i(Program.uSampler1, 1);
```

6. Next, we need to add the new sampler uniform to the fragment shader:

```
uniform sampler2D uSampler1;
```

7. Don't forget to add the corresponding string to the `uniformList` in the `configure` function.

8. Finally, we add the code to sample the new texture value and blend it with the first texture. In this case, since we want the second texture to simulate a light, we multiply the two values together as we did with the per-vertex lighting in the first texture example.

```
gl_FragColor = texture2D(uSampler, vTextureCoord) *
texture2D(uSampler1, vTextureCoord);
```

9. Note that we're re-using the same texture coordinate for both textures. It's convenient to do so in this case, but if needed, a second texture coordinate attribute could have been used, or we could even calculate a new texture coordinate from the vertex position or other criteria.

10. Assuming that everything works as intended, you should see a scene that looks like this when you open the file in your browser:

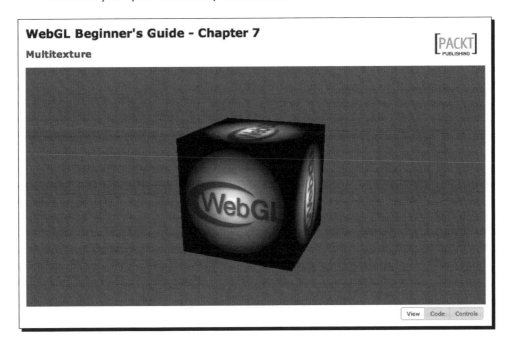

11. You can see the completed example in `ch7_Multitexture_Finished.html`.

What just happened?

We've added a second texture to the draw call and blended it with the first to create a new effect, in this case simulating a simple static spotlight.

It's important to realize that the colors sampled from a texture are treated just like any other color in the shader, that is as a generic 4-dimensional vector. As a result, we can combine textures together just like we would combine vertex and light colors, or any other color manipulation.

Have a go hero – moving beyond multiply

Multiplication is one of the most common ways to blend colors in a shader, but there's really no limit to how you can combine color values. Try experimenting with some different algorithms in the fragment shader and see what effect it has on the output. What happens when you add values instead of multiply? What if you use the red channel from one texture and the blue and green from the other? Or try out the following algorithm and see what the result is:

```
gl_FragColor = vec4(texture2D(uSampler2, vTextureCoord).rgb -
texture2D(uSampler, vTextureCoord).rgb, 1.0);
```

Cube maps

Earlier in this chapter, we mentioned that aside from 2D textures the functions we've been discussing can also be used for **cube maps**. But what are cube maps and how do we use them?

A **cube map** is, very much like it sounds, a cube of textures. Six individual textures are created, each assigned to a different face of the cube. The graphics hardware can sample them as a single entity, using a 3D texture coordinate.

The faces of the cube are identified by the axis they face and whether they are on the positive or negative side of that axis.

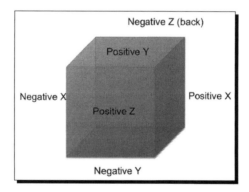

Up until this point, any time we have manipulated a texture, we have specified a texture target of TEXTURE_2D. Cube mapping introduces a few new texture targets that indicate that we are working with cube maps, and which face of the cube map we're manipulating:

◆   TEXTURE_CUBE_MAP

◆   TEXTURE_CUBE_MAP_POSITIVE_X

◆   TEXTURE_CUBE_MAP_NEGATIVE_X

◆ TEXTURE_CUBE_MAP_POSITIVE_Y

◆ TEXTURE_CUBE_MAP_NEGATIVE_Y

◆ TEXTURE_CUBE_MAP_POSITIVE_Z

◆ TEXTURE_CUBE_MAP_NEGATIVE_Z

These targets are collectively known as the `gl.TEXTURE_CUBE_MAP_*` targets. Which one you use depends on the function you are calling.

Cube maps are created like a normal texture, but binding and property manipulation happen with the `TEXTURE_CUBE_MAP` target, as shown here:

```
var cubeTexture = gl.createTexture();
gl.bindTexture(gl.TEXTURE_CUBE_MAP, cubeTexture);
gl.texParameteri(gl.TEXTURE_CUBE_MAP, gl.TEXTURE_MAG_FILTER,
gl.LINEAR);
gl.texParameteri(gl.TEXTURE_CUBE_MAP, gl.TEXTURE_MIN_FILTER,
gl.LINEAR);
```

When uploading the image data for the texture, however, you specify the side that you are manipulating as shown here:

```
gl.texImage2D(gl.TEXTURE_CUBE_MAP_POSITIVE_X, 0, gl.RGBA, gl.RGBA,
gl.UNSIGNED_BYTE, positiveXImage);
gl.texImage2D(gl.TEXTURE_CUBE_MAP_NEGATIVE_X, 0, gl.RGBA, gl.RGBA,
gl.UNSIGNED_BYTE, negativeXImage);
gl.texImage2D(gl.TEXTURE_CUBE_MAP_POSITIVE_Y, 0, gl.RGBA, gl.RGBA,
gl.UNSIGNED_BYTE, positiveYImage);
// Etc.
```

Exposing the cube map texture to the shader is done in the same way as a normal texture, just with the cube map target:

```
gl.activeTexture(gl.TEXTURE0);
gl.bindTexture(gl.TEXTURE_CUBE_MAP, cubeTexture);
gl.uniform1i(Program.uCubeSampler, 0);
```

However, the uniform type within the shader is specific to cube maps:

```
uniform samplerCube uCubeSampler;
```

When sampling from the cube map, you also use a cube map-specific function:

```
gl_FragColor = textureCube(uCubeSampler, vCubeTextureCoord);
```

The 3D coordinates that you provide is normalized by the graphics hardware into a unit vector, which specifies a direction from the center of the "cube". A ray is traced along that vector and where it intersects the cube face is where the texture is sampled.

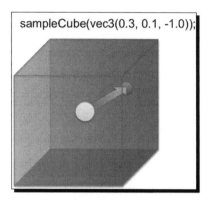

sampleCube(vec3(0.3, 0.1, -1.0));

Time for action – trying out cube maps

1. Open the file `ch7_Cubemap.html` using your HTML5 internet browser. Once again, this contains a simple textured cube example on top of which we'll build the cube map example. We want to use the cube map to create a reflective-looking surface.

2. Creating the cube map is a bit more complicated than the textures we've loaded in the past, so this time we'll use a function to simplify the asynchronous loading of individual cube faces. It's called `loadCubemapFace` and has already been added to the `configure` function. Below that function, add the following code which creates and loads the cube map faces:

```
cubeTexture = gl.createTexture();

gl.bindTexture(gl.TEXTURE_CUBE_MAP, cubeTexture);
gl.texParameteri(gl.TEXTURE_CUBE_MAP, gl.TEXTURE_MAG_FILTER,
gl.LINEAR);
gl.texParameteri(gl.TEXTURE_CUBE_MAP, gl.TEXTURE_MIN_FILTER,
gl.LINEAR);
loadCubemapFace(gl, gl.TEXTURE_CUBE_MAP_POSITIVE_X, cubeTexture,
'textures/cubemap/positive_x.png');
loadCubemapFace(gl, gl.TEXTURE_CUBE_MAP_NEGATIVE_X, cubeTexture,
'textures/cubemap/negative_x.png');
loadCubemapFace(gl, gl.TEXTURE_CUBE_MAP_POSITIVE_Y, cubeTexture,
```

```
'textures/cubemap/positive_y.png');
loadCubemapFace(gl, gl.TEXTURE_CUBE_MAP_NEGATIVE_Y, cubeTexture,
'textures/cubemap/negative_y.png');
loadCubemapFace(gl, gl.TEXTURE_CUBE_MAP_POSITIVE_Z, cubeTexture,
'textures/cubemap/positive_z.png');
loadCubemapFace(gl, gl.TEXTURE_CUBE_MAP_NEGATIVE_Z, cubeTexture,
'textures/cubemap/negative_z.png');
```

3. In the `draw` function, add the code to bind the cube map to the appropriate sampler:

```
gl.activeTexture(gl.TEXTURE1);
gl.bindTexture(gl.TEXTURE_CUBE_MAP, cubeTexture);
gl.uniform1i(Program.uCubeSampler, 1);
```

4. Turning to the shader now, first off we want to add a new `varying` to the vertex and fragment shader:

```
varying vec3 vVertexNormal;
```

5. We'll be using the vertex normals instead of a dedicated texture coordinate to do the cube map sampling, which will give us the mirror effect that we're looking for. Unfortunately, the actual normals of each face on the cube point straight out. If we were to use them, we would only get a single color per face from the cube map. In this case, we can "cheat" and use the vertex position as the normal instead. (For most models, using the normals would be appropriate).

```
vVertexNormal = (uNMatrix * vec4(-aVertexPosition, 1.0)).xyz;
```

6. In the fragment shader, we need to add the new sampler uniform:

```
uniform samplerCube uCubeSampler;
```

7. And then in the fragment shader's main function, add the code to actually sample the cubemap and blend it with the base texture:

```
gl_FragColor = texture2D(uSampler, vTextureCoord) *
textureCube(uCubeSampler, vVertexNormal);
```

8. We should now be able to reload the file in a browser and see the scene shown in the next screenshot:

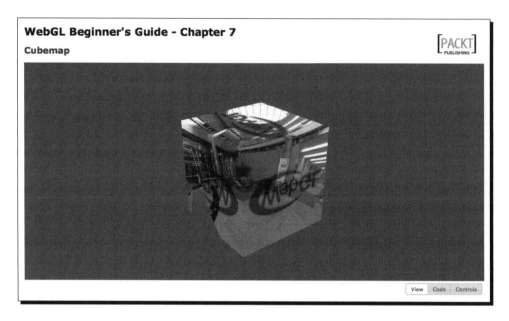

9. The completed example is available in `ch7_Cubemap_Finished.html`.

What just happened?

As you rotate the cube, you should notice that the scene portrayed in the cube map does not rotate along with it, which creates a "mirror" effect in the cube faces. This is due to multiplication of the normals by the normal matrix when assigning the `vVertexNormal` varying, which puts the normals in world space.

Using cube maps for reflective surfaces like this is a very common technique, but not the only use for cube maps. Other common uses are for skyboxes or advanced lighting models.

Have a go hero – shiny logo

In this example, we've created a completely reflective "mirrored" cube, but what if the only part of the cube we wanted to be reflective was the logo? How could we constrain the cube map to only display within the red portion of the texture?

Summary

In this chapter we learned how to use textures to add a new level of detail to our scenes. We covered how to create and manage texture objects, and use HTML images as textures. We examined the various filter modes and how they affect the texture appearance and usage, as well as the available texture wrapping modes and how they alter the way texture coordinates are interpreted. We learned how to use multiple textures in a single draw call, and how to combine them in a shader. Finally, we learned how to create and render cube maps, and saw how they can be used to simulate reflective surfaces.

Coming up in the next chapter, we'll look at selecting and interacting with objects in the WebGL scene with your mouse, otherwise known as picking.

8
Picking

Picking refers to the ability of selecting objects in a 3D scene by pointing at them. The most common device used for picking is the mouse. However, picking can also be performed using other human computer interfaces such as tactile screens and haptic devices. In this chapter we will see how picking can be implemented in WebGL.

This chapter talks about:

◆ Selecting objects in a WebGL scene using the mouse

◆ Creating and using offscreen framebuffers

◆ What renderbuffers are and how they are used by framebuffers

◆ Reading pixels from framebuffers

◆ Using color labels to perform object selection based on color

Picking

Virtually any 3D computer graphics application needs to provide mechanisms for the user to interact with the scene being displayed on the screen. For instance, you are writing a game you want to point at your target and perform an action upon it. Similarly, if you are writing a CAD system, you want to be able to select an object in your scene to modify its properties. In this chapter, we will see the basis of implementing these kinds of interactions in WebGL.

We could select objects by casting a ray (vector) from the camera position (also known as eye position) into the scene and calculate what objects lie along the ray path. This is known as **ray casting** and it involves detecting intersections between the ray and object surfaces in the scene. However, because of its complexity it is beyond the scope of this beginner's guide. Instead, we will use picking based on object colors. This method is easier to implement and it is a good starting point to help you understand how picking works.

The basic idea is to assign a different color to every object in the scene and render the scene to an offscreen framebuffer. Then, when the user clicks on the scene, we go to the offscreen framebuffer and read the color for the correspondent click coordinates. As we assigned beforehand the object colors in the offscreen buffer, we can identify the object that has been selected and perform an action upon it. The following figure depicts this idea:

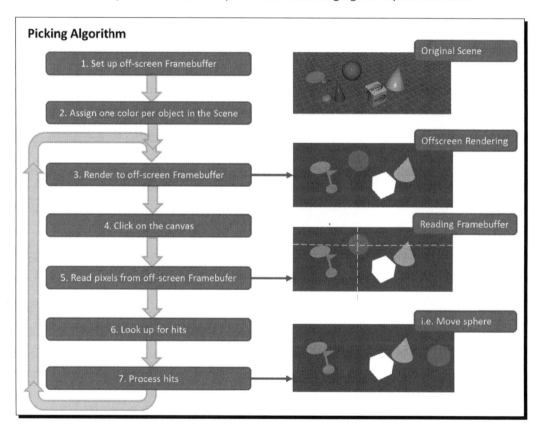

Let's break it down into the steps that we need to take.

Setting up an offscreen framebuffer

As shown in *Chapter 2*, *Rendering Geometry*, the framebuffer is the final rendering destination in WebGL. When you visualize a scene on your screen, you are looking at the framebuffer contents. Assuming that `gl` is our WebGL context, every call to `gl.drawArrays`, `gl.drawElements`, and `gl.clear` will change the contents of the framebuffer.

Instead of rendering to the default framebuffer, we can also render our scene offscreen. This will be the first step for implementing picking. To do so, we need to set up a new framebuffer and tell WebGL that we want to use it instead of the default one. Let's see how to do that.

To set up a framebuffer, we need to be able to create storage for at least two things: colors and depth information. We need to be able to store the color for every fragment that is rendered in the framebuffer so we can create an image; in contrast, we need depth information to make sure that we have a scene where overlapping objects look consistent. If we did not have depth information, then we would not be able to tell, in the case of two overlapping objects, which object is in front and which one is at the back.

To store colors we will use a WebGL texture, and to store depth information we will use a renderbuffer.

Creating a texture to store colors

The code to create a texture is pretty straightforward after reading *Chapter 7*, *Textures*. If you have not read it, you can go back there and review that chapter.

```
var canvas = document.getElementById('canvas-element-id');
var width = canvas.width;
var height = canvas.height;
var texture = gl.createTexture();
gl.bindTexture(gl.TEXTURE_2D, texture);
gl.texImage2D(gl.TEXTURE_2D, 0, gl.RGBA, width, height, 0, gl.RGBA,
gl.UNSIGNED_BYTE, null);
```

The only difference here is that we do not have an image to bind to the texture so when we call `gl.texImage2D`, the last argument is `null`. This is ok, as we are just allocating the space to store colors for the offscreen framebuffer.

Also, please notice that the width and height of the texture are set to the canvas size.

Creating a Renderbuffer to store depth information

Renderbuffers are used to provide storage for the individual buffers used in a framebuffer. The depth buffer (z-buffer) is an example of a renderbuffer. It is always attached to the screen framebuffer which is the default rendering destination in WebGL.

The code to create a renderbuffer looks like the following code:

```
var renderbuffer = gl.createRenderbuffer();
gl.bindRenderbuffer(gl.RENDERBUFFER, renderbuffer);
gl.renderbufferStorage(gl.RENDERBUFFER, gl.DEPTH_COMPONENT16, width,
height);
```

The first line of code creates the renderbuffer. Similar to other WebGL buffers, the renderbuffer needs to be bound before we can operate on it. The third line of code determines the storage size of the renderbuffer.

Please notice that the size of the storage is the same as with the texture. This way we make sure that for every fragment (pixel) in the framebuffer, we can have a color (stored in the texture) and a depth value (stored in the renderbuffer).

Creating a framebuffer for offscreen rendering

We need to create a framebuffer and attach the texture and the renderbuffer that we created in the two previous steps to it. Let's see how this works in code.

First, we create a new framebuffer using a line of code like this:

```
var framebuffer = gl.createFramebuffer();
```

Similar to the VBO manipulation, we will tell WebGL that we are going to operate on this framebuffer by making it the currently bound framebuffer. We do so with the following instruction:

```
gl.bindFramebuffer(gl.FRAMEBUFFER, framebuffer);
```

With the framebuffer bound, the texture is attached by calling the following method:

```
gl.framebufferTexture2D(gl.FRAMEBUFFER, gl.COLOR_ATTACHMENT0,
gl.TEXTURE_2D, texture, 0);
```

Then, the renderbuffer is attached to the bound framebuffer using:

```
gl.framebufferRenderbuffer(gl.FRAMEBUFFER, gl.DEPTH_ATTACHMENT,
gl.RENDERBUFFER, renderbuffer);
```

Finally, we do a bit of cleaning up as usual:

```
gl.bindTexture(gl.TEXTURE_2D, null);
gl.bindRenderbuffer(gl.RENDERBUFFER, null);
gl.bindFramebuffer(gl.FRAMEBUFFER, null);
```

When the previously created framebuffer is unbound, the WebGL state machine goes back to rendering into the screen framebuffer.

Assigning one color per object in the scene

We will pick an object based on its color. If the object has shiny reflections or shadows, then the color throughout it will not be uniform. Therefore, to pick an object based on its color we need to make sure that the color is constant per object and that each object has a different color.

We achieve constant coloring by telling the fragment shader to use only the material diffuse property to set the ESSL gl_FragColor variable. Here we are assuming that each object has a unique diffuse property.

When there are objects sharing the same diffuse color, then we need to create a new ESSL uniform to store the picking color and make it unique for every object that is rendered into the offscreen framebuffer. This way, the objects will look the same when they are rendered on screen but every time we render them into the offscreen framebuffer, their colors will be unique. This is something that we will do later on in this chapter.

For now, let's assume that the objects in our scene have unique diffuse colors as shown in the following diagram:

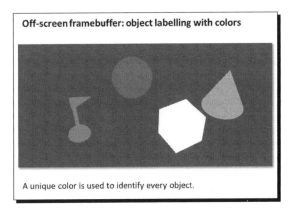

Off-screen framebuffer: object labelling with colors

A unique color is used to identify every object.

Let's see how to render the scene offscreen using the framebuffer that we just set up.

Rendering to an offscreen framebuffer

In order to perform object selection using the offscreen framebuffer, this one has to be synchronized with the onscreen default framebuffer every time that this last one receives an update. If the onscreen framebuffer and the offscreen framebuffer were not synchronized, then we could be missing addition or deletion of objects, or updates in the camera position between buffers. As a result of it there would not be a correspondence.

A lack of correspondence will hinder us from reading the picking colors from the offscreen framebuffer and use them to identify the objects in the scene. We can also refer to picking colors as object labels.

To implement this synchronicity, we will create the `render` function. This function calls the `draw` function twice. First when the offscreen buffer is bound and second time when onscreen default framebuffer is bound. The code looks like this:

```
function render(){
    //off-screen rendering
    gl.bindFramebuffer(gl.FRAMEBUFFER, framebuffer);
    gl.uniform1i(Program.uOffscreen, true);
    draw();

    //on-screen rendering
    gl.bindFramebuffer(gl.FRAMEBUFFER, null);
    gl.uniform1i(Program.uOffscreen, false);
    draw();
}
```

We tell the ESSL program to use only diffuse colors when rendering into the offscreen framebuffer using the `uOffscreen` uniform. The fragment shader looks like the following code:

```
void main(void) {
    if(uOffscreen){
        gl_FragColor = uMaterialDiffuse;
        return;
    }
    ...
}
```

The following diagram shows the behavior of the `render` function:

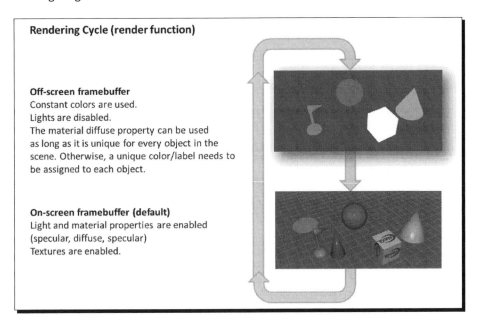

Rendering Cycle (render function)

Off-screen framebuffer
Constant colors are used.
Lights are disabled.
The material diffuse property can be used
as long as it is unique for every object in the
scene. Otherwise, a unique color/label needs to
be assigned to each object.

On-screen framebuffer (default)
Light and material properties are enabled
(specular, diffuse, specular)
Textures are enabled.

Consequently, every time that there is a scene update the `render` function should be called instead of calling the `draw` function.

We change this in the `runWebGLApp` function:

```
var app = null;
function runWebGLApp() {
    app = new WebGLApp("canvas-element-id");
    app.configureGLHook = configure;
    app.loadSceneHook   = load;
    app.drawSceneHook   = render;
    app.run();
}
```

In this way, the scene will be periodically updated using the `render` function instead of the original `draw` function.

We also need to update the function hook that the camera uses to render the scene whenever we interact with it. Originally, this hook is set to the `draw` function. If we do not change it, it points to the `render` function. We will have to wait until `WebGLApp.drawSceneHook` is invoked again to synchronize the offscreen and the onscreen framebuffers (every 500 ms by default as you can check in `WebGLApp.js`). During this time, picking will not work.

We change the camera render hook in the `configure` function:

```
function configure{
...
camera = new Camera(CAMERA_ORBITING_TYPE);
camera.goHome([0,0,40]);
camera.setFocus([0.0,0.0,0.0]);
camera.setElevation(-40);
camera.setAzimuth(-30);
camera.hookRenderer = render;

...
}
```

Clicking on the canvas

The next step is to capture the mouse coordinates when the user clicks on an object in the scene and reads the color value for these coordinates from the offscreen framebuffer.

For that, we use the standard `onmouseup` event from the `canvas` element in our webpage:

```
var canvas = document.getElementById('my-canvas-id');

canvas.onmouseup = function (ev){
    //capture coordinates from the ev event
    ...
}
```

There is an extra bit of work to do here given that the `ev` event does not return the mouse coordinates with respect to the canvas but with respect to the upper-left corner of the browser window (`ev.clientX` and `ev.clientY`). Then, we need to bubble up through the DOM getting the location of the elements that are in the DOM hierarchy to know the total offset that we have.

We do this with a code fragment like this inside the `canvas.onmouseup` function:

```
var x, y, top = 0, left = 0, obj = canvas;

while (obj&& && obj.tagName !== 'BODY') {
  top  += obj.offsetTop;
  left += obj.offsetLeft;
  obj   = obj.offsetParent;
}
```

The following diagram shows how we are going to use the offset calculation to obtain the clicked canvas coordinates:

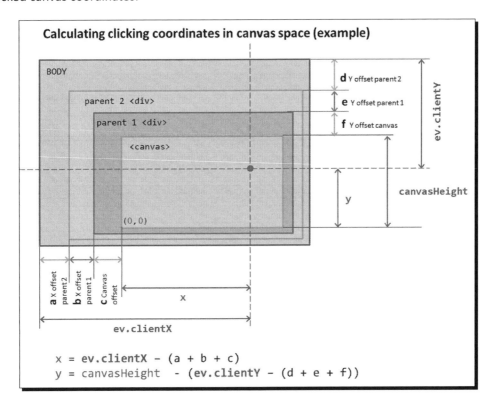

Also, we take into account any page offset if present. The page offset is the result of scrolling and affects the calculation of the coordinates. We want to obtain the same coordinates for the canvas every time regardless of any possible scrolling. For that we add the following two lines of code just before calculating the clicked canvas coordinates:

```
left += window.pageXOffset;
top  -= window.pageYOffset;
```

Finally, we calculate the canvas coordinates:

```
x = ev.clientX - left;
y = c_height - (ev.clientY - top);
```

Remember that unlike the browser window, the canvas coordinates (and also the framebuffer coordinates for this purpose) start in the lower-left corner as explained in the previous diagram.

c_height is a global variable that we are maintaining in the file codeview.js, it refers to the canvas height and it is updated along with c_width whenever we resize the browser's window. If you are developing your own application, codeview.js might not be available or applicable and then you might want to replace c_height in this snippet of code by something like clientHeight which is a standard canvas property. Also, notice that resizing the browser window will not resize your canvas. The exercises in this book do, because we have implemented this inside codeview.js.

Reading pixels from the offscreen framebuffer

We can go now to the offscreen buffer and read the color from the coordinates that we clicked on the canvas.

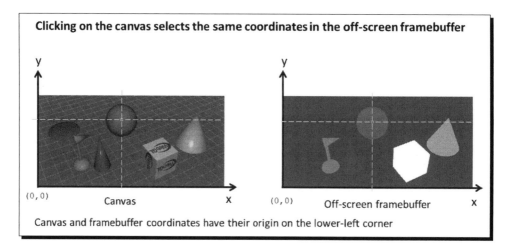

WebGL allows us to read back from a framebuffer using the readPixels function. As usual, having gl as the WebGL context variable:

Function	Description
`gl.readPixels(x, y, width, height, format, type, pixels)`	`x` and `y`: Starting coordinates.
	`width, height`: The extent of pixels to read from the framebuffer. In our example we are just reading one pixel (where the user clicks) so this will be `1, 1`.
	`format`: At the time of writing this book the only supported format is `gl.RGBA`.
	`type`: At the time of writing this book the only supported type is `gl.UNSIGNED_BYTE`.
	`pixels`: It is a typed array that will contain the results of querying the framebuffer. It needs to have sufficient space to store the results depending on the extent of the query (`x,y,width,height`).
	According to the WebGL specification at the time of writing this book it needs to be of type `Uint8Array`.

Remember that WebGL works as a state machine and many operations only make sense if this machine is in a valid state. In this case, we need to make sure that the framebuffer from which we want to read, the offscreen framebuffer, is the current one. To do that, we bind it using `bindFramebuffer`. Putting everything together, the code looks like this:

```
//read one pixel
var readout = new Uint8Array(1 * 1 * 4);

gl.bindFramebuffer(gl.FRAMEBUFFER, framebuffer);
gl.readPixels(coords.x,coords.y,1,1,gl.RGBA,gl.UNSIGNED_BYTE,readout);
gl.bindFramebuffer(gl.FRAMEBUFFER, null);
```

Here the size of the readout array is `1*1*4`. This means it has one pixel of width times one pixel height times four channels, as the format is RGBA. You do not need to specify the size this way; we just did it so that it was clear why the size is 4 when we are just retrieving one pixel.

Looking for hits

We are going to check now whether or not the color that was obtained from the off-screen framebuffer corresponds to any of the objects in the scene. Remember here that we are using colors as object labels. If the color matches one of the objects then we call it a **hit**. If it does not we call it a **miss**.

When looking for hits, we compare each object's diffuse color with the label obtained from the offscreen framebuffer. There is a consideration to make here: each color channel of the label is in the `[0,255]` range while the object diffuse colors are in the `[0,1]` range. So, we need to consider this before we can actually check for any possible hits. We do this in the `compare` function:

```
function compare(readout, color){
  return (Math.abs(Math.round(color[0]*255) - readout[0]) <= 1 &&
      Math.abs(Math.round(color[1]*255) - readout[1]) <= 1 &&
      Math.abs(Math.round(color[2]*255) - readout[2]) <= 1);
}
```

Here we are scaling the diffuse property to the `[0,255]` range and then we are comparing each channel individually. Note that we do not need to compare the alpha channel. If we had the two objects with the same color but different alpha channel, we would use the alpha channel in the comparison as well but in our example we do not have that scenario, therefore the comparison of the alpha channel is not relevant.

Also, note that the comparison is not precise because of the fact that we are dealing with decimal values in the `[0,1]` range. Therefore, we assume that after rescaling colors in this range and subtracting the readout (object label) if the difference is less than one for all the channels then we have a hit. The less then or equal to one comparison is a fudge factor.

Now, we just need to go through the object list in the `Scene` object and check if we have a miss or a hit. We are going to use two auxiliary variables here: `found`, which will be true in case of having a hit and `pickedObject` to retrieve the object that was hit.

```
var pickedObject = null, ob = null;
for(var i = 0, max = Scene.objects.length; i < max; i+=1){
    ob = Scene.objects[i];
    if (compare(readout, ob.diffuse)){
     pickedObject = ob;
        break;
    }
}
```

The previous snippet of code will tell us if we have had a hit or a miss, and also what object we hit.

Processing hits

Processing a hit is a very wide concept. It basically depends on the type of application that you are building. For instance if your application is a CAD system, you might want to retrieve on screen the properties of the object that you picked to edit them. You might also want to move the object or change its dimensions. In contrast, if you are developing a game, you could have selected the next target that your main character has to fight. We will leave this part of the code for you to decide. Nevertheless, we have included a simple example in the next *Time for action* section where you can drag-and-drop objects, which is one of the most common interactions you could have with your scene.

Architectural updates

The picking method described in this chapter has been implemented in our architecture:

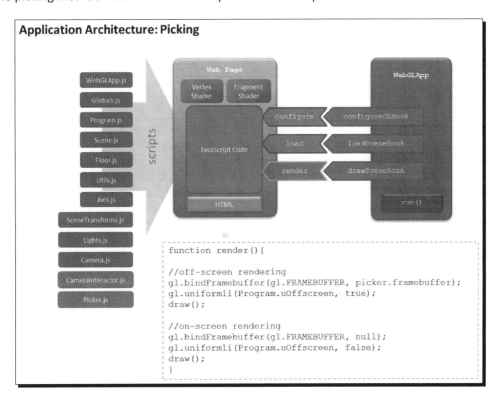

We have replaced the draw function with the render function. This function is the same that we previously described in the section *Rendering to an offscreen framebuffer*.

There is a new class: Picker. The source code for this class can be obtained from /js/webgl/Picker.js. This class encapsulates the offscreen framebuffer and encapsulates the code necessary to create it, configure it, and read from it.

We also updated the class CameraInteractor to notify the picker whenever the user clicks on the canvas. The following diagram explains how the picking algorithm is implemented using the Render function and the classes Picker and CameraInteractor:

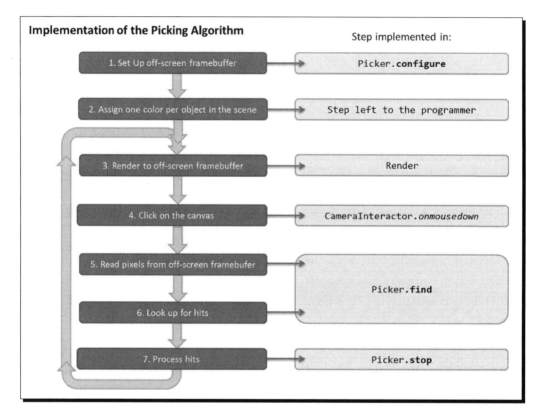

The source code for Picker and CameraInteractor can be found in the code accompanying this chapter under /js/webgl.

Now let's see picking in action!

Time for action – picking

1. Open the file ch8_Picking.html using your HTML5 Internet browser. You will see a screen similar to this:

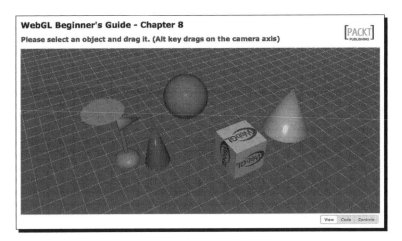

Here you have a set of objects, each one of which has a unique diffuse color property. As in the previous exercises you can rotate the camera around the scene. Please notice that the cube has a texture and that the flat disk is translucent. As you may expect, the code in the draw function handles textures coordinates and also transparencies, so it looks a bit more complex than before (you can check it out in the source code). This is a more realistic draw function. In a real application, you will have to handle these variables.

2. Click on the sphere and drag it around the scene. Notice that the object becomes translucent. Also, note that the displacement occurs along the axis of the camera. To make this evident, please go to your web browser's console and type:

```
camera.setElevation(0);
```

You will see that the camera updates its position to an elevation of zero degrees as shown in the following screenshot:

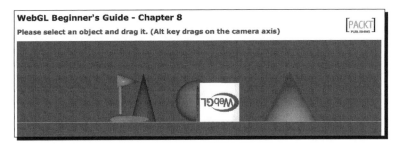

To access the console using:
Firefox go to **Tools | Web Developer | Web Console**
Safari go to **Develop | Show Web Inspector**
Chrome go to **Tools | Javascript Console**

3. Now when you click-and-drag objects in the scene from this perspective, you will see that they change their position according to the camera axis. In this case the up axis of the camera is aligned with the scene's y axis. If you move an object up and down, you will see that they change their position in the y coordinate. If you change the camera position (by clicking on the background and dragging the mouse around) and then you pick and move a different object, you will see that this moves according to the new camera axis.

    Try different camera angles and see what happens.

4. Now let's see what the offscreen framebuffer looks like. Click on the **Show Picking Image** button. Here we are instructing the fragment shader to use each of the object diffuse properties to color the fragments. You can also rotate the scene and pick objects in this mode. If you want to go back to the original shading method, click again **on Show Picking Image** to deactivate it.

5. To reset the scene, click on **Reset Scene**.

What just happened?

We have seen an example of picking in action. The source code uses the `Picker` object that we previously described in the architectural update section. Let's examine it a bit closer.

Picker architecture

The following diagram tells us what happens in the `Picker` object when the user clicks the mouse on the canvas, drags it, and releases it:

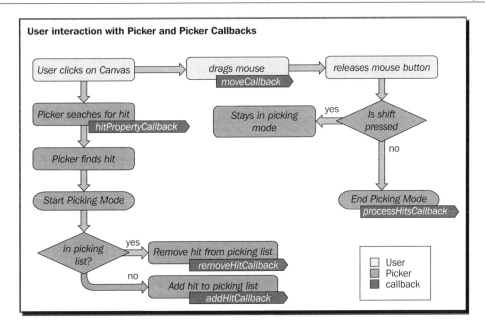

As you can see, every picker state has a callback function associated to it:

State	Callback
Picker searches for hit	`hitPropertyCallback(object)`: This callback informs the picker which object property we will use to make the comparison with the color retrieved from the offscreen framebuffer.
User drags mouse in picking mode	`moveCallback(hits, interactor, dx, dy)`: When the picking mode is activated (by having picked at least one object), this callback allows us to move the objects in the picking list (`hits`). This list is maintained internally by the `Picker` class.
Remove hit from picking list	`addHitCallback(object)`: If we click on an object and this object is not in the picking list, the picker notifies the application by triggering this callback.
Add hit to picking list	`removeHitCallback(object)`: If we click on an object and this object is already in the picking list, the picker will remove it from the list and then it will inform the application by triggering this callback.
End Picking Mode	`processHitsCallback(hits)`: if the user releases the mouse button and the *Shift* key is not pressed when this happens, then the picking mode finishes and the application is notified by triggering this callback. If the *Shift* key is pressed then the picking mode continues and the picker waits for a new click to continue looking for hits.

Implementing unique object labels

We previously mentioned that picking based on the diffuse property could be difficult if two or more objects in the scene share the same diffuse color. If that were the case and you selected one of them, how would you know which one is picked based on its color? In the next *Time for Action* section, we will implement unique object labels. The objects will be rendered in the offscreen framebuffer using these color labels instead of the diffuse colors. The scene will still be rendered on screen using the non-unique diffuse colors.

Time for action – unique object labels

This section is divided in two parts. In the first part you will develop the code to generate a random scene with cones and cylinders. Each object will be assigned a unique object label that will be used for coloring the object in the offscreen renderbuffer. In the second part, we will configure the picker to work with unique labels. Let's get started!

1. **Creating a random scene:** Open the ch8_Picking_Scene_Initial.html file in your HTML5 browser. As you can see this is a scene that is only showing the floor object. We are going to create a scene that contains multiple objects that can be either balls or cylinders.

2. Open ch8_Picking_Scene_Initial.html in a source code editor.

We will write code so each object in the scene can have:

- ❏ A position assigned randomly
- ❏ A unique object label color
- ❏ A non-unique diffuse color
- ❏ A scale factor that will determine the size of the object

3. We have provided empty functions that you will implement in this section.

4. Let's start by writing the positionGenerator function. Scroll down to it and add the following code:

```
function positionGenerator(){
    var x = Math.floor(Math.random()*60);
    var z = Math.floor(Math.random()*60);
    var flagX = Math.floor(Math.random()*10);
    var flagZ = Math.floor(Math.random()*10);

    if (flagX >= 5) {x=-x;}
    if (flagZ >= 5) {z=-z;}
    return [x,0,z];
}
```

Here we are using the `Math.random` function to generate the x and z coordinates for an object in the scene. Since `Math.random` always returns a positive number, we use the `flagX` and `flagZ` variables to randomly distribute the objects on the x-z plane (floor). Also, as we want all the objects to be on the x-z plane, the y component is set to zero in the `return` statement.

5. Now let's write a unique object label generator function. Scroll to the empty `objectLabelGenerator` function and add this code:

```
var colorset = {};
function objectLabelGenerator(){
    var color = [Math.random(), Math.random(),Math.random(),1.0];
    var key = color[0] + ':' + color[1] + ':' + color[2];

    if (key in colorset){
        return uniqueColorGenerator();
    }
    else {
        colorset[key] = true;
        return color;
    }
}
```

Here we are creating a random color using the `Math.random` function. If the `key` variable is already a property of the `colorset` object then we call the `objectLabelGenerator` function recursively; otherwise, we make `key` a property of `colorset` and then return the respective `color`. Notice how nicely the idea of handling JavaScript objects as sets allows here to resolve possible key collisions.

6. Now write the `diffuseColorGenerator` function. We will use this function to assign diffuse properties to the objects.

```
function diffuseColorGenerator(index){
    var c = (index % 30 / 60) + 0.2;
    return [c,c,c,1];
}
```

This function represents the case where we want to generate colors that are not unique. The `index` parameter represents the index of the object in the `Scene.objects` list to which we are assigning the diffuse color. In this function we are creating a gray-level color as the r, g, and b components in the `return` statement all have the same `c` value.

The `diffuseColorGenerator` function will create collisions every 30 indices. The remainder of the division of the index by 30 will create a loop in the sequence:

```
0 % 30 = 0
1 % 30 = 1
...
29 % 30 = 29
30 % 30 = 0
31 % 30 = 1
...
```

As this result is being divided by 60, the result will be a number in the $[0, 0.5]$ range. Then we add 0.2 to make sure that the minimum value that c has is 0.2. This way the objects will not look too dark during the onscreen rendering (they would be black if the calculated diffuse color were zero).

7. The last auxiliary function that we will write is the `scaleGenerator` function:

```
function scaleGenerator() {
    var f = Math.random()+0.3;
    return [f, f, f];
}
```

This function will allow us to have objects of different sizes. 0.3 is added to control the minimum scaling factor that any object will have in the scene.

Now let's load 100 objects to our scene. By the end of this section you will be able to test picking on any of them!

8. Go to the `load` function and edit it so it looks like this:

```
function load(){
    Floor.build(80,5);
    Floor.pcolor = [0.0,0.0,0.0,1.0];
    Scene.addObject(Floor);

    var positionValue,
    scaleFactor,
    objectLabel,
    objectType,
    diffuseColor;

    for (var i = 0; i < 100; i++){
        positionValue = positionGenerator();
        objectLabel = objectLabelGenerator();
        scaleFactor = scaleGenerator();
        diffuseColor = diffuseColorGenerator(i);
```

```
        objectType = Math.floor(Math.random()*2);

        switch (objectType){


            case 1: Scene.loadObject('models/geometry/sphere.
json',
                                'ball_'+i,
                                {
                                  position:positionValue,
                                  scale:scaleFactor,
                                  diffuse:diffuseColor,
                                pcolor:objectLabel
                                });
                    break;

            case 0: Scene.loadObject('models/geometry/cylinder.
json',
                                'cylinder_'+i,
                                {
                                  position:positionValue,
                                  scale:scaleFactor,
                                  diffuse:diffuseColor,
                                pcolor:objectLabel
                                });
                    break;
        }
    }
}
```

Note here that the picking color is represented by the pcolor attribute. This attribute is passed in a list of attributes to the loadObject function from the Scene object. Once the object is loaded (using the **JSON/Ajax** mechanism discussed in *Chapter 2*, *Rendering Geometry*), loadObject uses this list of attributes and adds them as object properties.

9. **Using unique labels in the fragment shader:** The shaders in this exercise have already been set up for you. The pcolor property that corresponds to the unique object label is mapped to the uPickingColor uniform and the uOffscreen uniform determines if it is used or not in the fragment shader:

```
uniform vec4 uPickingColor;
... //other uniforms and varyings
main(void){
if(uOffscreen){
```

```
        gl_FragColor = uPickingColor;
        return;
    }
    else {
    ... //on-screen rendering
    }
}
```

10. As mentioned before, we keep the offscreen and onscreen buffer in sync using the `render` function which looks like this:

```
function render(){
    //off-screen rendering
    gl.bindFramebuffer(gl.FRAMEBUFFER, picker.framebuffer);
    gl.uniform1i(Program.uOffscreen, true);
    draw();
    //on-screen rendering
    gl.uniform1i(Program.uOffscreen, showPickingImage);
    gl.bindFramebuffer(gl.FRAMEBUFFER, null);
    draw();
}
```

11. Save your work as `ch8_Picking_Scene_NoPicker.html`.

12. Open `ch8_Picking_Scene_Final_NoPicker.html` in your HTML5 Internet browser. As you can see the scene is generated as expected.

13. Click on **Show Picking Image**. What happens?

14. The scene is being rendered in the offscreen framebuffer and in the default (onscreen) framebuffer. However, we have not configured the `Picker` object callbacks yet.

15. **Configuring the picker to work with unique object labels:** Open `ch8_Picking_Scene_Final_NoPicker.html` in your source code editor.

16. Scroll down to the `configure` function. As you can see, the picker is already set up for you:

```
picker = new Picker(canvas);
picker.hitPropertyCallback = hitProperty;
picker.addHitCallback = addHit;
picker.removeHitCallback = removeHit;
picker.processHitsCallback = processHits;
picker.moveCallback = movePickedObjects;
```

This code fragment maps functions in the web page to picker callback hooks. These callbacks are invoked according to the picking state. If you need to review how this works, please go back to the *Picker Architecture* section.

In this part of the section, we are going to implement these callbacks. Again, we have provided empty functions that you will need to code.

17. Let's create the hitProperty function. Scroll down to the empty hitProperty function and add this code:

```
function hitProperty(ob){
    return ob.pcolor;
}
```

Here we are telling the picker to use the pcolor property to make the comparison with the color that will be read from the offscreen framebuffer. If these colors match then we have a hit.

18. Now we are going to write the addHit and removeHit functions. We want to create the effect where the diffuse color is changed to the picking color during picking. For that we need an extra property to save temporarily the original diffuse color so we can restore it later :

```
function addHit(ob){
    ob.previous = ob.diffuse.slice(0);
    ob.diffuse = ob.pcolor;
    render();
}
```

The addHit function stores the current diffuse color in an auxiliary property named previous. Then it changes the diffuse color to pcolor, the object picking label.

```
function removeHit(ob){
    ob.diffuse = ob.previous.slice(0);
    render();
}
```

The removeHit function restores the diffuse color. In both functions we are calling render which we will implement later.

19. Now let's write the code for processHits:

```
function processHits(hits){
    var ob;
    for(var i = 0; i< hits.length; i+=1){
        ob = hits[i];
        ob.diffuse = ob.previous;
    }
    render();
}
```

Remember that `processHits` is called upon exiting picking mode. This function will receive one parameter: the `hits` that the picker detected. Each element of the `hits` list is an object in the scene. In this case, we want to give back the hits their diffuse color. For that we use the `previous` property that we set in the `addHit` function.

20. The last picker callback that we need to implement is the `movePickedObjects` function:

```
function movePickedObjects(hits,interactor,dx,dy){
    if (hits == 0) return;
    var camera = interactor.camera;
    var depth = interactor.alt;
    var factor = Math.max(Math.max(
                                camera.position[0],
                                camera.position[1]),
                                camera.position[2])/1000;

    var scaleX, scaleY;
    for (var i = 0, max = hits.length; i < max; i+=1){
        scaleX = vec3.create();
        scaleY = vec3.create();
        if (depth){
            //moving along the camera normal vector
            vec3.scale(camera.normal, dy * factor, scaleY);
        }
        else{
            //moving along the plane defined by the up and right
            //camera vectors
            vec3.scale(camera.up, -dy * factor, scaleY);
            vec3.scale(camera.right, dx * factor, scaleX);
        }
        vec3.add(hits[i].position, scaleY);
        vec3.add(hits[i].position, scaleX);

    }
    render();
}
```

This function allows us to move the objects in the `hits` list interactively. The parameters that this callback function receives are:

- ❑ `hits`: The list of objects that have been picked
- ❑ `interactor`: The camera interactor object that is set up in the `configure` function

    ❑   dx: Displacement in the horizontal direction obtained from the mouse when it is dragged on the canvas

    ❑   dy: Displacement in the vertical direction obtained from the mouse when it is dragged on the canvas.

Let's analyze the code. First, if there are no hits the function returns immediately.

```
if (hits == 0) return;
```

Otherwise, we obtain a reference to the camera and we determine if the user is pressing the *Alt* key.

```
var camera = interactor.camera;
var depth =  interactor.alt;
```

We calculate a weighing factor that we will use later (fudge factor):

```
factor = Math.max(Math.max(
                        camera.position[0],
                        camera.position[1]),
                        camera.position[2])/1000;
```

Next we create a loop to go through the hits list so we can update each object position:

```
Var scaleX, scaleY;
for (var i = 0, max = hits.length; i < max; i+=1){
        scaleX = vec3.create();
        scaleY = vec3.create();
```

The `scaleX` and `scaleY` variables are initialized for every hit.

As we have seen in previous exercises, the *Alt* key is being used to perform dollying (move the camera along its normal). In this case we want to move the objects that are in the picking list along the camera normal direction when the user is pressing the *Alt* key to provide a consistent user experience.

To move the hits along the camera normal we use the `dy` (up-down) displacement as follows:

```
if (depth){
    vec3.scale(camera.normal, dy * factor, scaleY);
}
```

This creates a scaled version of `camera.normal` and stores it into the `scaleY` variable. Notice that `vec3.scale` is an operation available in the `glMatrix` library.

If the user is not pressing the *Alt* key then we use dx (left-right) and dy (up-down) to move the hits in the camera plane. Here we use the camera up and $right$ vectors like this to calculate the $scaleX$ and $scaleY$ parameters:

```
else {
    vec3.scale(camera.right, dx * factor, scaleX);
    vec3.scale(camera.up,   -dy * factor, scaleY);
}
```

Finally we update the position of the hit:

```
vec3.add(hits[i].position, scaleY);
vec3.add(hits[i].position, scaleX);
}
```

After calculating the new position for all hits we call render:

```
render();
}
```

21. **Testing the scene:** Save the page as `ch8_Picking_Scene_Final.html` and open it using your HTML5 web browser.

22. You will see a scene as shown in the following screenshot:

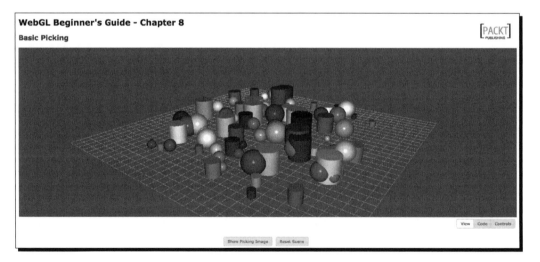

23. Click on **Reset Scene** several times and verify that you get a new scene every time.

24. In this scene, all the objects have very similar colors. However, each one has a unique picking color. To verify that click on the **Show Picking Image** button. You will see on screen what it is being rendered in the offscreen buffer:

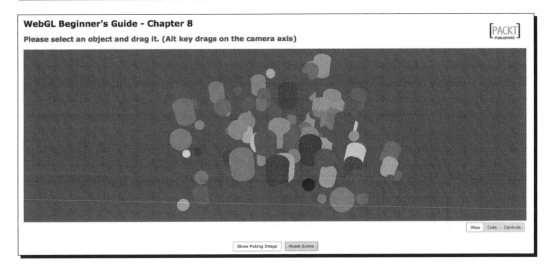

25. Now let's validate the changes that we made to the picker callbacks. Let's start by picking one object. As you see, the object diffuse color becomes its picking color (this was the change you implemented in the addHit function):

26. When the mouse is released, the object goes back to the original color! This is the change that was implemented in the processHits function.

27. While the mouse button is held down over an object, you can drag it around. While this is done, the movePickedObjects is being invoked.

28. If the *Shift* key is pressed while objects are being selected, you will be telling the picker not to exit **picking mode**. This way you can select and move more than one object at once:

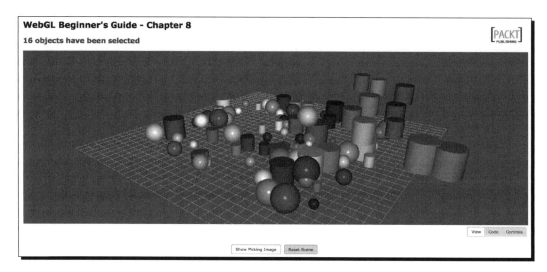

29. You will exit picking mode if you select an object and the *Shift* key is no longer pressed or if your next click does not produce any hits (in other words: clicking anywhere else).

If you have any problems with the exercise or you missed one of the steps, we have included the complete exercise in the files ch8_Picking_Scene_NoPicker.html and ch8_Picking_Scene_Final.html.

What just happened?

We have done the following:

♦ Created the property picking color. This property is unique for every object in the scene and allows us to implement picking based on it.

♦ Modified the fragment shader to use the picking color property by including a new uniform: uPickingColor and mapping this uniform to the pcolor object property.

♦ Learned about the different picking states. We have also learned how to modify the Picker callbacks to perform specific application logic such as removing picked objects from the scene.

Have a go hero – clearing the scene

Rewrite the `processHits` function to remove the balls in the hit list from the scene. If the user has removed all the balls from the scene then display a message telling the elapsed time accomplishing this task.

Hint 1: Use `Scene.removeObject(ob.alias)` in the `processHits` function if `alias` starts with `ball_`.

Hint 2: Once the hits are removed from the scene, go again through the `Scene.objects` list and make sure that there are no objects whose alias starts with `ball_`.

Hint 3: Use a JavaScript timer to measure and display the elapsed time until task completion.

Summary

In this chapter, we have learned how to implement color-based picking in WebGL. Picking based on a diffuse color is a bad idea because there could be scenarios where several objects have the same diffuse color. It is better to assign a new color property that is unique for every object to perform picking. We called this property picking color/object label.

Through the discussion of the picking implementation, we learned that WebGL provides mechanisms to create offscreen framebuffers and that what we see on screen when we render a scene corresponds to the default framebuffer contents.

We also studied the difference between a framebuffer and a renderbuffer. We saw that a renderbuffer is a special buffer that is attached to a framebuffer. Renderbuffers are used to store information that does not have a texture representation such as depth values. In contrast, textures can be used to store colors.

We saw too that a framebuffer needs at least one texture to store colors and a renderbuffer to store depth information.

We discussed how to convert from clicking coordinates in the page to canvas coordinates. We said also that the framebuffer coordinates and the canvas coordinates originate in the lower-left corner with a (0,0) origin.

The architecture of the picker implementation was discussed. We saw that picking can have different states and that each state can be associated to a callback function. Picker callbacks allow coding-specific logic application that will determine what we see in our scene when picking is in progress.

In the next chapter, we will develop a car showroom application. We will see how to import car models from Blender into a WebGL application.

9
Putting It All Together

In this chapter, we will apply the concepts and use the infrastructure code that we have previously developed to build a Virtual Car Showroom. During the development of this demo application, we will use models, lights, cameras, animation, colors, and textures. We will also see how we can integrate these elements with a simple yet powerful graphical user interface.

This chapter talks about:

- ◆ The architecture that we have developed throughout the book
- ◆ Creating a virtual car showroom application using our architecture
- ◆ Importing car models from Blender into a WebGL scene
- ◆ Setting up several light sources
- ◆ Creating robust shaders to handle multiple materials
- ◆ The OBJ and MTL file formats
- ◆ Programming the camera to fly through the scene

Creating a WebGL application

At this point, we have covered the basic topics that you need to be familiar with in order to create a WebGL application. These topics have been implemented in the infrastructure code that we have iteratively built up throughout the book. Let's see what we have learned so far.

In *Chapter 3*, *Lights!*, we introduced WebGL and learned how to enable it in our browser. We also learned that WebGL behaves as a state machine and that we can query the different variables that determine the current state using `gl.getParameter`.

After that, we studied in *Chapter 2, Rendering Geometry*, that the objects of a WebGL scene are defined by vertices. We said that usually we use indices to label those vertices so we can quickly tell WebGL how to 'connect the dots' to render the object. We studied the functions that manipulate buffers and the two main functions to render geometry `drawArrays` (no indices) and `drawElements` (with indices). We also learned about the JSON format to represent geometry and how we can download models from a web server using AJAX.

In *Chapter 3, Lights!*, we studied about lights. We learned about normal vectors and the physics of light reflection. We saw how to implement different lighting models using shaders in ESSL.

We learned in *Chapter 4, Camera*, that WebGL does not have cameras and that we need to define our own cameras. We studied the Camera matrix and we showed that the Camera matrix is the inverse of the Model-View matrix. In other words, rotation, translation, and scaling in the world space produce the inverse operations in camera space.

The basics of animation were covered in *Chapter 5, Action*. We discussed the matrix stack with its push and pop operations to represent local object transformations. We also analyzed how to set up an animation cycle that is independent from the rendering cycle. We also studied different types of interpolation and saw examples of how interpolation is used to create animations.

In *Chapter 6, Colors, Depth Testing, and Alpha Blending*, we discussed a bit deeper about color representation and how we can use colors in objects, in lights, and in the scene. We also studied blending and the use of transparencies.

Chapter 7, Textures, covered textures and we saw an implementation for picking in *Chapter 8, Picking*.

In this chapter, we will use our knowledge to create a simple application. Fortunately, we are going to use all the infrastructure code that we have developed so far. Let's review it.

Architectural review

The following diagram presents the architecture that has been built throughout the book:

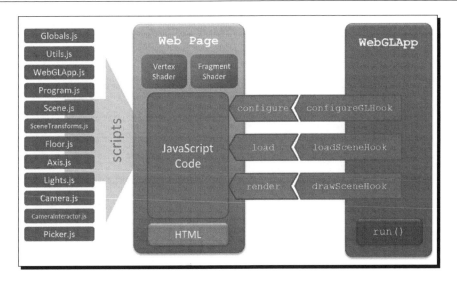

`Globals.js`: Defines the global variables `gl` (WebGL context), `prg` (ESSL program), and the canvas width (`c_width`) and height (`c_height`).

`Utils.js`: Contains auxiliary functions such as `getGLContext` which tries to create a WebGL context for a given HTML5 canvas.

`WebGLApp.js`: It provides three function hooks, namely: `configureGLHook`, `loadSceneHook`, and `drawSceneHook` that define the life cycle of a WebGL application.

As the previous diagram shows these hooks are mapped to JavaScript functions in our web page:

- `configure`: Here we create cameras, lights, and instantiate the `Program.object`.
- `load`: Here we request objects from the web server by calling `Scene.loadObject`. We can also add locally generated geometry (such as the `Floor`) by calling `Scene.addObject`.
- `render` (or `draw`): This is the function that is called every time when the rendering timer goes off. Here we will retrieve the objects from the Scene, one by one, and we will render them paying attention to their location (applying local transforms using the matrix stack), and their properties (passing the respective uniforms to the Program).

`Program.js`: Is composed of the functions that handle programs, shaders, and the mapping between JavaScript variables and ESSL uniforms.

`Scene.js`: Contains a list of objects to be rendered by WebGL.

`SceneTransform.js`: Contains the matrices discussed in the book: The Model-View matrix, the Camera matrix, the Perspective matrix, and the Normal matrix. It implements the matrix stack with the operations push and pop.

`Floor.js`: Auxiliary object that when rendered appears like a rectangular mesh providing the floor reference for the scene.

`Axis.js`: Auxiliary object that represents the center of the scene.

`Lights.js`: Simplifies the creation and managing of lights in the scene.

`Camera.js`: Contains a camera representation. We have developed two types of camera: orbiting and tracking.

`CameraInteractor.js`: Listens for mouse and keyboard events on the HTML5 canvas that it is being used. It interprets these events and then transforms them into camera actions.

`Picker.js`: Provides color-based object picking.

Let's see how we can put everything together to create a Virtual Car Showroom.

Virtual Car Showroom application

Using our WebGL skills and the infrastructure code that we have developed, we will create an application that allows visualizing different 3D car models. The final result will look like this:

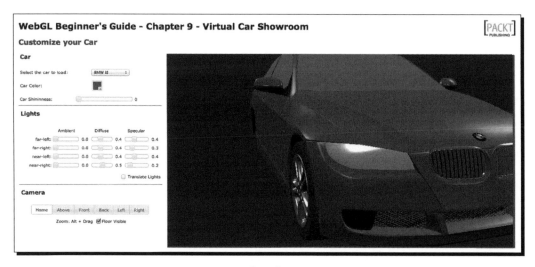

First of all, we need to define what the graphical user interface (GUI) is going to look like. Then, we will be adding WebGL support by creating a canvas element and obtaining the correspondent WebGL context. Simultaneously, we need to define and implement the Vertex Shader and Fragment Shader using ESSL. After that, we need to implement the three functions that constitute the lifecycle of our application: `configure`, `load`, and `render`.

First, let's consider some particularities of our virtual showroom application.

Complexity of the models

A real-world application is different from a proof of concept demo in that the models that we will be loading are much more detailed than simple spheres, cones, and other geometric figures. Usually, models have lots of vertices conforming very complicated configurations that give the level of detail and realism that people would expect. Also, in many cases, these models are accompanied by one or more textures. Creating the geometry and the texture mapping *by hand* in JSON files is nothing less than a daunting task.

Hopefully, we can use 3D design software to create our own models and then import them into a WebGL scene. For the Virtual Car Showroom we will use models created with Blender.

Blender is an open-source 3D computer graphics software that allows you to create animations, games, and other interactive applications. Blender provides numerous features to create complex models. In this chapter, we will import car models created with Blender into a WebGL scene. To do so, we will export them to an intermediary file format called OBJ and then we will parse OBJ files into JSON files.

Shader quality

Because we will be using complex models, such as cars, we will see that there is a need to develop shaders that can render the different materials that our models are made of. This is not a big deal for us since the shaders that we previously developed can handle diffuse, specular, and ambient components for materials. In Blender, we will select the option to export materials when generating the OBJ files. When we do so, Blender will generate a second file known as the **Material Template Library** (**MTL**). Also, our shaders will use Phong shading, Phong lighting, and will support multiple lights.

Network delays and bandwidth consumption

Due to the nature of WebGL, we will need to download the geometry and the textures from a web server. Depending on the quality of the network connection and the amount of data that needs to be transferred this can take a while. There are several strategies that you could investigate, such as geometry compression. Another alternative is background data downloading (using AJAX for example) while the application is idle or the user is busy and not waiting for something to download.

With these considerations in mind let's get started.

Defining what the GUI will look like

We will define a very simple layout for our application. The title will go on top, and then we have two `div` tags. The `div` on the left will contain the instructions and the tools we can use on the scene. The canvas will be placed inside the `div` on the right, shown as follows:

The code to achieve this layout looks like this (`css/cars.css`):

```
#header
{
    height: 50px;
    background-color: #ccc;
    margin-bottom: 10px;
}

#nav
{
    float: left;
    width: 28%;
    height: 80%;
    background-color: #ccc;
    margin-bottom: 1px;
}

#content
{
    float: right;
```

```
        margin-left: 1%;
        width: 70%;
        height: 80%;
        background-color: #ccc;
        margin-bottom: 1px;
    }
```

And we can use it like this (taken from `ch9_GUI.html`):

```
<body>
<div id="header">
<h1>Show Room</h1>
</div>

<div id="nav">
<b>Instructions</b>
</div>

<div id="content">
<h2>canvas goes here</h2>
</div>
</body>
```

Please make sure that you include `cars.css` in your page. As you can see in `ch9_GUI.html`, `cars.css` has been included in the header section:

```
<link href='css/cars.css' type='text/css' rel='stylesheet' />
```

Now let's add the canvas. Replace:

```
<h2>canvas goes here</h2>
```

With:

```
<canvas id='the-canvas'></canvas>
```

inside the `content` div.

Adding WebGL support

Now, please check the source code for `ch9_Scaffolding.html`. We have taken `ch9_GUI.html` which defines the basic layout and we have added the following:

◆ References to the elements defined in our architecture: `Globals.js`, `Utils.js`, `Program.js`, and so on.

◆ A reference to `glMatrix.js`, the matrix manipulation library that we use in our architecture.

- ◆ References to JQuery and JQuery UI.

- ◆ References to the JQuery UI customized theme that we used in the book.

- ◆ We have created the scaffolding for the three main functions that we will need to develop in our application: configure, load and render.

- ◆ Using JQuery we have included a function that allows resizing the canvas to its container:

```
function resizeCanvas(){
    c_width = $('#content').width();
    c_height = $('#content').height();
    $('#the-canvas').attr('width',c_width);
    $('#the-canvas').attr('height',c_height);
}
```

We bind this function to the `resize` event of the `window` here:

```
$(window).resize(function(){resizeCanvas();});
```

This function is very useful because it allows us adapt the size of the canvas automatically to the available window space. Also, we do not need to hardcode the size of the canvas.

- ◆ As in all previous exercises, we need to define the entry point for the application. We do this here:

```
var app;
function runShowRoom(){
    app = new WebGLApp("the-canvas");
    app.configureGLHook = configure;
    app.loadSceneHook   = load;
    app.drawSceneHook    = render;
    app.run();
}
```

And we bind it to the `onLoad` event:

```
<body onLoad='runShowRoom()'>
```

Now if you run `ch9_Scaffolding.html` in your HTML5-enabled web browser, you will see that the canvas resizes according to the current size of content, its parent container, shown as follows:

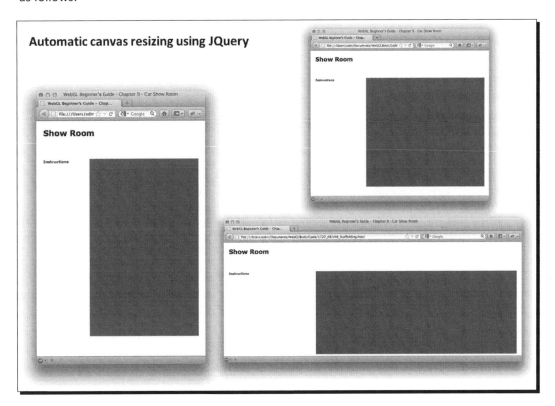

Implementing the shaders

The shaders in this chapter will implement **Phong shading** and the **Phong reflection** model. Remember that Phong shading interpolates vertex normals and creates a normal for every fragment. After that, the Phong reflection model describes the light that an object reflects as the addition of the ambient, diffuse, and specular interaction of the object with the light sources present in the scene.

To keep consistency with the Material Template Library (MTL) format, we will use the following convention for the uniforms that refer to material properties:

Material Uniform	Description
uKa	Ambient property
uKd	Diffuse property
uKs	Specular property
uNi	Optical density. We will not use this feature but you will see it on the MTL file.
uNs	Specular exponent. A high exponent results in a tight, concentrated highlight. Ns values normally range from 0 to 1000.
d	Transparency (alpha channel)
illum	Determines the illumination model for the object being rendered. Unlike previous chapters where we had one model for all the objects, here we let the object to decide how it is going to reflect the light.
	According to the MTL file format specification illum can be:
	0: Diffuse on and Ambient off (purely diffuse)
	1: Diffuse on and Ambient on
	2: Highlight on (Phong illumination model)
	There are other values that are defined in the MTL specification that we mention here for completeness but that our shaders will not implement. These values are:
	3: Reflection on and Ray trace on
	4: Transparency: Glass on, Reflection: Ray trace on
	5: Reflection: Fresnel on and Ray trace on
	6: Transparency: Refraction on, Reflection: Fresnel off and Ray trace on
	7: Transparency: Refraction on, Reflection: Fresnel on and Ray trace on
	8: Reflection on and Ray trace off
	9: Transparency: Glass on, Reflection: Ray trace off
	10: Casts shadows onto invisible surfaces

The shaders that we will use support multiple lights using uniform arrays as we saw in *Chapter 6, Colors, Depth Testing, and Alpha Blending*. The number of lights is defined by a constant in both the Vertex and the Fragment shaders:

```
const int NUM_LIGHTS = 4;
```

We will use the following uniform arrays to work with lights:

Light Uniform Array	Description
uLa[NUM_LIGHTS]	Ambient property
uLd[NUM_LIGHTS]	Diffuse property
uLs[NUM_LIGHTS]	Specular property

 Please refer to ch9_Car_Showroom.html to explore the source code for the shaders in this chapter.

Next, we are going to work on the three main functions that constitute the lifecycle of our WebGL application. These are the configure, load, and render functions.

Setting up the scene

We set up the scene by writing the code for the configure function. Let's analyze it line by line:

```
var camera = null, transforms = null;
function configure(){
```

At this stage, we want to set some of the WebGL properties such as the clear color and the depth test. After that, we need to create a camera and set its original position and orientation. Also we need to create a camera interactor so that we can update the camera position when we click and drag on the HTML5 canvas in our web page. Finally, we want to define the JavaScript variables that will be mapped to the shaders. We can also initialize some of them at this point.

To accomplish the aforementioned tasks we will use Camera.js, CameraInteractor.js, and Program.js and SceneTransforms.js from our architecture.

Configuring some WebGL properties

Here we set the background color and the depth test properties as follows:

```
gl.clearColor(0.3,0.3,0.3, 1.0);
gl.clearDepth(1.0);
gl.enable(gl.DEPTH_TEST);
gl.depthFunc(gl.LEQUAL);
```

Setting up the camera

The `camera` variable needs to be global so we can access it later on from the GUI functions that we will write. For instance, we want to be able to click on a button (different function in the code) and use the `camera` variable to update the `camera` position:

```
camera = new Camera(CAMERA_ORBITING_TYPE);
camera.goHome([0,0,7]);
camera.setFocus([0.0,0.0,0.0]);
camera.setAzimuth(25);
camera.setElevation(-30);
```

The azimuth and elevation of the camera are relative to the negative z-axis, which will be the default pose if you do not specify any other. An azimuth of 25 degrees and elevation of -30 degrees will give you a nice initial angle to see the cars. However, you can set any combination that you prefer as the default pose in here.

Here we make sure that the camera's rendering callback is our rendering function:

```
camera.hookRenderer = render;
```

Creating the Camera Interactor

We create a `CameraInteractor` that will bind the mouse gestures to camera actions. The first argument here is the camera we are controlling and the second element is a DOM reference to the canvas in our webpage:

```
var interactor = new CameraInteractor(camera, document.
getElementById('the-canvas');
```

The SceneTransforms object

Once we have instantiated the camera, we create a new `SceneTransforms` object passing the camera to the `SceneTransforms` constructor as follows:

```
transforms = new SceneTransforms(camera);
transforms.init();
```

The `transforms` variable is also declared globally so we can use it later in the rendering function to retrieve the current matrix transformations and pass them to the shaders.

Creating the lights

We will create four lights using the `Light` object from our infrastructure code. The scene will look like in the following image:

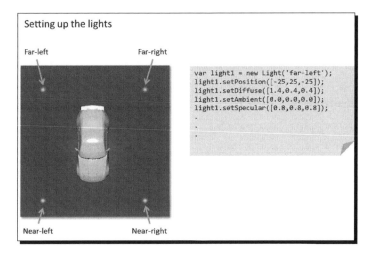

For each light we will create a `Light` object:

```
var light1 = new Light('far-left');
light1.setPosition([-25,25,-25]);
light1.setDiffuse([1.4,0.4,0.4]);
light1.setAmbient([0.0,0.0,0.0]);
light1.setSpecular([0.8,0.8,0.8]);

var light2 = new Light('far-right');
light2.setPosition([25,25,-25]);
light2.setDiffuse([0.4,1.4,0.4]);
light2.setAmbient([0.0,0.0,0.0]);
light2.setSpecular([0.8,0.8,0.8]);

var light3 = new Light('near-left');
light3.setPosition([-25,25,25]);
light3.setDiffuse([0.5,0.5,1.5]);
light3.setAmbient([0.0,0.0,0.0]);
light3.setSpecular([0.8,0.38,0.38]);

var light4 = new Light('near-right');
light4.setPosition([25,25,25]);
light4.setDiffuse([0.2,0.2,0.2]);
light4.setAmbient([0.0,0.0,0.0]);
light4.setSpecular([0.38,0.38,0.38]);
```

Then, we add them to the `Lights` list (also defined in `Lights.js`):

```
Lights.add(light1);
Lights.add(light2);
Lights.add(light3);
Lights.add(light4);
```

Mapping the Program attributes and uniforms

The last thing to do inside `configure` function is to map the JavaScript variables that we will use in our code to the attributes and uniforms that we will use in the shaders.

Using the `Program` object from our infrastructure code, we will set up the JavaScript variables that we will use to map attributes and uniforms to the shaders. The code looks like this:

```
var attributeList = ["aVertexPosition",
                     "aVertexNormal",
                     "aVertexColor"];

var uniformList = [ "uPMatrix",
                    "uMVMatrix",
                    "uNMatrix",
                    "uLightPosition",
                    "uWireframe",
                    "uLa",
                    "uLd",
                    "uLs",
                    "uKa",
                    "uKd",
                    "uKs",
                    "uNs",
                    "d",
                    "illum"];

Program.load(attributeList, uniformList);
```

 When creating your own shaders, make sure that the shader attributes and uniforms are properly mapped to JavaScript variables. Remember that this mapping step allows us referring to attributes and uniforms through their location. In this way, we can pass attribute and uniform values to the shaders. Please check the methods `setAttributeLocations` and `setUniformLocations`, which are called by `load` in the `Program` object (`Program.js`) to see how we do the mapping in the infrastructure code.

Uniform initialization

After the mapping, we can initialize shader uniforms such as lights:

```
gl.uniform3fv(Program.uLightPosition, Lights.getArray('position'));
gl.uniform3fv(Program.uLa, Lights.getArray('ambient'));
gl.uniform3fv(Program.uLd, Lights.getArray('diffuse'));
gl.uniform3fv(Program.uLs, Lights.getArray('specular'));
```

The default material properties are as follows:

```
gl.uniform3fv(Program.uKa , [1.0,1.0,1.0]);
gl.uniform3fv(Program.uKd , [1.0,1.0,1.0]);
gl.uniform3fv(Program.uKs , [1.0,1.0,1.0]);
gl.uniform1f(Program.uNs , 1.0);
}
```

With that, we have finished setting up the scene.

Loading the cars

Next, we need to implement the `load` function. Here is where we usually use AJAX to download the objects that will appear on the scene.

When we have the JSON files corresponding to the cars the procedure is really simple, we just use the `Scene` object to load these files. However, most commonly than not, you will not have ready-to-use JSON files. As mentioned at the beginning of this chapter, there are specialized design tools such as Blender that allow creating these models.

Nonetheless, we are assuming that you are not an expert 3D modeler (neither we are). So we will use pre-built models. We will use cars from `blendswap.org`, these models are publically available, free of charge, and free to distribute.

Before we can use the models, we need to export them to an intermediate file format from where we can extract the geometry and the material properties so we can create our corresponding JSON files. The file format that we are going to use is **Wavefront OBJ**.

Exporting the Blender models

Here we are using the current Blender version (2.6). Once you have loaded the car that you want to render in WebGL you need to export it as an OBJ file. To do so go to **File | Export | Wavefront (.obj)** as shown in the following screenshot:

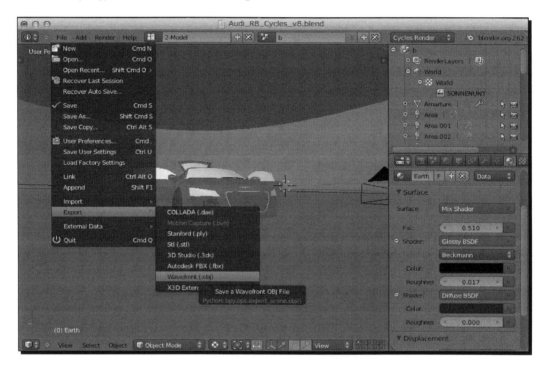

In the **Export OBJ** panel, make sure that the following options are active:

- ◆ **Apply Modifiers**: This will write the vertices in the scene that are the result of a mathematical operation instead of direct modeling. For instance, reflections, smoothing, and so on. If you do not check this option, the model may appear incomplete in the WebGL scene.

- ◆ **Write Materials**: Blender will create the correspondent Material Template Library (MTL file). More about this in the following section.

- ◆ **Triangulate Faces**: Blender will write the indices as triangles. Ideal for WebGL rendering.

- ◆ **Objects as OBJ Objects**: This configuration will identify every object in the Blender scene as an object in the OBJ file.

◆ **Material Groups**: If an object in the Blender scene has several materials, for instance a car tire can have aluminum and rubber, then the object will be subdivided into groups, one per material in the OBJ file. Once you have checked these export parameters, select the directory and the name for your OBJ file and then click on **Export**.

Understanding the OBJ format

There are several types of definitions in an OBJ file. Let's see them with a line-by-line example. We are going to dissect the file `square.obj` that we have exported from the Blender file `square.blend`. This file represents a square divided into two parts, one painted in red and the other painted in blue, as shown in the following image:

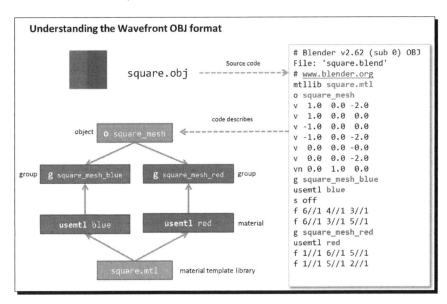

When we export Blender models to the OBJ format, the resulting file would normally start with a comment:

```
# Blender v2.62 (sub 0) OBJ File: 'squares.blend'
# www.blender.org
```

As we can see here, comments are denoted with a hash (#) symbol at the beginning of the line.

Next, we will usually find a line referring to the Material Template Library that this OBJ file is using. Such line will start with the keyword `mtllib` followed by the name of the materials library file:

```
mtllib square.mtl
```

There are several ways in which geometries can be grouped into entities in an OBJ file. We can find lines starting with the prefix `o` followed by the object name; or by the prefix `g`, followed again by the group name:

```
o squares_mesh
```

After an object declaration, the following lines will refer to vertices (`v`) and optionally to vertex normals (`vn`) and texture coordinates (`vt`). It is important to mention that vertices are shared by all the groups in an object in the OBJ format. That is, you will not find lines referring to vertices when defining a group because it is assumed that all vertex data was defined first when the object was defined:

```
v    1.0     0.0     -2.0
v    1.0     0.0      0.0
v  -1.0      0.0      0.0
v  -1.0      0.0     -2.0
v    0.0     0.0      0.0
v    0.0     0.0     -2.0
vn 0.0      1.0       0.0
```

In our case, we have instructed Blender to export group materials. This means that each part of the object that has different set of material properties will appear in the OBJ file as a group. In this example, we are defining an object with two groups (`squares_mesh_blue` and `squares_mesh_red`) and two corresponding materials (blue and red):

```
g squares_mesh_blue
```

If materials are being used, the line after the group declaration will be the material that is being used for that group. Here only the name of the material is required. It is assumed that the material properties for this material are defined in the Material Template Library file that was declared at the beginning of the OBJ file:

```
usemtl blue
```

The lines that start with the prefix `s` refer to smooth shading across polygons. We mention it here in case you see it on your files but we will not be using this definition when parsing the OBJ files into JSON files:

```
s off
```

The lines that start with `f` refer to faces. There are different ways to represent faces. Let's see them:

- **Vertex**:

  ```
  f i1 i2 i3...
  ```

  In this configuration, every face element corresponds to a vertex index. Depending on the number of indices per face, you could have triangular, rectangular, or polygonal faces. However, we have instructed Blender to use triangular faces to create the OBJ file. Otherwise, we would need to decompose the polygons into triangles before we could call `drawElements`.

- **Vertex / Texture Coordinate**:

  ```
  f i1/t1 i2/t2 i3/t3...
  ```

  In this combination, every vertex index appears followed by a slash sign and a texture coordinate index. You will normally find this combination when texture coordinates are defined at the object level with `vt`.

- **Vertex / Texture Coordinate / Normal**:

  ```
  f i1/t1/n1 i2/t2/n2 i3/t3/n3...
  ```

  Here a normal index has been added as the third element of the configuration. If both texture coordinates and vertex normals are defined at the object level, you most likely see this configuration at the group level.

- **Vertex // Normal**:

  There could also be a case where normals are defined but not texture coordinates. In this case, the second part of the face configuration is missing:

  ```
  f i1//n1 i2//n2 i3//n3...
  ```

  This is the case for `square.obj`, which looks like this:

  ```
  f 6//1 4//1 3//1
  f 6//1 3//1 5//1
  ```

 Please notice that faces are defined using indices. In our example, we have defined a square divided in two parts. Here we can see that all vertices share the same normal identified with index 1.

The remaining lines in this file represent the red group:

```
g squares_mesh_red
usemtl red
f 1//1 6//1 5//1
f 1//1 5//1 2//1
```

As mentioned before, groups belonging to the same object share indices.

Parsing the OBJ files

After exporting our cars to the OBJ format, the next step is parse the OBJ files to create WebGL JSON files that we can load into our scene. We have included the parser that we developed for this step into the code files accompanying this chapter. This parser has the following features:

◆ It is written in python and can be called on the command line like this:

```
obj_parser.py arg1 arg2
```

Where `arg1` is the name of the `obj` file to parse and `arg2` is the name of the Material Template Library. The file extension is needed in both cases. For example:

```
obj_parser.py square.obj square.mtl
```

◆ It creates one JSON file per OBJ group.

◆ It searches into the Material Template Library (if defined) for the material properties for each group and adds them to the correspondent JSON file.

◆ It will calculate the appropriate indices for each group. Remember that OBJ groups share indices. Since we are creating one independent WebGL object per group, each object needs to have indices starting in zero. The parser takes care of this for you.

 If you do not have python installed in your system you can get it from: `http://www.python.org/`

The following diagram summarizes the procedure to create JSON files from Blender scenes:

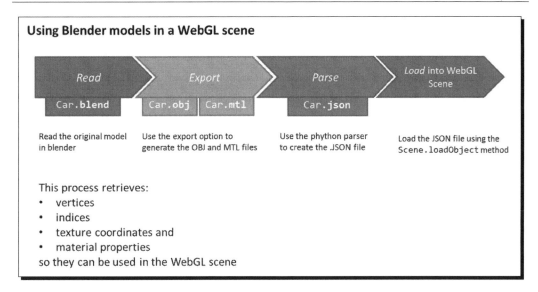

Load cars into our WebGL scene

Now we have cars stored as JSON files, ready to be used in our WebGL scene. Now we have to let the user tell us which car he wants to visualize. We could, however, load by default one of the cars so our GUI looks more attractive. To do so, we will write the following code inside the load function (finally!):

```
function load(){

    loadBMW();
}

// The bmw model has 24 parts. We retrieve them all in a loop
function loadBMW(){
for(var i = 1; i <= 24; i+=1){
        Scene.loadObject('models/cars/bmw/part'+i+'.json');
    }
}
```

We will add other cases later on.

Rendering

Let's take a step back to take a look at the big picture. We mentioned before that in our architecture we have defined three main functions that define the lifecycle of our WebGL application. These functions are: `configure`, `load`, and `render`.

Up to this point, we have set up the scene writing the code for the `configure` function. After that, we have created our JSON cars and loaded them by writing the code for the `load` function. Now, we will implement the code for the third function: the `render` function.

The code is pretty standard and almost identical to the `draw/render` functions that we have written in previous chapters. As we can see in the following diagram, we set and clear the area that we are going to draw on, then we check on the camera perspective and then we process every object in `Scene.objects`.

The only consideration that we need to have here is to make sure that we are mapping correctly the material properties defined in our JSON objects to the appropriate shader uniforms. The code that takes care of this in the `render` function looks like this:

```
gl.uniform3fv(Program.uKa, object.Ka);
gl.uniform3fv(Program.uKd, object.Kd);
gl.uniform3fv(Program.uKs, object.Ks);
gl.uniform1f(Program.uNi, object.Ni);
gl.uniform1f(Program.uNs, object.Ns);
gl.uniform1f(Program.d, object.d);
gl.uniform1i(Program.illum, object.illum);
```

If you want, please take a look at the list of uniforms that was defined in the section *Implementing the shaders*. We need to make sure that all the shader uniforms are paired with object attributes.

The following diagram shows the process inside the `render` function:

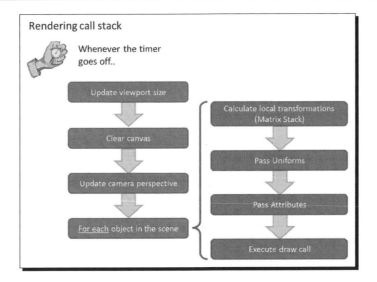

Each car part is a different JSON file. The `render` function goes through all the parts stored as JSON objects inside the `Scene` object. For each part, the material properties are passed as uniforms to the shaders and the geometry is passed as attributes (reading data from the respective VBOs). Finally, the draw call (`drawElements`) is executed. The result looks something like this:

The file `ch9_Car_Showroom.html` contains all the code described up to now.

Time for action – customizing the application

1. Open the file `ch9_Car_Showroom.html` using your favorite code editor.

2. We will assign a different home for the camera when we load the Ford Mustang. To do so, please check the `cameraHome`, `cameraAzimuth`, and `cameraElevation` global variables. We set up the camera home position by using this variable inside the `configure` function like this:

```
camera.goHome(cameraHome);
camera.setAzimuth(cameraAzimuth);
camera.setElevation(cameraElevation);
```

Let's use this code to configure the default pose for the camera when we load the Ford Mustang. Go to the `loadMustang` function and append these lines:

```
cameraHome = [0,0,10];
cameraAzimuth = -25;
cameraElevation = -15;
camera.goHome(cameraHome);
camera.setAzimuth(cameraAzimuth);
camera.setElevation(cameraElevation);
```

3. Now save your work and load the page in your web browser. Check that the camera appears in the indicated position when you load the Ford Mustang.

4. We can also set up the lighting scheme on a car-per-car basis. For instance, while low-diffusive, high-specular lights work well for the BMW I8, these configurations are not as good for the Audi R8. Let's take for example `light1` in the `configure` function. First we set the light attributes like this:

```
light1.setPosition([-25,25,-25]);
light1.setDiffuse([0.4,0.4,0.4]);
light1.setAmbient([0.0,0.0,0.0]);
light1.setSpecular([0.8,0.8,0.8]);
```

Then, we add `light1` to the `Lights` object:

```
Lights.add(light1);
```

Finally, we map the light arrays contained in the `Lights` object to the respective uniform arrays in our shaders:

```
gl.uniform3fv(Program.uLightPosition, Lights.
getArray('position'));
gl.uniform3fv(Program.uLa ,    Lights.getArray('ambient'));
gl.uniform3fv(Program.uLd,     Lights.getArray('diffuse'));
gl.uniform3fv(Program.uLs,     Lights.getArray('specular'));
```

Notice though that we need to add light1 to Lights only once. Now check the code for the one in the updateLightProperty function at the bottom of the page:

```
function updateLightProperty(index,property){
    var v = $('#slider-l'+property+''+index).slider('value');
    $('#slider-l'+property+''+index+'-value').html(v);
    var light;
    switch(index){
                case 1: light = light1; break;
                case 2: light = light2; break;
                case 3: light = light3; break;
                case 4: light = light4; break;
    }

    switch(property){
        case 'a':light.setAmbient([v,v,v]);
        gl.uniform3fv(Program.uLa, Lights.getArray('ambient'));
        break;
        case 'd':light.setDiffuse([v,v,v]);
        gl.uniform3fv(Program.uLd, Lights.getArray('diffuse'));
        break;
        case 's':light.setSpecular([v,v,v]);
        gl.uniform3fv(Program.uLs, Lights.getArray('specular'));
        break;
    }

    render();
}
```

Here we are detecting what slider changed and we are updating the correspondent light. Notice that we refer to light1, light2, light3, or light4 directly as these are global variables. We update the light that corresponds to the slider that changed and then we map the Lights object arrays to the correspondent uniform arrays. Notice that here we are not adding light1 or any other light again to the Lights object. The reason we do not need to do this is that the Lights object keeps a reference to light1 and the other lights. This saves us from having to clear the Lights object and mapping all the lights again every time we want to update one of them.

Using the same mechanism described in `updateLightProperty`, update the `loadAudi` function to set the diffuse terms of all four lights to `[0.7,0.7,0.7]` and the specular terms to `[0.4,0.4,0.4]`.

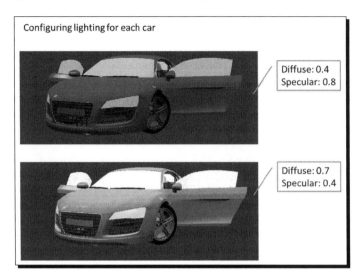

Configuring lighting for each car

Diffuse: 0.4
Specular: 0.8

Diffuse: 0.7
Specular: 0.4

5. Save your work and reload the page on your web browser. Try different lighting schemes for different cars.

What just happened?

We have built a demo that uses many of the elements that we have discussed in the book. For that purpose, we have used the infrastructure code writing three main functions: `configure`, `load`, and `render`. These functions define the lifecycle of our application.

On each of these functions, we have used the objects defined by the architecture of the examples in the book. For example, we have used a camera object, several light objects, the program, and the scene object among others.

Have a go Hero – flying through the scene

We want to animate the camera to produce a fly-through effect. You will need to consider three variables to be interpolated: the camera position, elevation, and azimuth. Start by defining the key frames, these are the intermediate poses that you want the camera to have. One could start for instance by looking at the car in the front view and then flying by one of the sides. You could also try a fly-through starting from a 45 degree angle in the back view. In both cases, you want to make sure that the camera *follows* the car. To achieve that effect, you need to make sure to update the azimuth and elevation on each key frame so the car keeps in focus.

Hint: Take a look at the code for the `animCamera` function and the functions that we have defined for the `click` events on the **Camera** buttons:

Summary

In this chapter, we have reviewed the concepts and the code developed throughout the book. We have also built a simple application that shows how all the elements fit together.

We have learned that designing complex models requires specialized tools such as Blender. We also saw that most of the current 3D graphics formats require the definition of vertices, indices, normals, and texture coordinates. We studied how to obtain these elements from a Blender model and parse them into JSON files that we can load into a WebGL scene.

In the next and final chapter, we will give you a sneak peak of some of the advanced techniques that are used regularly in 3D computer graphic systems including games, simulations, and other 3D applications in general. We will see how to implement these techniques in WebGL.

10
Advanced Techniques

At this point, you have all the information you need to create rich 3D applications with WebGL. However, we've only just scratched the surface of what's possible with the API! Creative use of shaders, textures, and vertex attributes can yield fantastic results. The possibilities are, literally, limitless! In this final chapter, we'll provide a few glimpses into some advanced WebGL techniques, and hopefully leave you eager to explore more on your own.

In this chapter, we'll learn the following topics:

- Post-process effects
- Point sprites
- Normal mapping
- Ray tracing in fragment shaders

Post-processing

Post-processing effects are the effects that are created by re-rendering the image of the scene with a shader that alters the final image somehow. Think of it as if you took a screenshot of your scene, opened it up in your favorite image editor, and applied some filters. The difference is that we can do it in real time!

Examples of some simple post-processing effects are:

◆ Grayscale

◆ Sepia tone

◆ Inverted color

◆ Film grain

◆ Blur

◆ Wavy/dizzy effect

The basic technique for creating these effects is relatively simple: A framebuffer is created that is of the same dimensions as the canvas. At the beginning of the draw cycle, the framebuffer is set as the render target, and the entire scene is rendered normally to it. Next, a full-screen quad is rendered to the default framebuffer using the texture that makes up the framebuffer's color attachment. The shader used during the rendering of the quad is what contains the post-process effect. It can transform the color values of the rendered scene as they get written to the quad to produce the desired visuals.

Let's look at the individual steps of this process more closely.

Creating the framebuffer

The code that we use to create the framebuffer is largely same as the code used in *Chapter 8*, *Picking*, for the picking system. However, there is a key difference worth noting:

```
var width = canvas.width;
var height = canvas.height;

//1. Init Color Texture
var texture = gl.createTexture();
gl.bindTexture(gl.TEXTURE_2D, texture);
gl.texParameteri(gl.TEXTURE_2D, gl.TEXTURE_MAG_FILTER, gl.NEAREST);
gl.texParameteri(gl.TEXTURE_2D, gl.TEXTURE_MIN_FILTER, gl.NEAREST);
gl.texParameteri(gl.TEXTURE_2D, gl.TEXTURE_WRAP_S, gl.CLAMP_TO_EDGE);
gl.texParameteri(gl.TEXTURE_2D, gl.TEXTURE_WRAP_T, gl.CLAMP_TO_EDGE);
gl.texImage2D(gl.TEXTURE_2D, 0, gl.RGBA, width, height, 0, gl.RGBA,
gl.UNSIGNED_BYTE, null);

//2. Init Render Buffer
var renderbuffer = gl.createRenderbuffer();
gl.bindRenderbuffer(gl.RENDERBUFFER, renderbuffer);
gl.renderbufferStorage(gl.RENDERBUFFER, gl.DEPTH_COMPONENT16, width,
height);
```

```
//3. Init Frame Buffer
var framebuffer = gl.createFramebuffer();
gl.bindFramebuffer(gl.FRAMEBUFFER, framebuffer);
gl.framebufferTexture2D(gl.FRAMEBUFFER, gl.COLOR_ATTACHMENT0,
gl.TEXTURE_2D, texture, 0);
gl.framebufferRenderbuffer(gl.FRAMEBUFFER, gl.DEPTH_ATTACHMENT,
gl.RENDERBUFFER, renderbuffer);
```

The change is that we are now using the canvas width and height to determine our buffer size instead of the arbitrary values that we used for the picker. This is because the content of the picker buffer was not meant to be rendered to the screen, and as such didn't need to worry too much about resolution. For the post-process buffer, however, we'll get the best results if the output matches the dimensions of the canvas exactly.

The canvas size won't always be a power of two, and as such we can't use the mipmapped texture filtering modes on it. However, in this case that won't matter. Since the texture will be exactly the same size as the canvas, and we'll be rendering it as a full-screen quad we have one of the rare situations where most of the time the texture will be displayed at exactly a 1:1 ratio on the screen, which means no filters need to be applied. This means that we could use the NEAREST filtering with no visual artifacts, though in the case of post-process effects that warp the texture coordinates (such as the wavy effect described later) we will still benefit from using LINEAR filtering. We also need to use a wrap mode of CLAMP_TO_EDGE, but again this won't pose many issues for our intended use.

Otherwise, the code is identical to the picker framebuffer creation.

Creating the geometry

While we could load the quad from a file, in this case the geometry is simple enough that we can put it directly into our code. All that's needed in this case is the vertex positions and texture coordinates:

```
//1. Define the geometry for the fullscreen quad
var vertices = [
    -1.0,-1.0,
     1.0,-1.0,
    -1.0, 1.0,

    -1.0, 1.0,
     1.0,-1.0,
     1.0, 1.0
];

var textureCoords = [
    0.0, 0.0,
```

```
        1.0, 0.0,
        0.0, 1.0,

        0.0, 1.0,
        1.0, 0.0,
        1.0, 1.0
];

//2. Init the buffers
this.vertexBuffer = gl.createBuffer();
gl.bindBuffer(gl.ARRAY_BUFFER, this.vertexBuffer);
gl.bufferData(gl.ARRAY_BUFFER, new Float32Array(vertices), gl.STATIC_
DRAW);

this.textureBuffer = gl.createBuffer();
gl.bindBuffer(gl.ARRAY_BUFFER, this.textureBuffer);
gl.bufferData(gl.ARRAY_BUFFER, new Float32Array(textureCoords),
gl.STATIC_DRAW);

//3. Clean up
gl.bindBuffer(gl.ARRAY_BUFFER, null);
```

Setting up the shader

The vertex shader for the post-process draw is the simplest one you are likely to see
in a WebGL application:

```
attribute vec2 aVertexPosition;
attribute vec2 aVertexTextureCoords;

varying vec2 vTextureCoord;

void main(void) {
    vTextureCoord = aVertexTextureCoords;
    gl_Position = vec4(aVertexPosition, 0.0, 1.0);
}
```

Something to note here is that unlike every other vertex shader that we've worked with so
far, this one doesn't make use of any matrices. That's because the vertices that we declared
in the previous step are **pre-transformed**.

Recall from *Chapter 4, Camera*, that typically we retrieve normalized device coordinates by multiplying the vertex position by the Perspective matrix, which maps the positions to a [-1,1] range on each axis, representing the full extents of the viewport. In this case our vertex positions are already mapped to that [-1,1] range, and as such no transformation is needed. They will map perfectly to the viewport bounds when we render.

The fragment shader is where most of the interesting work happens, and will be different based on the post-process effect that is desired. Let's look at a simple grayscale shader as an example:

```
uniform sampler2D uSampler;
varying vec2 vTextureCoord;

void main(void)
{
    vec4 frameColor = texture2D(uSampler, vTextureCoord);
    float luminance = frameColor.r * 0.3 + frameColor.g * 0.59 +
frameColor.b * 0.11;
    gl_FragColor = vec4(luminance, luminance, luminance,
frameColor.a);
}
```

Here we are sampling the original color rendered by our scene (available through uSampler), taking a weighted average of the red, green, and blue channels, and outputting the averaged result to all color channels. The output is a simple grayscale version of the original scene.

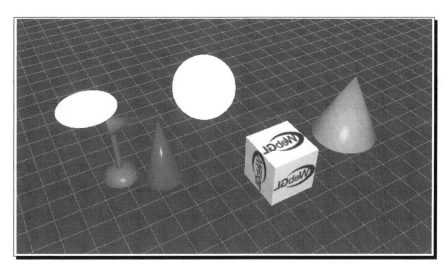

Architectural updates

We've added a new class, `PostProcess`, to our architecture to assist in applying post-process effects. The code can be found in `js/webgl/PostProcess.js`. This class will create the appropriate framebuffer and quad geometry for us, compile the post-process shader, and perform the appropriate render setup needed to draw the scene out to the quad.

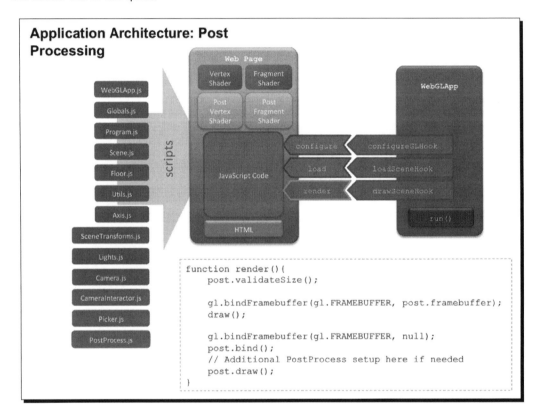

Application Architecture: Post Processing

```
function render(){
    post.validateSize();

    gl.bindFramebuffer(gl.FRAMEBUFFER, post.framebuffer);
    draw();

    gl.bindFramebuffer(gl.FRAMEBUFFER, null);
    post.bind();
    // Additional PostProcess setup here if needed
    post.draw();
}
```

Let's see it in action!

Time for action – testing some post-process effects

1. Open the file `ch10_PostProcess.html` in an HTML5 browser.

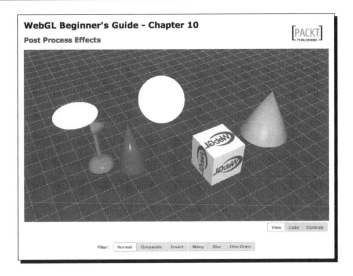

The buttons at the bottom allow you to switch between several sample effects. Try each of them to get a feel for the effect they have on the scene. We've already looked at grayscale, so let's examine the rest of filters individually.

2. The invert effect is similar to grayscale, in that it only modifies the color output; this time inverting each color channel.

```
uniform sampler2D uSampler;
varying vec2 vTextureCoord;

void main(void)
{
    vec4 frameColor = texture2D(uSampler, vTextureCoord);
    gl_FragColor = vec4(1.0-frameColor.r, 1.0-frameColor.g,
1.0-frameColor.b, frameColor.a);
}
```

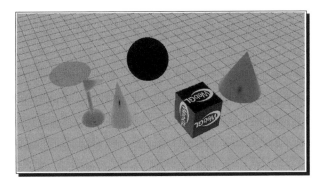

3. The wavy effect manipulates the texture coordinates to make the scene swirl and sway. In this effect, we also provide the current time to allow the distortion to change as time progresses.

```
uniform sampler2D uSampler;
uniform float uTime;
varying vec2 vTextureCoord;

const float speed = 15.0;
const float magnitude = 0.015;

void main(void)
{
    vec2 wavyCoord;
    wavyCoord.s = vTextureCoord.s + (sin(uTime+vTextureCoord.t*spe
ed) * magnitude);
    wavyCoord.t = vTextureCoord.t + (cos(uTime+vTextureCoord.s*spe
ed) * magnitude);
    vec4 frameColor = texture2D(uSampler, wavyCoord);
    gl_FragColor = frameColor;
}
```

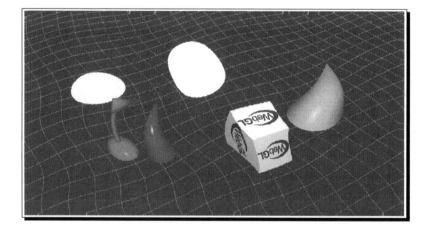

4. The blur effect samples several pixels to either side of the current one and uses a weighted blend to produce a fragment output that is the average of it's neighbors. This gives a blurry feel to the scene.

A new uniform used here is `uInverseTextureSize`, which is 1 over the width and height of the viewport, respectively. We can use this to accurately target individual pixels within the texture. For example, `vTextureCoord.x + 2*uInverseTextureSize.x` will be exactly two pixels to the left of the original texture coordinate.

```glsl
uniform sampler2D uSampler;
uniform vec2 uInverseTextureSize;
varying vec2 vTextureCoord;

vec4 offsetLookup(float xOff, float yOff) {
    return texture2D(uSampler, vec2(vTextureCoord.x
+ xOff*uInverseTextureSize.x, vTextureCoord.y +
yOff*uInverseTextureSize.y));
}

void main(void)
{
    vec4 frameColor = offsetLookup(-4.0, 0.0) * 0.05;
    frameColor += offsetLookup(-3.0, 0.0) * 0.09;
    frameColor += offsetLookup(-2.0, 0.0) * 0.12;
    frameColor += offsetLookup(-1.0, 0.0) * 0.15;
    frameColor += offsetLookup(0.0, 0.0) * 0.16;
    frameColor += offsetLookup(1.0, 0.0) * 0.15;
    frameColor += offsetLookup(2.0, 0.0) * 0.12;
    frameColor += offsetLookup(3.0, 0.0) * 0.09;
    frameColor += offsetLookup(4.0, 0.0) * 0.05;

    gl_FragColor = frameColor;
}
```

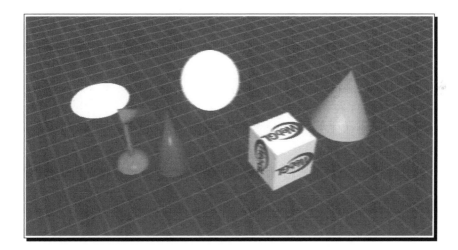

5. Our final example is a film grain effect. This uses a noisy texture to create a grainy look to the scene, which simulates the use of an old camera. This example is significant because it shows the use of a second texture besides the framebuffer when rendering.

```
uniform sampler2D uSampler;
uniform sampler2D uNoiseSampler;
uniform vec2 uInverseTextureSize;
uniform float uTime;
varying vec2 vTextureCoord;

const float grainIntensity = 0.1;
const float scrollSpeed = 4000.0;

void main(void)
{
    vec4 frameColor = texture2D(uSampler, vTextureCoord);
    vec4 grain = texture2D(uNoiseSampler, vTextureCoord * 2.0 +
uTime * scrollSpeed * uInverseTextureSize);
    gl_FragColor = frameColor - (grain * grainIntensity);
}
```

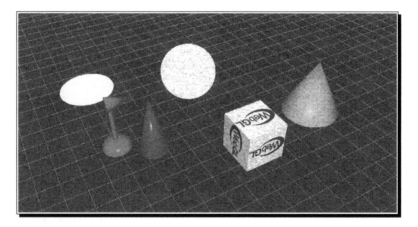

What just happened?

All of these effects are achieved by manipulating the rendered image before it is output to the screen. Since the amount of geometry processed for these effects is quite small, they can often be performed very quickly regardless of the complexity of the scene itself. Performance may still be affected by the size of the canvas or the complexity of the post-process shader.

Have a go hero – funhouse mirror effect

What would it take to create a post-process effect that stretches the image near the center of the viewport and squashes it towards the edges?

Point sprites

Common techniques in many 3D applications and games are **particle effects**. A particle effect is a generic term for any special effect created by rendering groups of **particles** (displayed as points, textured quads, or repeated geometry), typically with some simple form of physics simulation acting on the individual particles. They can be used for simulating smoke, fire, bullets, explosions, water, sparks, and many other effects that are difficult to represent as a single geometric model.

One very efficient way of rendering the particles is to use **point sprites**. Typically, if you render vertices with the POINTS primitive type each vertex will be rendered as a single pixel on the screen. A point sprite is an extension of the POINTS primitive rendering where each point is provided a size and textured in the shader.

A point sprite is created by setting the gl_PointSize value in the vertex shader. It can be set to either a constant value or a value calculated from shader inputs. If it is set to a number greater than one, the point is rendered as a quad which always faces the screen (also known as a **billboard**). The quad is centered on the original point, and has a width and height equal to the gl_PointSize in pixels.

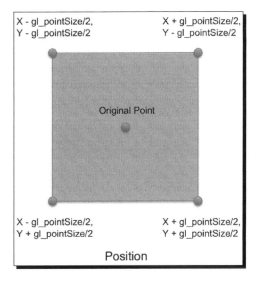

When the point sprite is rendered, it also generates texture coordinates for the quad automatically, covering a simple 0-1 range from upper left to lower right.

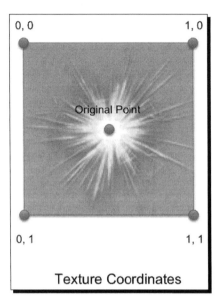

The texture coordinates are accessible in the fragment shader as the built-in vec2 gl_PointCoord. Combining these properties gives us a simple point sprite shader that looks like this:

```
//Vertex Shader
attribute vec4 aVertexPosition;

uniform mat4 uMVMatrix;
uniform mat4 uPMatrix;

void main(void) {
    gl_Position = uPMatrix * uMVMatrix * vec4(aVertexPosition, 1.0);
    gl_PointSize = 16.0;
}

//Fragment Shader
precision highp float;

uniform sampler2D uSampler;

void main(void) {
    gl_FragColor = texture2D(uSampler, gl_PointCoord);
}
```

This could be used to render any vertex buffer with the following call:

```
gl.drawArrays(gl.POINTS, 0, vertexCount);
```

As you can see, this would render each point in the vertex buffer as a 16 x 16 texture.

Time for action – using point sprites to create a fountain of sparks

1. Open the file `ch10_PointSprites.html` in an HTML5 browser.

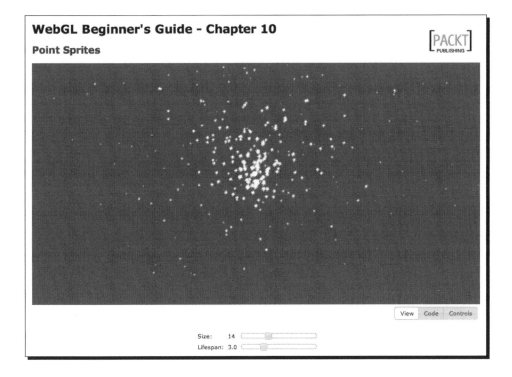

2. This sample creates a simple *fountain of sparks* effect with point sprites. You can adjust the size and lifetime of the particles using the sliders at the bottom. Play with them to see the effect it has on the particles.

3. The particle simulation is performed by maintaining a list of particles that comprises of a position, velocity, and lifespan. This list is iterated over every frame and updated, moving the particle position according to the velocity and applying gravity while reducing the remaining lifespan. Once a particle's lifespan has reached zero, it gets reset to the origin with a new randomized velocity and a replenished lifespan.

4. With every iteration of the particle simulation, the particle positions and lifespans are copied to an array which is then used to update a vertex buffer. That vertex buffer is what is rendered to produce the onscreen sprites.

5. Let's play with some of the other values that control the simulation and see how they affect the scene. Open up `ch10_PointSprites.html` in an editor.

6. First, locate the call to `configureParticles` at the bottom of the `configure` function. The number passed into it, initially set to `1024`, determines how many particles are created. Try manipulating it to lower or higher values to see the effect it has on the particle system. Be careful, as extremely high values (for example, in the millions) could cause performance issues for your page!

7. Next, find the `resetParticle` function. This function is called any time a particle is created or reset. There are several values here that can have a significant effect on how the scene renders.

```
function resetParticle(p) {
    p.pos = [0.0, 0.0, 0.0];

    p.vel = [
        (Math.random() * 20.0) - 10.0,
        (Math.random() * 20.0),
        (Math.random() * 20.0) - 10.0,
    ];

    p.lifespan = Math.random() * particleLifespan;
    p.remainingLife = p.lifespan;
}
```

8. The `p.pos` is the *x*, *y*, *z* starting coordinates for the particle. Initially all points start at the world origin (0, 0, 0), but this could be set to anything. Often it is desirable to have the particles originate from the location of another object in the scene, to make it appear as if that object is producing the particles. You can also randomize the position to make the particles appear within a given area.

9. `p.vel` is the initial velocity of the particle. You can see here that it's randomized so that particles spread out as they move away from the origin. Particles that move in random directions tend to look more like explosions or sprays, while those that move in the same direction give the appearance of a steady stream. In this case, the *y* value is designed to always be positive, while the *x* and *z* values may be either positive or negative. Experiment with what happens when you increase or decrease any of the values in the velocity, or if you remove the random element from one of the components.

10. Finally, `p.lifespan` determines how long a particle is displayed before being reset. This uses the value from the slider on the page, but it's also randomized to provide visual variety. If you remove the random element from the particle lifespan all the particles will expire and reset at the same time, resulting in fireworks-like *bursts* of particles.

11. Next, find the `updateParticles` function. This function is called once per frame to update the position and velocity of all particles and push the new values to the vertex buffer. The interesting part here, in terms of manipulating the simulation behavior, is the application of gravity to the particle velocity mid way through the function:

```
// Apply gravity to the velocity
p.vel[1] -= 9.8 * elapsed;
if(p.pos[1] < 0) {
    p.vel[1] *= -0.75; // Allow particles to bounce off the floor
    p.pos[1] = 0;
}
```

The `9.8` here is the acceleration applied to the *y* component over time. In other words, gravity. We can remove this calculation entirely to create an environment where the particles float indefinitely along their original trajectories. We can increase the value to make the particles fall very quickly (giving them a *heavy* appearance), or we could change the component that the deceleration is applied to change the direction of gravity. For example, subtracting from `vel[0]` makes the particles *fall* sideways.

12. This is also where we apply simple collision response for the *floor*. Any particles with a *y* position less than `0` (below the floor) have their velocities reversed and reduced. This gives us a realistic bouncing motion. We can make the particles less bouncy by reducing the multiplier (that is, `0.25` instead of `0.75`) or even eliminate bouncing altogether by simply setting the *y* velocity to 0 at that point. Additionally, we can remove the floor by taking away the check for `y < 0`, which would allow the particles to fall indefinitely.

13. It's also worth seeing the different effects that can be achieved with different textures. Try changing path for the `spriteTexture` in the `configure` function to see what it looks like when you use different images.

What just happened?

We've seen how point sprites can be used to efficiently render particle effects, and seen some of the ways we can manipulate the particle simulation to achieve different effects.

Have a go hero – bubbles!

The particle system in place here could be used to simulate bubbles or smoke floating upward just as easily as bouncing sparks. How would you need to change the simulation to make the particles float rather than fall?

Normal mapping

One technique that is very popular among real-time 3D applications today is **normal mapping**. Normal mapping creates the illusion of highly detailed geometry on a low-poly model by storing surface normals in a texture map, which is then used to calculate the lighting of the mesh. This method is especially popular in modern games, where it allows developers to strike a balance between high performance and detailed scenes.

Typically, lighting is calculated using nothing but the surface normal of the triangle being rendered, meaning that the entire polygon will be lit as a continuous, smooth surface.

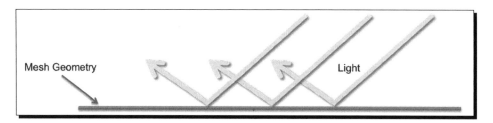

With normal mapping, the surface normals are replaced by normals encoded within a texture, which can give the appearance of a rough or bumpy surface. Note that the actual geometry is not changed when using a normal map, only how it is lit. If you look at a normal mapped polygon from the side, it will still appear perfectly flat.

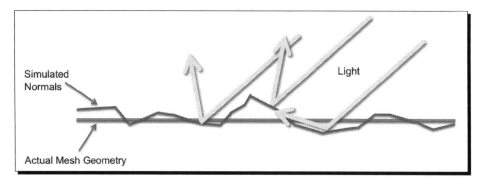

The texture used to store the normals is called a **normal map**, and is typically paired with a specific diffuse texture that complements the surface the normal map is trying to simulate. For example, here is a diffuse texture of some flagstones and the corresponding normal map:

 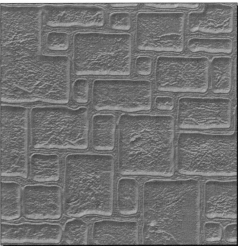

You can see that the normal map contains a similar pattern to the diffuse texture. The two textures work in tandem to give the appearance that the stones are raised and rough, while the grout between them is sunk in.

The normal map contains very specifically formatted color information that can be interpreted by the shader at runtime as a fragment normal. A fragment normal is essentially the same as the vertex normals that we are already familiar with: a three-component vector that points away from the surface. The normal texture encodes the three components of the normal vector into the three channels of the texture's texel color. Red represents the X axis, green the Y axis, and blue the Z axis.

The normal encoded in the map is typically stored in **tangent space** as opposed to world or object space. Tangent space is the coordinate system that the texture coordinates for a face are defined in. Normal maps are almost always predominantly blue, since the normals they represent generally point away from the surface and thus have larger Z components.

Time for action – normal mapping in action

1. Open the file `ch10_NormalMap.html` in an HTML5 browser.

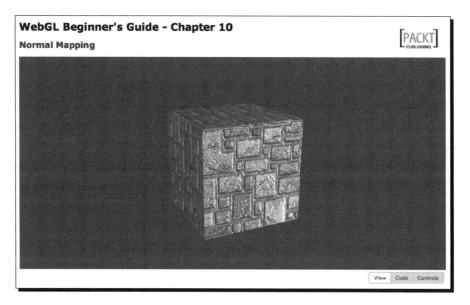

2. Rotate the cube to see the effect that the normal map has on how the cube is lit. Also observe how the profile of the cube has not changed. Let's examine how this effect is achieved.

3. First, we need to add a new attribute to our vertex buffers. There are actually three vectors that are needed to calculate the tangent space coordinates that the lighting is calculated in: the normal, the **tangent**, and **bitangent**.

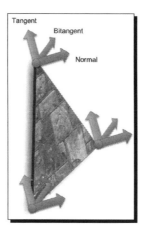

We already know what the normal represents, so let's look at the other two vectors. The tangent essentially represents the *up* (positive Y) vector for the texture relative to the polygon surface. Likewise, the bitangent represents the *left* (positive X) vector for the texture relative to the polygon surface.

We only need to provide two of the three vectors as vertex attributes, traditionally the normal and tangent. The third vector can be calculated as the cross-product of the other two in the vertex shader code.

4. Many times 3D modeling packages will generate tangents for you, but if they aren't provided, they can be calculated from the vertex positions and texture coordinates, similar to how we can calculate the vertex normals. We won't cover the algorithm here, but it has been implemented in `js/webgl/Utils.js` as `calculateTangents` and used in `Scene.addObject`.

```
var tangentBufferObject = gl.createBuffer();
gl.bindBuffer(gl.ARRAY_BUFFER, tangentBufferObject);
gl.bufferData(gl.ARRAY_BUFFER, new Float32Array(Utils.
calculateTangents(object.vertices, object.texture_coords, object.
indices)), gl.STATIC_DRAW);
```

5. In the vertex shader, seen at the top of `ch10_NormalMap.html`, the tangent needs to be transformed by the Normal matrix just like the normal does to ensure that it's appropriately oriented relative to the world-space mesh. The two transformed vectors can be used to calculate the third as mentioned earlier.

```
vec3 normal = vec3(uNMatrix * vec4(aVertexNormal, 1.0));
vec3 tangent = vec3(uNMatrix * vec4(aVertexTangent, 1.0));
vec3 bitangent = cross(normal, tangent);
```

The three vectors can then be used to create a matrix that transforms vectors into tangent space.

```
mat3 tbnMatrix = mat3(
    tangent.x, bitangent.x, normal.x,
    tangent.y, bitangent.y, normal.y,
    tangent.z, bitangent.z, normal.z
);
```

6. Instead of applying lighting in the vertex shader, as we did previously, the bulk of the lighting calculations need to happen in the fragment shader here so that they can incorporate the normals from the texture. We do transform the light direction into tangent space in the vertex shader, however, and pass it to the fragment shader as a varying.

```
//light direction, from light position to vertex
vec3 lightDirection = uLightPosition - vertex.xyz;
vTangentLightDir = lightDirection * tbnMatrix;
```

7. In the fragment shader, first we extract the tangent space normal from the normal map texture. Since textures texels don't store negative values, the normal components must be encoded to map from the `[-1,1]` range into the `[0,1]` range. Therefore, they must be *unpacked* back into the correct range before use in the shader. Fortunately, the algorithm to do so is simple to express in ESSL:

```
vec3 normal = normalize(2.0 * (texture2D(uNormalSampler,
vTextureCoord).rgb - 0.5));
```

8. At this point, lighting is calculated almost identically to the vertex-lit model, using the texture normal and tangent space light direction.

```
// Normalize the light direction and determine how much light is
hitting this point
vec3 lightDirection = normalize(vTangentLightDir);
float lambertTerm = max(dot(normal,lightDirection),0.20);

// Combine lighting and material colors
vec4 Ia = uLightAmbient * uMaterialAmbient;
vec4 Id = uLightDiffuse * uMaterialDiffuse * texture2D(uSampler,
vTextureCoord) * lambertTerm;
gl_FragColor = Ia + Id;
```

The code sample also includes calculation of a specular term, to help accentuate the normal mapping effect.

What just happened?

We've seen how to use normal information encoded into a texture to add a new level of complexity to our lit models without additional geometry.

Ray tracing in fragment shaders

A common (if somewhat impractical) technique used to show how powerful shaders can be is using them to **ray trace** a scene. Thus far, all of our rendering has been done with **polygon rasterization**, which is the technical term for the triangle-based rendering that WebGL operates with). Ray tracing is an alternate rendering technique that traces the path of light through a scene as it interacts with mathematically defined geometry.

Ray tracing has several advantages compared to polygonal rendering, the primary of which is that it can create more realistic scenes due to a more accurate lighting model that can easily account for things like reflection and reflected lighting. Ray tracing also tends to be far slower than polygonal rendering, which is why it's not used much for real-time applications.

Ray tracing a scene is done by creating a series of rays (represented by an origin and direction) that start at the camera's location and pass through each pixel in the viewport. These rays are then tested against every object in the scene to determine if there are any intersections, and if so the closest intersection to the ray origin is returned. That is then used to determine the color that pixel should be.

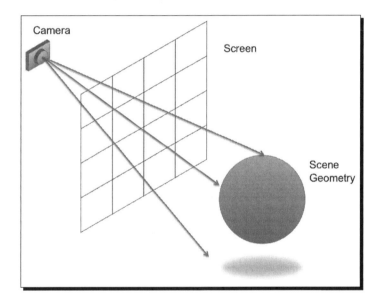

There are a lot of algorithms that can be used to determine the color of the intersection point, ranging from simple diffuse lighting to multiple bounces of rays off other objects to simulate reflection, but we'll be keeping it simple in our case. The key thing to remember is that everything about our scene will be entirely a product of the shader code.

Time for action – examining the ray traced scene

1. Open the file ch10_Raytracing.html in an HTML5 browser. You should
see a scene with a simple lit, bobbing sphere like the one shown in the
following screenshot:

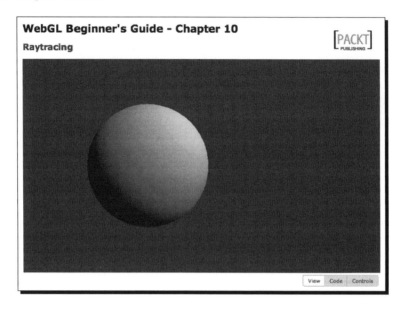

2. First, in order to give us a way of triggering the shader, we need to draw a full screen
quad. Luckily for us, we already have a class that helps us do exactly that from the
post-processing example earlier in this chapter! Since we don't have a scene to
process, we're able to cut a large part of the rendering code out, and the entirety
of our JavaScript drawing code becomes:

```
function render(){
    gl.viewport(0, 0, c_width, c_height);
    gl.clear(gl.COLOR_BUFFER_BIT | gl.DEPTH_BUFFER_BIT);

    //Checks to see if the framebuffer needs to be resized to
    match the canvas
    post.validateSize();
    post.bind();

    //Render the fullscreen quad
    post.draw();
}
```

3. That's it. The remainder of our scene will be built in the fragment shader.

4. At the core of our shader, there are two functions: One which determines if a ray is intersecting a sphere and one that determines the normal of a point on the sphere. We're using spheres because they're typically the easiest type of geometry to raycast, and they also happen to be a type of geometry that is difficult to represent accurately with polygons.

```
// ro is the ray origin, rd is the ray direction, and s is the
sphere
float sphereInter( vec3 ro, vec3 rd, vec4 s ) {
    // Transform the ray into object space
    vec3 oro = ro - s.xyz;

    float a = dot(rd, rd);
    float b = 2.0 * dot(oro, rd);
    float c = dot(oro, oro) - s.w * s.w; // w is the sphere radius

    float d = b * b - 4.0 * a * c;

    if(d < 0.0) { return d; }// No intersection

    return (-b - sqrt(d)) / 2.0; // Intersection occurred
}

vec3 sphereNorm( vec3 pt, vec4 s ) {
    return ( pt - s.xyz )/ s.w;

}
```

5. Next, we will use those two functions to determine where the ray is intersecting with a sphere (if at all) and what the normal and color of the sphere is at that point. In this case, the sphere information is hardcoded into a couple of global variables to make things easier, but they could just as easily be provided as uniforms from JavaScript.

```
vec4 sphere1 = vec4(0.0, 1.0, 0.0, 1.0);
vec3 sphere1Color = vec3(0.9, 0.8, 0.6);
float maxDist = 1024.0;

float intersect( vec3 ro, vec3 rd, out vec3 norm, out vec3 color )
{
    float dist = maxDist;
        float interDist = sphereInter( ro, rd, sphere1 );

    if ( interDist > 0.0 && interDist < dist ) {
```

```
                    dist = interDist;

                    vec3 pt = ro + dist * rd; // Point of intersection
                    norm = sphereNorm(pt, sphere1); // Get normal for that
                    point
                    color = sphere1Color; // Get color for the sphere
                }

            return dist;
        }
```

6. Now that we can determine the normal and color of a point with a ray, we need to generate the rays to test with. We do this by determining the pixel that the current fragment represents and creating a ray that points from the desired camera position through that pixel. To aid in this, we will utilize the uInverseTextureSize uniform that the PostProcess class provides to the shader.

```
vec2 uv = gl_FragCoord.xy * uInverseTextureSize;
float aspectRatio = uInverseTextureSize.y/uInverseTextureSize.x;

// Cast a ray out from the eye position into the scene
vec3 ro = vec3(0.0, 1.0, 4.0); // Eye position is slightly up and
back from the scene origin
// Ray we cast is tilted slightly downward to give a better view
of the scene
vec3 rd = normalize(vec3( -0.5 + uv * vec2(aspectRatio, 1.0),
-1.0));
```

7. Finally, using the ray that we just generated, we call the intersect function to get the information about the sphere intersection and then apply the same diffuse lighting calculations that we've been using all throughout the book! We're using directional lighting here for simplicity, but it would be trivial to convert to a point light or spotlight model if desired.

```
// Default color if we don't intersect with anything
vec3 rayColor = vec3(0.2, 0.2, 0.2);

// Direction the lighting is coming from
vec3 lightDir = normalize(vec3(0.5, 0.5, 0.5));

// Ambient light color
vec3 ambient = vec3(0.05, 0.1, 0.1);

// See if the ray intesects with any objects.
// Provides the normal of the nearest intersection point and color
vec3 objNorm, objColor;
```

```
float t = intersect(ro, rd, objNorm, objColor);

if ( t < maxDist ) {
    float diffuse = clamp(dot(objNorm, lightDir), 0.0, 1.0); //
diffuse factor
    rayColor = objColor * diffuse + ambient;
}

gl_FragColor = vec4(rayColor, 1.0);
```

8. Rendering with the preceding code will produce a static, lit sphere. That's great, but we'd also like to add a bit of motion to the scene to give us a better sense of how fast the scene renders and how the lighting interacts with the sphere. To add a simple looping circular motion to the sphere we use the `uTime` uniform to modify the X and Z coordinates at the beginning of the shader.

```
sphere1.x = sin(uTime);
sphere1.z = cos(uTime);
```

What just happened?

We've just seen how we can construct a scene, lighting and all, completely in a fragment shader. It's a simple scene, certainly, but also one that would be nearly impossible to render using polygon-based rendering. Perfect spheres can only be approximated with triangles.

Have a go hero – multiple spheres

For this example, we've kept things simple by having only a single sphere in the scene. However, all of the pieces needed to render several spheres in the same scene are in place! See if you can set up a scene with three of four spheres all with different coloring and movement.

As a hint: The main shader function that needs editing is `intersect`.

Summary

In this chapter, we tried out several advanced techniques and learned how we could use them to create more visually complex and compelling scenes. We learned how to apply post-process effects by rendering a framebuffer, created particle effects through the use of point sprites, created the illusion of complex geometry through the use of normal maps, and rendered a raycast scene using nothing but a fragment shader.

These effects are only a tiny preview of the vast variety of effects possible with WebGL. Given the power and flexibility of shaders, the possibilities are endless!

Index

B

C

camera, WebGL properties
  setting up 298
canvas
  about 10
  clicking on 264, 265
canvas element 264
canvas.onmouseup function 264
checkKey function 17
c_height 266
CLAMP_TO_EDGE 317
CLAMP_TO_EDGE wrap mode 244
clear function 17
client-based rendering 9
clientHeight 266
cMatrix. *See* camera matrix
colors
  constant coloring 179
  per-fragment coloring 181
  pre-vertex coloring 180, 181
  storing, by creating texture 259
  using, in lights 185
  using, in objects 179
  using, in scene 206
  using, in WebGL 178
colors, using in lights
  about 185
  getUniformLocation function 185
  uniform4fv function 185
compileShader function 91
Cone First button 223
configure function
  about 144, 184, 200, 248, 264, 278, 308
  updating 193, 194
configureGLHook 143
configure, JavaScript functions 289
configureParticles 328
constant coloring
  about 179
  and per-fragment coloring, comparing 181-184
context
  used, for accessing WebGL API 18
context attributes, WebGL
  setting up 15-18
copy operation 116
cosine emission law 66
createProgram(), WebGL function 91

createShader function 91
creation operation 116
cross product
  used, for calculating normals 61
cube
  texturing 231-233
cube maps
  about 250, 251
  cube map-specific function 251
  using 252-254

D

deleteBuffer(Object aBuffer) method 30
depth buffer 208
depth function
  about 210
  gl.ALWAYS parameter 210
  gl.EQUAL parameter 210
  gl.GEQUAL parameter 210
  gl.GREATER parameter 210
  gL.LEQUAL parameter 210
  gl.LESS parameter 210
  gl.NEVER parameter 210
  gl.NOTEQUAL parameter 210
depth information
  storing, by creating Renderbuffer 260
depth testing 208, 209
dest 137
diffuse 67
diffuseColorGenerator function 275, 276
diffuse material property 179
directional lights 99
directional point light 202-204
discard command 207
div tags 292
d, materials uniforms 296
doLagrangeInterpolation function 173
doLinearInterpolation function 173
drawArrays function
  about 33, 34, 288
  using 34, 35
drawElements function
  about 33, 43, 288
  using 36, 37

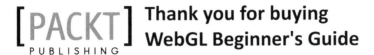

Thank you for buying
WebGL Beginner's Guide

About Packt Publishing

Packt, pronounced 'packed', published its first book "Mastering phpMyAdmin for Effective MySQL Management" in April 2004 and subsequently continued to specialize in publishing highly focused books on specific technologies and solutions.

Our books and publications share the experiences of your fellow IT professionals in adapting and customizing today's systems, applications, and frameworks. Our solution-based books give you the knowledge and power to customize the software and technologies you're using to get the job done. Packt books are more specific and less general than the IT books you have seen in the past. Our unique business model allows us to bring you more focused information, giving you more of what you need to know, and less of what you don't.

Packt is a modern, yet unique publishing company, which focuses on producing quality, cutting-edge books for communities of developers, administrators, and newbies alike. For more information, please visit our website: www.PacktPub.com.

Writing for Packt

We welcome all inquiries from people who are interested in authoring. Book proposals should be sent to author@packtpub.com. If your book idea is still at an early stage and you would like to discuss it first before writing a formal book proposal, contact us; one of our commissioning editors will get in touch with you.

We're not just looking for published authors; if you have strong technical skills but no writing experience, our experienced editors can help you develop a writing career, or simply get some additional reward for your expertise.

HTML5 Games Development by Example: Beginner's Guide

ISBN: 978-1-84969-126-0   Paperback:352 pages

Create six fun games using the latest HTML5, Canvas, CSS, and JavaScript techniques.

1. Learn HTML5 game development by building six fun example projects

2. Full, clear explanations of all the essential techniques

3. Covers puzzle games, action games, multiplayer, and Box 2D physics

4. Use the Canvas with multiple layers and sprite sheets for rich graphical games

HTML5 Canvas Cookbook

ISBN: 978-1-84969-136-9   Paperback: 348 pages

Over 80 recipes to revolutionize the web experience with HTML5 Canvas

1. The quickest way to get up to speed with HTML5 Canvas application and game development

2. Create stunning 3D visualizations and games without Flash

3. Written in a modern, unobtrusive, and objected oriented JavaScript style so that the code can be reused in your own applications.

Please check **www.PacktPub.com** for information on our titles

Quick answers to common problems

HTML5 Mobile Development Cookbook

Over 60 recipes for building fast, responsive HTML5 mobile websites for iPhone 5, Android, Windows Phone, and Blackberry

Shi Chuan   [   ]

HTML5 Mobile Development Cookbook

ISBN: 978-1-84969-196-3   Paperback:254 pages

Over 60 recipes for building fast, responsive HTML5 mobile websites for iPhone 5, Android, Windows Phone and Blackberry.

1. Solve your cross platform development issues by implementing device and content adaptation recipes.

2. Maximum action, minimum theory allowing you to dive straight into HTML5 mobile web development.

3. Incorporate HTML5-rich media and geo-location into your mobile websites.

Quick answers to common problems

HTML5 Multimedia Development Cookbook

Recipes for practical, real-world HTML5 multimedia-driven development

Dale Cruse   Lee Jordan   [   ]

HTML5 Multimedia Development Cookbook

ISBN: 978-1-84969-104-8   Paperback: 288 pages

Recipes for practical, real-world HTML5 multimedia-driven development

1. Use HTML5 to enhance JavaScript functionality. Display videos dynamically and create movable ads using JQuery.

2. Set up the canvas environment, process shapes dynamically and create interactive visualizations.

3. Enhance accessibility by testing browser support, providing alternative site views and displaying alternate content for non supported browsers.

Please check **www.PacktPub.com** for information on our titles

10403469R00212

Made in the USA
San Bernardino, CA
17 April 2014